"Centurion", Caesar's Palace, Las Vegas. Debased and commodified, the manly virtue identified with Romanness still has cultural currency in the late twentieth century, providing name recognition for a famous gambling casino in the Nevada desert. From *Learning from Las Vegas*, Robert Venturi, Denise Scott Brown and Steven Izenour.

FEMINIST READINGS OF SHAKESPEARE

Literary studies have been transformed in the last 20 years by a number of new approaches which have challenged traditional assumptions and traditional ways of reading. Critics of Shakespeare and English Renaissance literature have been at the forefront of these developments, and feminist criticism has proved to be one of the most important areas of productivity and change.

'Feminist Readings of Shakespeare' is a series of five generically based books by leading feminist critics from Britain, continental Europe and North America. Each book outlines and engages with the current positions and debates within the field of feminist criticism and in addition provides an original feminist reading of the texts in question. While the authors share a commitment to feminist values, the books are not uniform in their approach but rather exemplify the richness and diversity of feminist criticism today.

ENGENDERING A NATION: A FEMINIST ACCOUNT OF
SHAKESPEARE'S ENGLISH HISTORIES
Jean E. Howard and Phyllis Rackin

ROMAN SHAKESPEARE: WARRIORS,
WOUNDS, AND WOMEN
Coppélia Kahn

ROMAN SHAKESPEARE

In the first full-length feminist study of Shakespeare's Roman plays Coppélia Kahn brings to these texts a startling critical perspective which interrogates the gender ideologies that uphold "Roman virtue."

Roman Shakespeare offers fresh, detailed readings of *Lucrece, Titus Andronicus, Julius Caesar, Antony and Cleopatra, Coriolanus*, and *Cymbeline*, examining the image of the wound as a fetish of Roman masculinity. Setting the Roman works in the dual context of the popular theater and Renaissance humanism, the author identifies new sources and analyses them from a historicised feminist perspective.

Roman Shakespeare is written in an accessible style and will appeal to Shakespeare scholars and students and those interested in feminist theory, as well as Classicists.

Coppélia Kahn is Professor of English at Brown University. She is co-editor of *Changing Subjects: The Making of Feminist Literary Criticism* and *Making a Difference*, and author of *Man's Estate: Masculine Identity in Shakespeare*.

ROMAN SHAKESPEARE

Warriors, Wounds, and Women

Coppélia Kahn

London and New York

First published 1997
by Routledge
11 New Fetter Lane, London EC4P 4EE

Simultaneously published in the USA and Canada
by Routledge
29 West 35th Street, New York, NY 10001

© 1997 Coppélia Kahn

Typeset in Baskerville by Florencetype Ltd, Stoodleigh, Devon

Printed and bound in Great Britain by
Biddles Ltd, Guildford and King's Lynn

British Library Cataloguing in Publication Data
A catalogue record for this book is available from the British Library

Library of Congress Cataloguing in Publication Data
A catalogue record for this book has been requested

ISBN 0-415-05450-8 (hbk)
ISBN 0-415-05451-6 (pbk)

FOR GABRIEL
caro filio mio
and for
PHYLLIS
and
MARTY and NORMAN

CONTENTS

PLATES

SERIES EDITOR'S PREFACE

As I write this towards the end of 1996, feminist criticism of Shakespeare has just come of age. While we will no doubt continue to rediscover and celebrate notable pre-feminist and proto-feminist precursors, it is usually acknowledged that the genre as we know it began 'officially' just 21 years ago with Juliet Dusinberre's *Shakespeare and the Nature of Women* (London: Macmillan, 1975), a book taken as the obvious starting-point by Philip C. Kolin in his *Shakespeare and Feminist Criticism: An Annotated Bibliography and Commentary* (New York and London: Garland, 1991) which lists 439 items from 1975 to its cut-off date in 1988. A glance at any publisher's catalogue will reveal that the rate of publication has certainly not slowed down during the eight years since then; it is clear in fact that feminist criticism continues to be one of the most lively, productive and influential of the current approaches to Shakespeare.

Shakespeare and the Nature of Women has just been reissued (London: Macmillan, 1996) with a substantial new Preface by Dusinberre entitled 'Beyond the Battle?'. The interrogative mode seems appropriate both in relation to the state of feminist scholarship itself – *is* the battle lost or won? – and to the extent to which the whole enterprise has been about asking questions: asking *different* questions about the Shakespearean texts themselves and using those texts to interrogate 'women's place in culture, history, religion, society, the family'. It seems to me that these questions are now inescapably on the agenda of academic enquiry, and that they have moved from the margin to the centre. The growth and variety of feminist approaches in Shakespeare studies has been complemented and supported by work in feminist theory, women's history, the study of women's relationship to language and the study of women's writing. A summary of the achievements of feminist criticism of Shakespeare in its first 21 years would for me include the following:

1 Since *Shakespeare and the Nature of Women* looked at Shakespeare's works in the context of the history of contemporary ideas about women, drawing on non-literary texts to do so, feminist studies have contributed to the now widely accepted view that works of art can and should be treated within a social frame of reference.

2 While sharing some features of their work with new historicist critics, feminist critics have also provided a critique of new historicism, notably by objecting to its neglect of gender issues and its concentration on male power relationships, and by resisting the conservative idea that subversion is a calculated form of license, always in the end contained.

3 Feminist critics have changed what scholars and students read: there are many more texts by women of the Renaissance period available now, and more studies of women as writers, readers, performers, patrons and audiences. Publishers are responding to the demands of feminist critics and their students for more and different texts from those traditionally taught.

4 Feminist critics have changed how we read: women readers no longer have to pretend to be men. Reading is seen as a complex interaction between the writer, the text and the reader in which the gender of the reader is not necessarily irrelevant.

5 The performance tradition has been affected, with feminist approaches making new stage and screen interpretations possible. Supportive relationships exist between feminist scholars, directors and performers, and a female-centred study of Shakespeare in performance is burgeoning.

6 Our perceptions of dramatic texts have been changed by work on women's access to language and women' use of language. We are opening up the discussion of the gendering of rhetoric, public and private voices, the stereotypes of the 'bad' vocal shrew and the 'good' silent woman.

I believe of course that the five books in this series will help to consolidate these achievements and further the aims of feminist criticism of Shakespeare in a number of ways. The books are generically-based studies by authors who would define themselves as feminist critics but who would not see this as an exclusive or narrow label, preventing them from being, at the same time, traditional scholars, psychoanalytic critics, textual critics, new historicist critics, materialist critics and so forth.

When I first proposed the series in 1990 I wanted to commission

xiv

books which would on the one hand outline the current positions and debates within the field and on the other hand advance original feminist readings of the texts in question. I wanted the books to demonstrate the full range of possibilities offered by feminist criticism and to challenge the standard over-simplifications voiced by hostile critics, namely that feminist criticism is limited to the study of female characters and that it is driven by a desire to co-opt Shakespeare on behalf of the feminist movement.

Certainly the authors of the books in this series are not uninterested in female characters, but they are also interested in male characters. The first two books to appear are on the History plays and the Roman Tragedies – not on the whole noted for their wealth of substantial female roles. The authors are not asking 'Is this woman a good or bad role-model for women today?' as nineteenth-century writers did, or 'Is Shakespeare capable of creating strong females?' as some early feminist critics did, but 'How has theatrical and critical tradition re-presented and re-read these texts in relation to the issue of gender difference?' They accept that systems of gender differentiation are historically specific and they seek to relate the practices of Shakespeare's theatre to their contemporary context as well as to the range of literary and historical materials from which the narratives are derived. They feel no obligation to claim that Shakespeare was a feminist, or to berate him for not being one, but they are interested in exploring ways in which his work can at times seem feminist – or can be appropriated for feminist purposes – while still being totally consistent with Renaissance conceptions of patriarchy.

The study of Shakespeare in the late 1990s is a vigorous and exciting field to which feminism is making a major contribution. In just 21 years it has become quite difficult for anyone to perform, read, teach or study Shakespeare without an awareness of gender issues and I am confident that this will prove to be a permanent and positive change in our attitude to the plays and their extraordinarily rich afterlife in international culture.

Ann Thompson

ACKNOWLEDGEMENTS

This book has been a long time in the making, on two continents and in many planes, trains, libraries, and study sites. Despite its moderate length, it has a cast of thousands. Parts of it were written amidst deep personal sorrow and anguish; at that point, only a chorus of friends, almost daily chanting mantras of sympathy and understanding, kept me and the project going. Abandoning the usual decorum, I would like to put the personal before the professional, and thank those whose friendship and love mattered so much – but in many cases, friends are colleagues and vice versa. Besides those to whom the book is dedicated, these people sustained me: Janet Adelman, Christina Crosby and Elizabeth Weed, Stephen and Mary Jo Foley, Heide Gerritsen-Robertson, Carla Kaplan and John Brenkman, Dian Kriz, Bill and Emily Leider, David Savran, Henry and Sheli Wortis, Shaun Wortis and Suzi Lee.

I was lucky to be offered some lively intellectual forums at which to test out parts of the book. I gave the chapter on *Lucrece* as a talk at the Columbia University Shakespeare Seminar at the invitation of David Kastan; it was published in *Rape and Representation* edited by Lyn Higgins and Brenda Silver, and is printed here with the permission of Columbia University Press. The chapter on *Titus* was first a talk at the Roehampton Institute under the auspices of Ann Thompson, and later at the Shakespeare Seminar, chaired by William Carroll and Virginia Vaughan, at the Harvard Center for Literary and Cultural Studies. The chapter on *Julius Caesar* was heard in several versions at the following venues: Pennsylvania State University, in a lecture series sponsored by the Women's Studies Program; the University of Pittsburgh, at the invitation of the Honors Program and the English Department with Marianne Novy as host; the European Renaissance Conference organized by Jean Brink and held at the University of

Glasgow in 1990; the International Shakespeare Congress, Tokyo, 1991. A portion of it became the introduction to the Folger Shakespeare edition of the play, edited by Barbara Mowat, and is reprinted here with permission of the Folger Library. My reading of *Antony and Cleopatra* was also developed through many hearings: at the Shakespeare Association of America; the English Department, University of Notre Dame, at the invitation of Christopher Fox; the English Institute at which John Brenkman invited me to speak; the University of Bologna thanks to Massimo Riva and Vita Fortunati; and the University of Florence thanks to Keir Elam. The *Coriolanus* chapter received a hearing at ACCUTE (the Association of Canadian College and University Teachers of English), and is printed here with the permission of *differences*, where it was published at the invitation of Elizabeth Weed. My writing group at Brown University, Susan Bernstein, Christina Crosby, Mary Ann Doane, Karen Newman, Ellen Rooney and (in 1987–8) Naomi Schor, provided stringently sympathetic critiques of successive chapters. Kevin Wortis gave me a book that proved crucial to my thinking. Thérèse de Vet helped with some Latin translation, and Evvie Lincoln with an illustration. Duane Davies told me where to find pictures of Caesar's Palace. Ann Thompson, editor of Feminist Readings in Shakespeare, was patient with my delays and prompt with her own meticulous, astute reading of the manuscript.

Over the years, I have learned a great deal from a far-flung community of feminist Shakespeareans who share ideas with one another and whose work informs this book deeply. Some have already been named; others are Catherine Belsey, Lynda Boose, Peter Erickson, Gayle Greene, Carol Neely, Gail Paster, and Madelon Sprengnether. This list isn't comprehensive; the best record of my engagement with the collective endeavor of feminist Shakespeare criticism can be found in the pages to follow.

Fellowships at the Folger Library, the Center for the Humanities at Oregon State University, and the Huntington Library, as well as research support from Brown University, provided the money and time off that it takes to write a book. Brown also supplied me with efficient and congenial research assistants: Margie Zohn, Sianne Ngai, Tom Juvan, Ivan Kreilkamp, and Nicolle Jordan. Lorraine Mazza of the English Department, Nate Tassler who takes care of its computers, and Charlie Flynn of Rockefeller Library helped me in many ways. The errors are all my own.

Pasadena, California
22 March 1996

1

ROMAN VIRTUE ON
ENGLISH STAGES

His story requires Romans or kings, but he thinks only on men.

Samuel Johnson, *Preface to Shakespeare*

In 1765, when Samuel Johnson wrote the word "men" in the statement quoted above, he meant it in the sense of humankind, human
beings – but at the same time, he meant males. The benchmark of
literate, civilized humanity implied in this context rested in the possession of males. Males controlled the meaning of humanity; if the
term included qualities deemed "feminine," if women could possess
humanity, it was so by permission, as it were, from males. Kings, of
course, were men, and if a queen happened to rule instead of a king,
she did so because the laws of succession written by men allowed it.
Shakespeare's Romans were women as well as men: Lucrece, Lavinia,
Portia, Calphurnia, Octavia, Volumnia are all women. But when Dr
Johnson writes "Romans," he thinks of Romanness as male. And so,
I think, did Shakespeare – but with a difference. That is the central
claim of this book: that Shakespeare's Roman works articulate a
critique of the ideology of gender on which the Renaissance understanding of Rome was based.

In making this claim, my key premise is that gender is an ideology.
At least it works like ideology, in rendering something brought about
by human beings into something reified, transcendent, "natural" and
inaccessible to human intervention.[1] What Simone de Beauvoir said
of women almost fifty years ago is also true of the opposite sex: a
man is not born, but made (1989). The discursive practices of culture
make bodily and other differences between human beings into a
gender system that makes men as well as women.[2] Once the system
in is operation, it no longer seems humanly determined but rather
becomes "reality", "biology" or "common sense." Our word for one

1

of the world's oldest and most persistent gender systems, "patriarchy," comes from Latin, and the male dominance that it promotes is strongly associated with Rome, though it didn't originate there. Because Rome was a patriarchal society, Romanness *per se* is closely linked to an ideology of masculinity. For almost four centuries, within the English-speaking world and beyond, both the scholarly community and the general public have taken Shakespeare's Roman works to represent Romanness – reading them *within the terms of this ideology*. Thus the degree to which that Romanness is virtually identical with an ideology of masculinity has gone unnoticed, and it has been generally assumed that Shakespeare didn't notice it either. I hope to demonstrate that, on the contrary, he dramatized precisely this linkage and, in doing so, demystified its power.

In one sense, this book continues the work I began in *Man's Estate: Masculine Identity in Shakespeare* (1981) of identifying a gender-specific dimension – a preoccupation with the masculine subject – in Shakespeare. In another respect, however, this book differs importantly from *Man's Estate*: though I make some use of psychoanalytic theory, I no longer rely on it as a hermeneutic cornerstone. Rather, I have come to see masculinity in these works less as an intra-psychic phenomenon and more as an ideology discursively maintained through the appropriation of the Latin heritage for the early modern English stage. Thus I am concerned here with the social dimensions of *virtus* – its interdependence with political constructions of the state and the family, and with the intertextuality of Shakespeare and the Latin authors he read.

Mungo MacCallum was the first to designate the Roman play as a Shakespearean sub-genre, in *Shakespeare's Roman Plays and their Background* (1910). Since then, many book-length studies of them have appeared, and several significant articles defining the category or surveying the field.[3] All of them take for granted just what I want to identify and interpret: the centrality of a specifically Roman masculinity to Rome as represented in these texts. Though some pathbreaking essays over the past decade have employed gender as a category of analysis for individual Roman works, no comprehensive study of the ideological centrality of masculinity in Shakespeare's Rome exists.[4]

Before attending to men, however, I must attend to history. Though Rome is called "the Eternal City," the Rome I am concerned with is a city viewed at a specific – if extended – historical moment. What did "Rome" – the city, the republic, the empire, the culture, the history, the legend, and the Latin language that mediated them all – mean to Shakespeare? Obviously, its meanings came to him from many sources – texts he could read in Latin or in translation; writings in English that mediated Roman history and culture; paintings, engravings, and tapestries; oral traditions; and generally, the humanistic culture of early modern England, for which Latin was the key to privilege and authority, and Rome the model of civilization itself.[5] From the properties of Rome known to many he fashioned his versions of it. Readers have often debated how "authentic" Shakespeare's Rome is; bothered by clocks in *Julius Caesar* or billiards in *Antony and Cleopatra*, they have argued about the extent of Shakespeare's classical learning or historical consciousness: did he get the Romans "right"?[6] With equal critical energy they have also justified such anachronisms on the grounds of artistic coherence – as creating a persuasive dramatic world rather than a historically "accurate" one.[7]

For modern readers and audiences, Rome is definitively ancient; historically and culturally distant from the modern moment, retrievable only with effort and special instruments. Moreover, it is only one of several possible origins or historical orientation points for Euro-American civilization, along with, say, the biblical (Judeo-Christian) past, or classical Greece. For the Renaissance as a whole, however, "Roman history was a discourse that one could not afford to ignore ... one had to make use of it ... The meaning of Roman history had to be articulated in and for the Renaissance present" (Burt 1991: 112). Moreover, for the English Renaissance, "the Roman past was ... not simply *a* past but *the* past" (Hunter 1977: 95), legendarily linked to the moment in which Britain itself emerged into history.

In English chronicle histories, the founding of Britain was connected to the founding of Rome through Brutus, the grandson of Aeneas, founder of Rome. In his chronicle history of England, Richard Grafton, writing in 1569, declares: "When Brute ... first entred this Island and named it Briteyne: there beginneth mine History of this Realme" (1569: 31). Grafton was only following Geoffrey of Monmouth, who recorded the myth of Brutus in his *History of the Kings of Britain* (1136). Though Holinshed queried it, he too included the legend of Brute in the *Chronicles* (1577), as did William Camden in his *Britannia* (1610), though he also was skeptical. Other chroniclers such as Drayton (*Poly-Olbion*, 1613) and Stow (*Annales*, 1615) defended "the long traduced Brute" (MacDougall 1982: 22).[8] In addition, Henry VIII upheld another tradition connecting England to Rome: his descent from a half-British Emperor Constantine who

3

"had united British kingship with Roman emperorship" (MacDougall 1982: 17). And finally, there was Julius Caesar. Camden draws heavily on his account of the Roman occupation of Britain, which was part of the grammar school curriculum, and legend had it that he had built the Tower of London.[9] Indeed, the old Roman wall defined the boundaries of the city of London, and Hadrian's wall in the north was a well-known landmark linking Britain's past to Rome's. Even though historians had begun to question long-accepted textual authorities, and to develop a proto-modern sense of anachronism, the Roman connection in the Brute legend persisted. Camden and Grafton both reject it, but they still feel obliged to recount it and deal with it.

In relation to Renaissance England, Rome was as much a cultural parent as a cultural other.[10] Through a kind of cross-pollination that isn't simply anachronism, Englishness appears in Roman settings, and Romanness is anglicized. The well-known drawing (attributed to Henry Peacham) of characters from *Titus Andronicus*, the earliest known illustration of a Shakespeare play, conveys the ambiguous perception of Rome as both near and far from England that characterized popular theatrical representations of it (see Plate 1). While Titus wears Roman dress, the soldiers attending him wear Elizabethan military dress and carry halberds. At the Globe or the Fortune, Rome was not an occasion for the "humanist pathos . . . the sense of difference, of littleness, of exclusion, even of estrangement" from it felt by earlier Italian humanists (Greene 1982: 42). Rather, to a great extent, Rome was familiarized for the English by being represented in terms of its past kinship with Britain and as a model for England's present and future. As in Golding's unabashedly exuberant and irreverent English translation of Ovid, Rome onstage is as much assimilated to an English scene and an English sensibility as it is distanced to the antique past.[11] Examples abound. Chapman devotes a scene in his *Caesar and Pompey* (1605) to the "poor and ragged knave" Fronto, accosted by the demon Ophioneus as he prepares to hang himself. Like Autolycus, Fronto has exhausted the occupations available to an enterprising man of low birth in early seventeenth-century England; there is nothing Roman about him. In Thomas Heywood's *The Rape of Lucrece* (1609), Valerius, a former courtier now "Transeshapt to a meere Ballater," punctuates many episodes with bawdy songs such as "Shall I woe the lovely Molly," songs that seem designed specifically as English entertainments, diversions from Romanness. Similarly, Thomas Lodge's two "burghers" Poppey and Curtall, in *The Wounds*

4

of Civil War (1587), talk in comic *double-entendres* like Dogberry and Verges; they could easily fit into an English comedy.

On the one hand, a repertory of "Roman" stage conventions signified an ancient civilization different from England, through "the same motifs, ideas, verbal images, episodes, scenes, and physical gear . . . repeating the names of the same gods, places, customs, and political offices and . . . reenacting such stock 'Roman' situations as the suicide, the triumph, and the sudden fight in a political forum" (Ronan 1995: 32–3). On the other hand, the increasing familiarity of, for example, the senate and the capitol, tribunes and aediles, Caesar and Pompey made Rome less strange. It was becoming common knowledge and common property in early modern England; it could pop up anywhere. Public spectacles in the city of London, open to all, frequently invoked Rome and linked it to the political order of Britain. Royal entries and coronation pageants, Elizabeth's annual Accession Day pageants, celebrations of England's victory over the Armada, and the annual Lord Mayor's pageants, employed Roman motifs. For example, on November 24, 1588, to celebrate the defeat of the Armada, " 'imitating the ancient Romans' [Elizabeth] rode in triumph in a symbolic chariot" (Strong 1977: 120). James was welcomed to London in "imperial style": triumphal arches decked with Roman gods and Latin inscriptions, coins and medallions, panegyrics and masques represented him as "England's Caesar" (Goldberg 1983: 33–54).

The history of Rome, moreover, was a matter of current (even in some circles urgent) controversy, rather than a firmly contoured tradition. Rome served as a model for both "imperial ambitions and nascent republican sentiments" in England (Cantor 1976: 17). Portrayed as a time of "Continuall Factions, Tumults, and Massacres" (Fulbecke 1601), the republican era was nonetheless admired for the pristine virtue of Scipio, Regulus, and Brutus. Julius Caesar was lauded as the first Roman emperor, but also denigrated as a tyrant; Octavius Caesar was viewed as Rome's savior and as a crafty politician. In schools, compositions were written on such themes as "Vituperate Julius Caesar" or "That some friend persuades Cicero that he should not accept the condition offered by Antony" (Baldwin 1944: 88, 89), through which students engaged in the clash of viewpoints that shaped Roman history and its historians. Scholars have demonstrated that Shakespeare brought these ambiguities and contradictions into some of his Roman works to make dramatic meaning prismatic and indeterminate.[12]

5

Before turning to my specific interest in his representations of Roman virtue, I want to survey some of the forms in which Rome's legacy appeared to Shakespeare, and suggest how he intervened in the ongoing project of articulating its meaning for his present moment.

From among numerous scenes in the canon that evoke the ways English culture mediated Rome, let us turn to William Page's Latin grammar lesson in *The Merry Wives of Windsor*. Mistress Page, accompanied by Mistress Quickly, interrupts her pursuit of Falstaff to drop her son off at school. Young William, like thousands of other boys, is learning the fundamentals of Latin grammar, probably much as young William Shakespeare had. Mistress Page asks for some proof of her son's progress because, she claims, "my husband says my son profits nothing in the world at his book" (4.1.11–12).[13] Sir Hugh Evans, the Welsh schoolmaster, the catechizes William on the cases of nouns and pronouns as Mistress Quickly interjects with a series of bawdy misconstructions: "polecat" (prostitute) for *pulcher* (beautiful); "whore" for *horum* (the genitive plural); "Ginny's case" (a slang reference to Ginny's sexual parts) for genitive case, and the like. The audience can see that William has merely memorized the grammar book (probably one written by William Lilly and John Colet and commanded by Edward VI to be used in all schools) without understanding the principles of grammar at all. Nonetheless, his mother is reassured: "He is a better scholar than I thought he was," she declares fondly (4.1.69).

This modest comic scene dramatizes the state-authorized regimen that trained men, from village parsons such as Evans to princes such as Edward, to govern England. It also dramatizes the gender division built into early modern culture by means of that regimen.[14] The two women, sharp-witted and articulate elsewhere in the play, are ignorant outsiders here, and the humor of the whole scene turns on Mistress Quickly's persistent but unwitting interventions into what Ong persuasively terms "a Renaissance puberty rite" for men only (1959).[15] Undeterred by the schoolmaster's rebukes, she rattles on, reducing the chaste forms of correct Latin to obscenity, thus fostering the familiar association of woman with uncontrolled speech, the body in general, and sexuality in particular. But the joke is on the males as well: if William is being trained to run the state, "the state totters," for he is a slow and reluctant learner, as uncomprehending in his way as Mistress Quickly in hers. And Sir Hugh's Welsh pronunciation and idioms, however sure his command of the genitive case, in effect mark him as not fully assimilated to the Tudor establishment.

6

Thus the scene works to demystify the grand humanist project of making Latin the cachet to a universal, disinterested virtue.

Recently Anthony Grafton and Lisa Jardine have tried to demystify humanistic education in the Renaissance by distinguishing between the ideology of humanism itself – its claim to inculcate civic and moral virtue through the study of ancient texts – and its actual pedagogical practice. They argue that by the early sixteenth century, "an ideology of routine, order, and above all, 'method'" prevailed in schools, its purpose being "to produce a total routineness of imaginative writing by reducing its variety to a sequence . . . of specified (and supposedly key) types of verbal composition." Method and system were simply assumed to guarantee an education in virtue as well as in Latin; precise arguments for the connection were lacking (Grafton and Jardine 1986: 123, 131, 135).

This reliance on method is easily documented, and its basic characteristic is disintegration: cutting the text into discrete rhetorical units for the accumulation of *copia*. Erasmus's treatise *De Ratione Studii* guided the standard curriculum of English grammar schools, specifying a certain sequence of Latin authors imitated word for word, phrase for phrase: Terence, Plautus, Virgil, Horace, Cicero, Caesar, Sallust (Baldwin 1944: 80). These texts weren't studied whole and entire, for the sake of their intellectual or artistic cogency; indeed, any play by Terence or Plautus teemed with licentious matter deemed inappropriate for boys that humanists deplored and tried to excise or recast (Halpern 1991: 46). Rather, texts were broken up and broken down, turned into "inventories of rhetorical styles and tropes" for students to memorize (Halpern 1991: 46). Nicholas Udall's *Floures for Latine Spekynge, Selected and Gathered out of Terence* (1533), written for pupils at Eton and conveniently printed in octavo, exemplifies this pedagogical fragmentation. Scene by scene, Udall mines Terence for succinct, graceful, apt phrases: "*Bono animo es*. Be of good cheere, or take a good harte;" "*Quid ita?* Why so?" (Udall 1533).[16] The same fragmentation applied to writing as to speaking. As Ascham explains the method of double translation (Latin to English, English back to Latin) in *The Scholemaster*, by comparing their diction and syntax with that of Terence or Cicero, students were drilled, sentence after sentence, to imitate their Latin models (1570: 14–15).

The practice of extracting fragments from a text, rather than grasping it as a whole, wasn't restricted to the classroom. Gentlemen made a lifelong habit of writing marginalia in the books they read, extrapolating pithy statements pertinent to the conduct of life, or

7

copying them into commonplace books, from which they might draw similes and *sententiae* in writing letters or making speeches. Gabriel Harvey, lawyer and man of letters, friend of Sidney and Spenser, wrote in his copy of Morysine's translation of Frontinus's *Strategems* (a treatise on Roman military strategy), "Aphorisms and examples will speedily make you great and admirable. Of longer discourses and histories there is no end. They tire the body and confuse the intellect and the memory." Commenting on Livy's account of the fall of Saguntum to the Carthaginians, Harvey extracts his own aphorism from this historical moment: "Had Carthage not been Rome's bitter enemy, Rome would never have become the powerful mistress of the world. The harsher the ill fortune, the greater the favourable fortune in the end . . ." (quoted in Jardine and Grafton: 1990: 61, 62). It is well known that Elizabethans wrote and read histories, especially histories of Rome, precisely as a source of ethical and political lessons. In his history of Rome William Fulbecke, for example, reduces the causes of the fall of Rome solely to ambition, and further to a homely moral for Englishmen, who may avoid Rome's fate through "humble estimation of ourselves, by living well, not by lurking well" (1601: sig. A2).

Nothing could be farther from Shakespeare's approach to the Romans. The public theatre, because of its relative novelty as a cultural institution and its heterogeneous audience, was "a radically different discursive field" from humanistic scholarship or historiography (Rackin 1990: 21). As Karen Newman astutely remarks, "Drama stands in a liminal position, neither fully a part of the printed textual world of the elite nor wholly popular" (1991: 31). It had no established canon like the one on which the Latin curriculum was founded; playwrights found material for plays from every conceivable source, constantly experimenting and crossing such generic boundaries as there were. Roman history and legend competed, for example, with Italian novellas, medieval romances, English histories (and often combined with them in the same play) as matter for the stage; in the theatre Rome didn't command the priority it enjoyed elsewhere. Both the anonymous *Caesar's Revenge* (printed 1607) and Thomas Lodge's *Wounds* owe as much in structure and convention to the revenge play and the *de casibus* tragedy as they do to Roman history. And though many in the audience must have recognized and appreciated the quotations, allusions, appropriations and parodies of specific Latin authors that might pop up in any play, many more knew little or no Latin and were acquainted with Roman history only in a rudimentary way, as I shall argue below, through a select group of famed "noble Romans."

The public theatre, both as an art form and as a social milieu, allowed Shakespeare wide latitude in refashioning Romanness. As many scholars have shown, "The place of the stage was a marginal one" in that it was positioned betwixt and between established cultural categories and jurisdictions (Mullaney 1988: 9). Its physical location (outside the city walls, licensed by the court, yet often considered a threat to civic order) and social authorization (players were organized as joint stock companies for profit, but were also affiliated with royal or aristocratic households) made it anomalous. By constantly changing roles, the player – a beggar in one play, a prince in the next – mirrored the contradictions of a society obsessed with distinctions of rank while subject to unprecedented social mobility (Montrose 1980: 56–7 *et passim*). For the audience as well, "to go to the theatre was, in short, to be positioned at the crossroads of cultural change and contradiction," where "one's money, not one's blood or title" conferred on commoners a license to judge the doings of kings (Howard 1988: 440; Kastan 1986).

By comparing the sources on which Shakespeare drew for his English history plays with those he used for the Roman works, we can further appreciate the path he took in creating Rome for English audiences. The major Roman historians weren't translated into English until the last decade of the sixteenth century.[17] Thus nothing remotely comparable to the English chronicle histories, which began with the founding of Britain and ended with the founding of the Tudor dynasty, nothing that authoritatively covered the entire sweep of Roman history from Aeneas through the late empire, was available to Shakespeare. Accounts of Roman history in English were cursory as well as incomplete (Richard Reynoldes's imperial chronicle, 1571; William Fulbecke's history of the late republic, 1601). In their emphasis on the horrors and miseries of civil war and the benefits of the Augustan peace, they obscured divergent accounts and interpretations, and bore a general resemblance to the providential moralizing of Holinshed. It is just as well, perhaps, that Shakespeare doesn't seem to have used them.

Plutarch, however, offered him no coherent account or even a vague idea of the course of Roman history. Because the biographer's readers were living under Roman rule, he could assume they knew about the institutions, mores, political issues and events of Roman history, and plunge into the circumstantial details of each life without

9

any explicit contextualization. As important as Plutarch is to Shakespeare's Roman works, though, his role has been overemphasized. He supplied Shakespeare with three out of five narratives, for *Julius Caesar, Antony and Cleopatra,* and *Coriolanus.* For *Lucrece* the dramatist was indebted to Ovid and Livy, and for *Titus Andronicus,* to many influences but no single narrative source. While he wrote the English history plays in two tetralogies, linking the plays in each tetralogy chronologically and thematically, only *Julius Caesar* and *Antony and Cleopatra* fit into a historical sequence, and each stands on its own to a much greater extent than do the individual English history plays. Furthermore, the order of composition of the Roman works, unlike that of the English history plays, follows no chronological sequence.[18]

In making plays out of Roman history and legend, then, in one sense Shakespeare was much more on his own than he was with regard to English history. Furthermore, rather than breaking Roman materials down into the "small and manageable ethico-historical vignettes" beloved to readers of history (Hunter 1977: 101), he put together coherent playworlds from highly anecdotal and digressive Plutarchan narratives or, in the case of *Titus,* from even more disparate materials. Only the story of Lucrece came to him in tersely unified form, and that he made into a poem instead of a play. He approached the venerable figures of Roman history in the opportunistic spirit of a playwright, a cultural entrepreneur hoping to make a profitable entertainment from authors treated more reverently outside the theatre than within it.

When he began writing about Rome in the early 1590s, a tradition of plays drawing on Roman history and legend was already well established. Because of the unsystematic, fragmentary records of dramas written and performed, and because many plays were "minglemangles" of several genres and settings, it is hard to define the category "Roman play" consistently or determine with any certainty exactly how many such plays were written, published, or acted. In the several lists attempted by scholars, totals differ according to the time-span charted, the playing venues included (public theatres, academic dramas, closet dramas), the generic category (Roman plays are classified both as histories and as tragedies, and romances may have Roman characters and settings), and whether only extant plays are included or Roman-sounding titles of lost plays as well.[19] Clifford Ronan, author of the most recent and comprehensive study of Roman plays in English Renaissance drama, lists forty-three extant vernacular

Roman plays 1585–1635, including academic and closet drama (Ronan 1995: 2, 165–9). Such leading writers and dramatists as Marlowe, Lodge, Kyd, Middleton, Munday, Heywood, Massinger, Jonson, Webster, Chapman, and Fletcher wrote Roman plays for the public theatre. While the English history play can be called "largely Shakespeare's creation" (Rackin 1990: 31), the Roman play was not.

Just how much specificity and consistency can be claimed for this genre? Like other dramatic genres in this period, it can be quite elastic. Among Ronan's forty-three Roman plays we find, for example, Massinger's *Believe As You List* (1631), the "largely fictitious story of Seleucid king Antiochus the Great, persecuted by a Republican Roman ambassador," and Fletcher's *Bonduca* (1613), a "fairly historical account of Britons Caratacus, Boadicea, and her family – until he is sent to Rome to grace Claudius's triumph" (Ronan 1995: 165). Such plays bear little resemblance to Shakespeare's Roman plays, unless *Cymbeline* is our benchmark. Yet as I have already noted, blatantly comic English characters intrude into plays that otherwise treat large chunks of Roman history with high seriousness. For my purpose of situating Shakespeare's Roman works within the twin contexts of Renaissance humanism and the public theatre, however, I would define Roman plays as those whose plots and characters are based on Roman history and legend (thus including Dido and Aeneas) and set in Rome. Between 1564, when Shakespeare was born and one R. B.'s *Apius and Virginia* was performed, and 1642 when the public theatres closed, thirty-one plays titled after their Roman protagonists were written for and/or performed in the public theatre.[20] Caesar, Pompey, Dido, Aeneas, Sulla, Fabius, Scipio: this invocation of famous, resonant personages reveals, I think, an important continuity between the representation of Rome in humanistic studies and in the public theatre – and a crucial difference. I see Shakespeare's focus on Roman virtue in terms of both the continuity and the difference.

As Timothy Hampton explains, "The promotion of ancient images of virtue as patterns that aim to form or guide readers is a central feature of almost every major text in the Renaissance. . . . The heroic or virtuous figure offers a model of excellence, an icon after which the reader is to be formed . . . [who] can be seen as a marked sign that bears the moral and historical authority of antiquity" (1990: i, xi, 5). Such exemplars (mostly male) are meant to be imitated, in somewhat the same way as the humanist pedagogue was supposed to be a model – of Latinity, civility, virtue – for his students to emulate (Halpern 1991: 29). Richard Halpern interprets this kind of "mimetic

11

education" as "a set of practices that places the subject in an imaginary relation with a governing model," producing the ideological effect that Althusser calls interpellation, "wherein the subject comes both to recognize himself within and to depend upon a dominant specular image" (Halpern 1991: 29). No textual representation could ever command the interpellating power that the schoolmaster or scholar possessed through frequent if not daily interaction with his pupils. But schoolmasters and scholars actively promoted exemplars and their images were widely disseminated in humanistic culture as models of virtue.

Gabriel Harvey has left a fascinating record of how men of his educated class might emulate Roman models. Among the copious marginalia in his folio edition of Livy's history of Rome he wrote an account of a debate inspired by a deeply engaged reading of Livy, held at the estate of Sir Thomas Smith sometime in 1570–1. Two gentlemen took the side of Marcellus, two the side of Fabius Maximus, before an audience; Fabius seems to have won. But in Harvey's view,

> Both of them [were] worthy men, and judicious. Marcellus the more powerful; Fabius the more cunning. Neither was the latter unprepared [weak], nor the former imprudent: each as indispensible [*sic*] as the other in his place. There are times when I would rather be Marcellus, times when Fabius.
> (Quoted in Jardine and Grafton 1990: 40)

Harvey moves from reporting the debate, to taking his own position in it, to identifying himself with the objects of it: he would "be," imaginatively, Marcellus or Fabius. Jardine and Grafton argue that Harvey and his circle "persistently envisage action as the *outcome* of reading – not simply reading as active, but reading as trigger for action" (40). Elsewhere Harvey comments that a certain decade of Livy "should be studied by the best actors," meaning men of action, but the other meaning of the word also comes into play (quoted in Jardine and Grafton 1990: 38). As an opponent of Elizabeth's antiwar policy, like Sidney he hoped for military action in the field, but had to content himself instead with impersonations in debates or imaginary identification with exemplars through reading. Or he could go to the theatre and perhaps be "ravish'd . . . when Cesar would appeare, / And on the Stage at halfe-sworde parley were, / Brutus and Cassius," as a poet recalls shortly before the close of the theatres in 1642 (Digges, quoted in Ingleby *et al.* 1932: 456).

12

The exemplar's name served as "a single sign which contains folded within it the entire history of the hero's deeds" (Hampton 1990: 25). Not only men of Harvey's social rank and learning, but unlettered common folk could recognize the great exemplars from Roman history. "Julius Caesar" or "Pompey" signalled a puissant conqueror who commanded vast foreign territories and enjoyed universal fame, only to be brought down by a fellow Roman who had once been an ally; "Lucrece" stood for a narrative of rape, revenge, and revolution that culminated in the founding of the republic. When represented on the public stage, these exemplars "moved beyond the control of an elite" (Mullaney, quoted in Howard 1994: 83). No longer models of ideal virtue but rather characters played by actors, they became visibly, materially, vulnerably present as objects of judgment and vehicles for current concerns.

The pageant of the Nine Worthies in *Love's Labor's Lost* illustrates but also satirizes the easy currency of such names. The Nine Worthies, a conventional entertainment performed throughout Europe in the Middle Ages and the Renaissance, consisted simply of speeches by three trios of exemplars – biblical, Greco-Roman, and medieval martial heroes – describing their careers. In Renaissance England it represented a common denominator of high and low cultures, a minimal core of shared knowledge of the ancient world. As performed in *Love's Labor's Lost*, it suggests – in contrast to Harvey's deeply admiring identification with Roman exemplars – the kind of satirical detachment they could provoke, perhaps drawing on class resentment in those who lacked access to humanistic studies. Costard the clown plays Pompey, "surnam'd the Big" – his mistranslation of Pompey's unique cognomen *Magnus* or Great. When Pompey and Hector nearly come to blows, Berowne eggs the Roman hero on by shouting "Greater than great, great, great, great Pompey! Pompey the Huge!" (5.2.675–6), mocking glory and renown by confounding them with physical size.[21]

The heroes of three of Shakespeare's Roman plays are renowned exemplars of Roman history, and the fourth (Titus) is modelled on them; the heroine of his Roman poem, *Lucrece*, is an exemplar of chastity. Plutarch's *Parallel Lives of the Greeks and Romans* was a treasury of exemplars. These figures embodied what we might call an Elizabethan or Jacobean myth of Rome, an ethically orientated sense of *romanitas* well described by G. K. Hunter as "a set of virtues, thought of as characterizing Roman civilization – soldierly, severe, self-controlled, self-disciplined . . . transmitted to the Tudors, as to the

13

rest of Europe, and for century after century, in a series of images of virtue held up as models or secular *mirabilia*" (Hunter 1977: 94).

In making Roman plays, like his follow playwrights Shakespeare draws upon this stock of exemplars, but Rome is the testing ground rather than the backdrop of their virtues. He takes Rome more seriously and sees its heroes more critically than others do.[22] In Heywood or Lodge, exemplars are comparatively simple and pure. The antagonistic rivalries that Shakespeare holds up to critical scrutiny, for instance, are rendered unproblematic in other plays. Chapman clearly sides with Pompey in his *Caesar and Pompey*, as Lodge sides with Marius in his *The Wounds of Civil War*, simplifying the heroes' characters while taking rivalry itself for granted. Shakespeare, in contrast, creates particularized, coherent social worlds for his Romans; no bawdy balladeers or suicidal knaves break their consistency. Skillfully deploying details culled from Livy or Plutarch, he evokes the workings of a republic or an empire, making them intelligible to the subjects of a monarchy. In other Roman plays, ethical or psychological questions arising from the heroes' actions are subsumed into the overarching motif of Rome's fall from greatness understood as the inexorable turn of Fortune's wheel. As Cassius declares of Caesar in the anonymous *Caesar's Revenge*, "Thou placed art in top of fortunes wheele, / Her wheele must turne, thy glory must eclipse" (3.1.1148–9). In Shakespeare, the hero in effect turns that wheel himself. What he does brings about his fate, and his Romanness determines what he does.

Finally, in contradistinction to any of his contemporaries, Shakespeare made the gender-specific dimensions of exemplars dramatically interesting, by exposing them as not merely given characteristics in particular heroes but ideological constructions coterminous with the meaning of Rome itself. Hunter's summary description of the Roman virtues as "soldierly, severe, self-controlled, disciplined" quoted above is, in fact, a complex of traits and behaviours proper to men, making "Roman" virtue almost synonymous with masculinity. (Lucrece and Portia aspire to this virtue only through symbolic enactments of masculinity.) In fact, the very etymology of *virtus* is gender-specific. When in *Coriolanus* Cominius declares, "It is held / That valour is the chiefest virtue and / Most dignifies the haver" (*Coriolanus*, 2.2.83–5), Shakespeare plays on the derivation of virtue from *virtus*, in its turn derived from *vir* – Latin for man. In the fiercely martial Rome of *Coriolanus*, valor is the essence of manliness; in Shakespeare's other Roman works, manly virtue takes more varied forms, inflected, for example, by the role of the *paterfamilias*, or republicanism, or emulous rivalry, or

14

the preservation of female chastity, to name some of the important forces at work.[23] Whatever its specific form, however, *virtus* – Roman virtue – isn't a moral abstraction but rather a marker of sexual difference crucial to construction of the male subject – the Roman hero.

The past decade of feminist theory has demonstrated that "Gender identification, although it always appears coherent and fixed is, in fact, highly unstable," brought about through "processes of differentiation and distinction, requiring the suppression of ambiguities and opposite elements in order to ensure (create the illusion of) coherence and common understanding" (Scott 1988: 38). And the past decade of feminist criticism in the early modern period leads to the conclusion that "Gender is never grounded; there is no master discourse which is called upon to fix the essence of gender" (Jones and Stallybrass 1991: 81).[24] The strongly patriarchal milieu of the Roman works doesn't mean, therefore, that their representations of gender differences are any more clear-cut or unproblematical than in the comedies, histories, or tragedies. Like any discursive construction of gender difference, then, *virtus* proves to be at odds with itself, and its contradictions give these texts their complexity and energy.

In the title of this book, *Warriors, Wounds, and Women*, I have tried to suggest three main foci of Shakespeare's problematic of Roman virtue. To begin with, "warriors" evokes the central motif of the Greco-Roman heroic tradition – the agon, that "zero-sum game" of rivalry through which the hero wins his name by pitting himself against his likeness or equal in contests of courage and strength. From Achilles and Hector to Antony and Octavius, pairs of evenly matched heroes act out a mixture of admiration, imitation, and domination which the English Renaissance calls emulation. The *OED* defines emulation as "to copy or imitate with the object of equalling or excelling." In emulation, the admiration that generates a desire to imitate someone easily turns into rivalry, the desire to excel him, and finally to the desire to defeat or destroy him and take his place.[25] *Virtus* comes into being through emulation, a kind of agonistic rivalry that isn't exclusively martial in form; I will argue, for example, that Brutus and Cassius as political agents are defined by structures of emulation. Shakespeare's Roman heroes strive to prove themselves men not in relation to women, but against a rival whom they emulate in two senses – by imitating as the mirror-image of an ideal self, and by competing against with the aim of excelling and dominating. Emulation figures and enacts the differences *within* the masculine; thus it fractures a seemingly unified *virtus*.

15

Emulation as the imitation of approved Latin authors was integral to Renaissance pedagogy and poetics. Humanism depended on emulation as a mode of interpellating subjects into a governing class of literate men. In *The Boke Named the Governour* (1531), wherever Sir Thomas Elyot mentions the age of the (male) pupil working his way through the standard Latin curriculum, he links his linguistic proficiency to his developing "courage":

> the childes courage, inflamed by the frequent redynge of noble poetes, dayly more and more desireth to have experience in those things that they so vehemently do commende in them they write of.
>
> (Quoted in Ong 1959: 117)

Similarly, in a treatise on education written nearly a century later, John Brinsley urges schoolmasters to "nourish" in their students "that emulation mentioned, to strive who shall do best" (quoted in Halpern 1991: 30). Courtiership was virtually inseparable from forms of emulation, and the Elizabethan and Jacobean courts functioned through emulous faction and rivalry (Whigham 1984; Rebhorn 1990; Mallin 1990). Thus, through ancient fictions of heroes molded through competitive emulation of other heroes, the Roman works touch a cultural nerve and articulate contemporary anxieties about English "manly virtue".

Furthermore, insofar as Shakespeare draws on Plutarch, he is representing, with a difference, the "all-male power structure" of his own society. That society, as Bruce Smith explains, "fostered male bonds above all other emotional ties." In fact,

> For most sixteenth-century readers the very act of reading North's translation of Plutarch was an exercise in homosociality ... Noble men's lives are the *subject* of North's book, in more ways than one. Inspiring his readers to emulate 'the speciall actes of the best persons, of the famosest nations of the world' (1.3) is North's very purpose ...
>
> (Smith 1991: 56–7)

Thus North's readers not only read about emulation but also participated in it. In another, less benign, sense Plutarch's organization and presentation of comparisons – the "parallel lives" of North's title – interpellates his readers into emulation. By pairing Greek with Roman exemplars and then comparing the members of eighteen out of twenty-three pairs, Plutarch implicitly sets up rivalries between Greeks

16

and Romans, setting one against another. Shakespeare echoes this dyadic structure by pairing his Roman heroes with rivals: Tarquin and Collatine, Saturninus and Bassianus, Brutus and Cassius, Coriolanus and Aufidius, Antony and Octavius.

Through "wounds," the second word of the title, I want to suggest the most problematic, self-cancelling figuration of masculinity in the Roman works. The Latin word for wound is *vulnus*, the root of "vulnerability." In an obvious sense, wounds mark a kind of vulnerability easily associated with women: they show the flesh to be penetrable, they show that it can bleed, they make apertures in the body. But through the discursive operations of *virtus*, wounds become central to the signification of masculine virtue, and thus to the construction of the Roman hero. Lucrece's suicidal stab, for example, not only purifies the pollution she suffers through rape; it also authorizes her male kinsmen to rise against the Tarquins and reconfigure the Roman state as a republic. The generic codes of revenge tragedy make Lavinia's visible and invisible wounds into Titus's injury, reconstructing him into a revenge hero with a warrant for murder. In *Julius Caesar*, Caesar's punctured body is the feminized object through which the conspirators try to restore their manly virtue as citizens of the republic. When this effort fails, they have recourse to suicide. Portia's "voluntary wound . . . in the thigh," however, suggests the artificiality of such constructions. When Antony reaches "the very heart of loss" at Actium, his voluntary wound signifies not his defeat at Caesar's hands, but rather his conquest over Caesar. In *Coriolanus*, the pure, overt equation of the hero's many gashes with valor as "the chiefest virtue" leads to Shakespeare's most searching critique of gender construction in the Roman state. Wounds aren't equally prominent in all these texts. But they are a central, recurring image that invariably signifies instabilities underlying the apparent firmness of Roman virtue, instabilities that involve constructions of the feminine as well. As Joan Wallach Scott explains, "The principle of masculinity rests on the necessary repression of feminine aspects – of the subject's potential for bisexuality – and introduces conflict into the opposition of masculine and feminine" (Scott 1988: 38).

More precisely, the wound works like a fetish of masculinity, in several respects. The word fetish is derived from the Portuguese *feticheria*, a term used by European traders for a material object "worn about the body which itself embodied an actual power," and which could be used to obtain a concrete effect, in the African societies they encountered. *Feticheria*, in turn, derives from the Latin *facticius*,

17

meaning man-made, unnatural, and thus specious in contrast to the God-given, natural or "true" objects of Christian worship (Pietz 1987: 36, 25–6). In critical discourse, the concept of the fetish makes it possible to identify "the artifice present in virtually all forms of cultural representation" (Apter and Pietz 1993: 2–3) – especially in representations of sexual difference.

In feminist critiques or appropriations of Freudian theory, the fetish has become "a knife that cuts both ways" (Jacobus 1986: 111): Freud conceived it within the oedipal scenario that establishes gender difference, but feminist theory appropriates it to deconstruct that scenario.[26] According to Freud, the fetish is created in response to the boy's first sight of the female genitals, upon which he "sees nothing or disowns what he has seen, he softens it down or looks about for expedients for bringing it into line with his expectations." Later, "when some threat of castration has obtained a hold on him," he interprets the female's lack of a penis as castration and constructs the fetish as a compromise formation to defend against that anxiety (1925: 252):

> He retains this belief [that she is castrated, and that he could be too] but he also gives it up; during the conflict between the dead weight of the unwelcome perception and the force of the opposite wish [that the mother have a penis, thus refuting castration], a compromise is constructed . . . the woman still has a penis in spite of all, but this penis is no longer the same . . . Something else has taken its place . . . the fetish itself has become the vehicle both of denying and of asseverating the fact [sic] of castration.
>
> (Freud 1927: 154)

Thus the fetish constitutes "the mark at once of sexual difference and of indecideability: the 'site' where something (the feminine) is hidden by what comes to stand for it" (Jacobus 1986: 136). In the Roman works, the wound attests to a (feminine) vulnerability but at the same time, serves as a cultural marker of manly virtue; like a fetish, it both declares and disavows the feminine. The kind of manly virtue that it signifies is socially determined, by various ideologies and institutions (the family, the military state, the republic, the empire) that have the power to naturalize it. Poised, as it were, between "warriors" (men locked in agonistic structures of rivalry), and "women," the wound in these texts is always a site of anxiety and indeterminacy; a point at which it is possible to identify an ideology of gender difference in process.

That ideology is built on the binary oppositions of male to female, public to private, *forum* to *domus*. "Women," the third element in Shakespeare's problematic of manly virtue, though subordinated and inferiorized by this opposition, are nonetheless basic to the construction of male subjects as Romans, in several ways. In these texts heroic male subjectivity is, for the most part, configured through the stigmatization or sacrifice of the feminized private realm of emotion, interiority, and dependency. As I will argue, some of Shakespeare's Roman women provide, in effect, an alibi for the heroes with whom they are paired – in that, when impulses inimical to manly virtue are associated with women, such impulses can be disavowed. Or, when woman provides the occasion for a division in the male subject – as Lucrece does for Tarquin, or Cleopatra for Antony, or Volumnia for Coriolanus – that division serves as grounds for tragic conflict and heroic status. But the text can be read, I believe, to reveal this very operation, to show how the feminine refuses its assigned position "outside the masculine, [as] its reassuring canny *opposite*," and stubbornly remains "inside the masculine, its uncanny *difference from itself*" (Felman 1981: 41).

In Shakespeare's Rome, women are "symbolically central, though socially peripheral" (Babcock 1978: 32). Their centrality lies in their sexuality; specifically, in their wombs. Through the national cult of Vesta, Rome sacralized virgin chastity and identified it with the very continuity of the state. Lucrece and Lavinia are both conceived within this Vesta principle; they hold Rome's future within their wombs. Lucrece articulates that principle as the basis of her identity but also sacrifices herself to preserve it for the sake of the patriarchal order. Lavinia, deprived of speech, enacts a more unsettling tension between the erasure of the female subject and its distorted self-representation. Finally, in his most unsparing critique of manly virtue, Shakespeare shows in Volumnia the awesome power of the mother, once she is complicit with the ideology of *virtus*, to mold her son into a sword.

Kathleen McLuskie has argued persuasively for a feminist criticism that "[makes] a text reveal the conditions in which a particular ideology of femininity functions" (1985: 106). In this book I have tried to do the same for a particular ideology of masculinity – *virtus*, the manly virtue of Rome. Among the many "conditions" that made manly virtue interesting to Shakespeare, his audience, and his readers, I emphasize the Roman cultural legacy that formed the core of Renaissance humanism, and through humanistic education interpellated the governing classes of Tudor and Stuart England. Their

19

conception of Rome as the matrix of civility informed Shakespeare's world. Through exemplars such as the noble Romans whom Shakespeare took as his heroes, humanism made Romanness as manly virtue a widely known ideal of masculinity. When Shakespeare "translated" that ideal to the public theatre, he opened it up for critical scrutiny by a socially diverse audience that had long been encouraged to consider Rome as a mirror of England.

In the following pages, I take account of humanism whenever I deal with the many competing subtexts from Latin literature, history, myth, and legend that find their way into Shakespeare. What used to be conceived as "source study," determined by assumptions about the author's intention and focused on Plutarch, has now become a more sophisticated sense of Shakespeare's diverse options for appropriating other texts.[27] In particular, feminist critics have begun to problematize source study, questioning the assumed objectivity of the scholarship that identifies sources, and discovering elements of gender bias in Shakespeare's choice and treatment of his sources. For example, Stephanie Jed (1989) identifies as "chaste thinking" the similar logic by which humanist scholars prepared classical texts for publication and appropriated the legend of Lucrece. In both operations, she argues, they legitimized sexual violence: in their criteria for textual authenticity and purity, and as a condition for republican laws and institutions. Patricia Klindienst Joplin locates in the myth of Philomel social structures that establish sexual difference and hierarchy through violence against women, and textual operations that efface women's collective resistance and individual agency. In weaving the tapestry that narrates her rape and mutilation, says Joplin, Philomel speaks with "the voice of the shuttle," to avenge the injuries done to her (1984).

With specific regard to Shakespeare, Jane O. Newman urges us to question "how [he] read his sources" – such as the story of Philomel, which figures in both *Lucrece* and *Titus Andronicus* – "and how he intervened in the ideology inscribed in them." By challenging (in much the same way as Jed) the supposed disinterestedness of both Shakespeare's appropriation of Latin texts and of source study by Shakespeare scholars, Newman finds (as did Joplin) "an ideology of gender that represses . . . alternate forms of women's political agency not complicit in the reproduction of patriarchy" (1994: 307, 308). Whether Shakespeare questions, ignores, or confirms this or other ideologies of gender in his Roman sources is a complex question: the answers differ from text to text and within each text. Here I have tried to open up this question by problematizing both the Roman fictions on which he drew, and the fictions of *virtus* that he made.

NOTES

1 I am drawing on Louis Althusser's conception of ideology in "Ideology and Ideological State Apparatuses" (1971). For an explication of gender conceived as ideology, see Greene and Kahn (1985: 2–5). For a succinct restatement of Althusserian ideology, summation of critiques, and application of it to the ideological work performed by the theatre in English Renaissance culture, see Howard (1994). She emphasizes that "no subject ever occupies only one subject position [within ideology], but rather is entangled in a network of competing and contestatory ideologies" (81).

2 Here I alter Gayle Rubin's notion of a "sex-gender system" as "the set of arrangements by which a society transforms biological sexuality into products of human activity, and in which these transformed sexual needs are satisfied" (1975: 158) in agreement with Judith Butler's critique of Rubin. Butler argues that "Rubin's essay remains committed to a distinction between sex and gender which assumes the discrete and prior ontological reality of a 'sex' which is done over in the name of the law, that is, transformed subsequently into 'gender'" (1990: 74).

3 MacCallum, however, included in this sub-genre only the three plays based on Plutarch: *Julius Caesar*, *Antony and Cleopatra*, and *Coriolanus*. Accordion-like, it has been subsequently compressed and expanded, reaching its firmest generic definition in Miola (1983). Charney (1961), Traversi (1963), and Simmons (1973) followed MacCallum in excluding *Titus Andronicus* and *Lucrece*, Charney on the grounds that what makes Roman plays Roman is the use of Roman stage costume on the Elizabethan stage, praise of suicide, and a common source in North's Plutarch (Charney 1961: 207). Simmons conceives the three plays as sharing a common setting in the pagan world "as seen in the light of Christian historiography . . . with no reference beyond the Earthly City" (7, 8). Cantor (1976) discusses only *Coriolanus* and *Antony and Cleopatra*, contrasting them as representations of the republic and the empire. Similarly taking conceptions of the state as an organizing principle, Phillips (1940) compares the three Plutarchan plays to *Troilus and Cressida* and *Timon of Athens* as based on Greek ideas of the *polis*. Platt (1983) includes *Lucrece* along with the three Plutarchan plays but omits *Titus*, and views them as a sequence running from the founding of the republic in *Lucrece* to the inception of empire in *Antony*. Thomas (1989) includes *Titus* with the Plutarchan plays, focusing on "the sense of a social universe" conveyed in the group: "the values, attitudes, aspirations, and idiosyncrasies of the different Romes" portrayed (1). Siegel (1986) and Leggatt (1988) both group the English history plays with the Roman plays. Like Platt, Siegel conceives them as a sequence representing "the rise, decline, and slide to collapse" of Rome (100). Leggatt considers the two kinds of drama as "political plays," in terms of "the ordering and enforcing, the gaining and losing, of public power in the state" (ix). Brower (1971) and Knight (1931)

place the Roman plays under even broader headings. Brower sees them in the light of "the Greco-Roman heroic tradition" of Homer and Virgil that also influences Shakespeare's tragedies, while Knight groups them with *Hamlet* and *Macbeth* in what is primarily a study of Shakespearean tragedy. Miola (1983) is the first to treat as a group all four Roman plays along with *Lucrece*, including *Cymbeline* as well. He takes "an organic approach," seeing the plays as connected by a "network of images, ideas, gestures, and scenes," and by the ideals of "constancy, honor, and *pietas*" (16, 17). Articles by Spencer (1957) and Velz (1978) discuss criteria for considering them as a group. The bibliography by Velz (1968a) is essential, and amply supplemented by more recent bibliography in Ronan (1995). In a perceptive chapter on the three Plutarchan plays, Paster (1985) concurs with Velz's view that "To Shakespeare Rome is above all *urbs* in its etymological sense" (11), commenting that "Shakespeare is particularly drawn to those moments in the Roman past which brought the internal order of the city to a point of critical change, when one kind of city was giving way to another" (58).

4 On *Lucrece*, see Kahn (1976) and Vickers (1985, 1986). On *Titus*, see Green (1989). On *Julius Caesar*, see Paster (1993). On *Antony and Cleopatra*, see Fitz (1977); Erickson (1985); Neely (1985); Sprengnether (1989). On *Coriolanus*, see Adelman (1980, 1992); Kahn (1981); Sprengnether (1986). Ronan comments, "'Roman' meant 'man' to the superlative degree: stereotypically masculine man the ruler, the killer, the Stoic, the builder, the wielder of words," but doesn't develop this insight or employ gender as a category of analysis in his study of Roman plays (1995: 41).

5 See Miola's useful survey of the diverse forms in which Roman history and literature circulated in early modern England; he doesn't consider, however, popular as well as elite discourses of Rome.

6 The question of Shakespeare's "accuracy" has now been superseded by the question of how his conception of Rome differed from any prevailing notions of it in Tudor–Stuart culture. Disagreements arise between those who locate Tudor–Stuart conceptions of Rome in different textual sources. Spencer stresses the extent to which Elizabethans deplored the civil strife of the republican era, and sought in the empire lessons for the princes of their own time, thus creating "Elizabethan Romans." Arguing that Shakespeare went against the prevailing tendency in taking Plutarch – most of whose Romans were republicans – as a source, he regards *Titus*, set in the late empire, with its violence, bloodshed, and mixed political institutions, as "a more characteristic piece of Roman history" for its time than the Plutarchan plays (1957: 32). He doesn't compare it, however, to other Roman plays by Shakespeare's contemporaries. Hunter links dramatic representation of Rome to the lack of translations of those Roman historians who would have conveyed the full sweep of Rome's history (Tacitus and Livy weren't translated until, respectively, 1591 and 1600). Thus he holds that "The animation of *Romanitas* in the theatre remained obstinately fixed on the ethical models that the Republic provided" (1977: 102). Ronan disagrees, arguing that no such predominance of republic over empire existed (1995: 172–3). Miles (1989) believes "Shakespeare's distinctive interest in the inner life of his

characters" to be at odds with Plutarch's essentially Roman conception of character as expressed and defined by public action (279), but slights the degree to which Renaissance notions of place and reputation also constructed individuals through public action.

7 For a superb interpretation of clocks in *Julius Caesar* as signifying that Brutus has "failed to "take account of the time and the temper of the people," and thus "is guilty of an anachronism," see Burckhardt (1968: 9). For helpful distinctions between involuntary, pro forma, and intentional anachronisms, and an interesting discussion of how the latter can make "a drama bear on pressing contemporary issues," see Ronan (1995: 11–35). For the argument that Shakespeare uses "double-edged" anachronism in the English history plays to create both alienation from and identification with the past, see Rackin (1990: 94).

8 For some Tudor chroniclers, the question of Brute and the origin of Britain was bound up with a desire to imagine the nation as virile and to repress mythic associations of Britain with aggressive women. Camden ultimately allows the Brute legend to stand, even though he believes that Geoffrey of Monmouth merely "produced" (invented) it, because "it is manhood only, that ennobleth a nation" and "such originals as these, fetched from the gods, [are] profitable; that valorous men may believe, although untimely, that they are descended from the gods" (1610: 7, 9). Both Camden and Grafton are at great pains to deny an alternate myth explaining the name and origin of Britain that traces them not to valorous men but to murderous women, the thirty-two daughters of Diocletian, king of Syria, who all slew their husbands on the same night. To punish them, their father turned them out to sea; they arrived in England and called it Albion after the eldest sister, Albina. They then cohabited with devils and gave birth to giants and monsters, the first natives of Britain. Grafton denounces this story as "fabulous and foolishe," then cites another version of it in Thomas Cooper's *Dictionarium Linguae Latinae* (1565) and denounces that. See Mikalachki (1995) for an interesting discussion of the savage queens in early British historiography that disrupt the linkage of Britishness with manliness.

9 In *Richard III*, Shakespeare problematizes the validity of this legend when young Prince Edward asks, with regard to the Tower, "Did Julius Caesar build that place?" followed by further queries: "Is it upon record, or else reported / Successively from age to age, he built it?" (3.1.69–78). See Rackin (1990: 12–16) on the emergent desire of sixteenth-century historians to check written records, physical relics, and oral tradition against each other in a new effort to ascertain historical "truth".

10 Greece, in comparison, was far less known to Renaissance Englishmen than was Rome, and no legends connected it to the founding or history of Britain. Translations of Greek writers lagged far behind those of Latin ones: no translations of Aeschylus existed, probably none of Sophocles, only one of Aristophanes and of Euripides. Only the first two books of Herodotus and a few doubtful and minor works of Plato were translated, in contrast to a fair number of Aristotle's works (Palmer 1911). Greek grammar was taught beginning in the fifth form of grammar school, but the curriculum remained centered on Latin authors.

11 Obviously, even within the milieu of the popular stage, representations and perceptions of Rome varied greatly from play to play. Critical opinion as to Shakespeare's sense of its cultural proximity also differs. Compare, for example, MacCallum's judgment that "Shakespeare . . . does not give the notes that mark off Rome from every other civilization, but rather those that it possessed in common with the rest, and especially with his own" (1910: 84–5) to that of Charles and Michelle Martindale: in Shakespeare, "Roman society is seen as 'other,' an object of contemplation more than direct involvement" (1990: 144).

12 See especially Adelman on *Antony and Cleopatra*: "In this play, Shakespeare exploits the conflicts of opinion which are built into the traditional accounts of the lovers . . . [He] can count on the audience to know the story and the traditional interpretations of it; and the conflict of interpretation that the audience brings to the theater becomes part of the play" (1973: 53). Similarly, with regard to the ambiguity of the title character in *Julius Caesar*, Schanzer remarks, "Shakespeare seems to me to be playing on his audience's varied and divided views of Caesar, encouraging and discouraging in turn each man's preoccupations" (1963: 33).

13 This and all subsequent quotations are taken from *The Merry Wives of Windsor*, ed. H. J. Oliver (London: Methuen, 1971).

14 On this issue, see Joan Kelly's groundbreaking essay, "Did Women Have a Renaissance?" (1977, rpt. 1984); Grafton and Jardine (1986: 29–57); Ong (1959); Halpern (1991: 27); Ferguson *et al.* (1986a: xvi–xxxvi).

15 Ong quotes Sir Thomas Elyot advising that boys "be taken from the company of women" at the age of seven, the age at which they entered grammar school, and comments: "In cultivating the young boy's ability to speak Latin, women, not being part of the Latin world, were commonly of no use to a child after the age of seven . . . if there were too many women around, the child would speak English, not Latin. He would slip back into the vernacular family circle instead of being forced out already at this tender age into the world of the 'tribe,' of men" (Ong 1959: 110).

16 The text of the play is preceded by *Loquendi formulae*, selected phrases suitable for conversation, translated into English, followed by *Applicatio seu imitatio Grammatica*, the same phrases grammatically reworked, with changes of noun, verb, etc.

17 Livy's history of the founding of Rome through the republic was represented only in Antony Cope's account of Hannibal and Scipio (1544) until Philemon Holland's complete translation, which appeared in 1600. Appian's history, which focuses on military campaigns and goes up to the reign of Augustus, came out in English in 1578. Translations of imperial history came even later: four books of Tacitus by Henry Savile in 1591; the complete Suetonius, by Philemon Holland, in 1606.

18 For the compositional order of the Roman works, I follow the dating given by Bevington (1992), as follows: *Lucrece*, 1593–4; *Titus*, 1589–92; *Julius Caesar*, 1599; *Antony and Cleopatra*, 1606–7; *Coriolanus*, 1608. The dating proposed by Wells and Taylor (1987) differs with regard to two plays. They place *Titus* in mid-1592 (but find "the only feasible alternative" to be 1590 or before), and *Antony and Cleopatra* in 1606. It isn't

24

possible to ascertain whether *Lucrece* or *Titus* was written first: both are
listed in the Stationers' Register in 1594. In terms of historical time,
Lucrece is set at the end of the monarchy and the inception of the republic,
in 509 BC; *Titus* around the fourth century AD, in the late empire; *Julius
Caesar* covers events from 45 to 42 BC; *Antony and Cleopatra*, from 40 to
30 BC; the setting of *Coriolanus* reverts in time to the early republic,
494–491 BC.

19   Lists of Roman plays vary as follows: 1566–1635, thirty-nine extant out
of "more than fifty recorded" (Martindale 1990: 130); 1564–1611, forty-
one plays, twenty extant (Hunter 1977: 118). Cf. the several tabulations,
especially the exhaustive "Annals of English Roman Plays, 1100–1700,"
in Ronan (1995: 180–5).

20   This total is based on the plays listed in Harbage (1989); in addition, six
closet dramas based on Roman history were written during this period.

21   Compare a similar joke in *Measure for Measure*, when Pompey the bawd
gives his surname as "Bum," and Escalus exclaims, "Troth, and your
bum is greatest thing about you; so that, in the beastliest sense, you
are Pompey the Great" (2.1.214–16). Again, as in Mistress Quickly's
mistranslations, something venerable in Latin is travestied by association
with what Bakhtin calls "the lower bodily stratum."

22   It is a critical truism that Jonson also took Rome seriously, signalling his
knowledge of Latin texts and Roman history in nearly every line of his
two Roman plays *Sejanus* (1603) and *Catiline* (1611). Katharine Maus
(1984) describes Jonson's orientation toward his Latin models in a way
that clearly indicates the key differences between him and Shakespeare.
Jonson, she holds, favors and emulates "a select group": Seneca, Horace,
Tacitus, Cicero, Juvenal, and Quintilian (3) who endorse the "austere"
virtues of "Temperance, self-reliance, fortitude, altruistic self-sacrifice" (5).
No such ethical agenda underlies Shakespeare's eclectic appropriation of
Ovid, Plutarch, and Livy. Commenting on the "stubborn fixedness, a
refusal to change or grow" in Jonson's historical characters, Jonas Barish
suggests another revealing difference between the two playwrights' treatment of Rome: "Jonson aims at exemplary characters, from whom audiences may take their own moral bearings" (1965: 9), while Shakespeare,
I maintain, strikes a critical and ironic stance toward exemplars that
precludes audiences from taking them as models for conduct. See
Goldberg (1983) for an interesting treatment of "a particular kind of
hero" in Jonson's Roman plays who mirrors James's style of absolutism.

23   Thomas Cooper's *Thesaurus Linguae Romanae et Britannicae* (1565), the
standard Latin dictionary used in schools and homes until 1595, lists as
its first definition of *vir*, "A man: a valiaunte man of good courage: an
husbande," and defines the adjectival form *virilis* as "Of a man: manly:
valiaunt: stoute." Among the numerous phrases from Latin authors using
vir that he lists, references to valor predominate, suggesting that the association of Romanness with masculinity and military action was a strong
one.

24   The "one-sex model" of gender as teleologically male proposed by
Laqueur (1990) assumes that medicine is just such a "master discourse."
Such assumptions are challenged, implicitly or explicitly, by several recent

studies exploring the fragility and fluidity of binary gender differences in early modern culture. On the fluidity of gender difference in seventeenth-century Quakerism and other radical sects, see Mack (1992); on anti-theatrical treatises and witchcraft as barometers of male anxiety about feminization, see Levine (1994); on fantasies of the maternal body, especially in medical discourse, as both origin of and threat to male identity, see Adelman (1992); on construction of gendered bodies and selves within humoral discourse, see Paster (1993).

25 Rebhorn brings out the ambivalence integral to emulation:

> This concept really contains two motives that, in pure form, are totally in opposition to one another. In Renaissance rhetorical and educational theory, emulation is classified as a form of imitation, an identification with one's model at the same time that one attempts to surpass it . . . on the one hand, then, emulation means *identification* with another person, a model, or an ideal; it can indicate a form of brotherhood or comradeship or even love. On the other hand, it simultaneously means *rivalry*; it is a competitive urge that necessarily involves struggle, but which can also, when taken to an extreme, entail feelings of hatred and envy or jealousy which that adjective might suggest. (1990: 77)

26 Schor states, "What is pertinent to women in fetishism is the paradigm of undecideability that it offers," in which fetishism isn't perversion but rather a "strategy designed to turn the so-called 'riddle of femininity' to women's account" (1986: 369). Bernheimer calls Freud's castration theory itself a fetish, in that "The fetishist embraces castration as a defense against what he finds still more 'uncanny and intolerable' – that is, woman's otherness, her specific difference. It is this difference that his fetish at once obscures and reveals, not the 'fact' of female mutilation" (1993: 81). Garber argues that in the fetish, the anatomical penis "becomes re-literalized as a stage prop, a detachable object," and cites the codpiece as an example of such "artifactuality" (1990: 47, 53).

27 Miola describes a new conception of the source as "an intermediate text (i.e., a tradition) that manifests its presence in verbal or stylistic echo or adaptation . . . allowing for a wide range of possible interactions between sources, intermediaries, and texts . . . deep source, resource, influence, confluence, tradition, heritage, origin, antecedent, precursor, background, milieu, subtext, context, intertext, affinity, and analogue" (1990: 49).

2

THE SEXUAL POLITICS OF SUBJECTIVITY IN *LUCRECE*

Representation of the world, like the world itself, is the work of men; they describe it from their own point of view, which they confuse with the absolute truth.

Simone de Beauvoir, The Second Sex

[T]he feminine . . . is not *outside* the masculine, its reassuring canny *opposite*, it is *inside* the masculine, its uncanny difference from itself.

Shoshana Felman, "Re-reading Femininity"

The story of Lucrece, celebrated by Livy, Ovid, Chaucer, and Shakespeare, is one of the founding myths of patriarchy. Like so many of those myths. it entails the heroine's death, in this case accomplished by her own hand. While suicide marks Lucrece's exit from the story, though, it does not constitute narrative closure; that is accomplished with the expulsion of the Tarquins (the royal dynasty, to which the heroine's assailant belongs) from Rome, the abolition of the monarchy, and the inauguration of the Roman republic. Rape authorizes revenge; revenge comprises revolution; revolution establishes legitimate government. In Lucrece's story, the personal is surely the political. Shakespeare's version of it is by far the longest, most fully dramatized one, in which the motives of Tarquin and the responses of Lucrece are given ampler representation and are subjected to keen moral scrutiny through richly elaborated language.

In this chapter, I want to consider the representation of male and female subjectivities within a feminist problematic of rape, by looking closely at the language of power and the power of language with regard to the poem's two main characters, Lucrece and Tarquin. Lucrece is notorious for her loquacity; while in comparison to Tarquin she says little before the rape, Shakespeare virtually turns the poem over to her after it. In copious lament, in apostrophe, sententiae, and ekphrasis, she explores the meaning of what has happened to her and her feelings about it. Yet, as I have argued elsewhere, Lucrece sees herself as a "patterne," a paradigm for all ages of the meaning of female chastity in a patriarchy (Kahn 1976: 45–72). Given the stridently patriarchal ideology in which the character is coded, then, it is supremely pertinent to ask the question Mary Jacobus asks: "Is there a woman in this text?" (1982: 117–41). Or, to paraphrase similar questions asked by Jonathan Goldberg about "the Shakespearean text," who or what speaks in the character we call Lucrece (1985: 116–37)?

Does Lucrece as a female subject nonetheless speak like a man, for men and the world they control? Or does she voice a contending point of view not strictly framed by the dominant discourse? In her searching analysis of the play's language, Nancy J. Vickers treats Lucrece as the voiceless creation of a rhetorical tradition through which the male gaze verbalizes itself, a tradition shaped by and shaping the linguistic and political rivalry of men, as exemplified in the blazon. She deals with that part of the poem, however, in which Lucrece is simply an object of description, before Tarquin enters her chamber, and not at all with the language Shakespeare gives the character herself (1985: 95–115).[1]

Before feminist criticism developed, for the most part readers avoided confronting the rape directly. They were also made uneasy by the poem's rhetorical luxuriance, particularly by the rhetoric accorded to Lucrece. This comment by F. T. Prince, the Arden editor of Shakespeare's poems, is representative: "Not only is she a less *interesting* character than Tarquin; she is forced to express herself in a way which dissipates the real pathos of her situation . . . After her violation. Lucrece loses our sympathy exactly in proportion as she gives *tongue* (emphasis mine)" (Prince 1969: xxxvi). Prince's phrase links Lucrece's speech with a physical organ and makes it sound unseemly (even faintly obscene) for her to use that organ to speak about her violation. That violation, of course, also brought into prominence physical organs about which it was unseemly to speak; to be raped and to speak about it are thus similarly indecorous, alluding to matters about which women in particular ought to be silent. In giving Lucrece a tongue, Shakespeare perforce works *against* the patriarchal codes that, at the same time, he puts into her mouth. The text of *Lucrece* is a site of struggle between Tarquin and Lucrece, between lust and chastity, between male force and female resistance. The paradigm of all these

28

struggles, however, is the struggle between speech and suppression of speech, a struggle in which Lucrece figures not so much as Tarquin's but as a telltale sign of *his* subjectivity rather than her own.[2]

While I agree with Jonathan Goldberg that "it is not necessarily a sign of power to have a voice, not necessarily a sign of subjection to lose it," I do not consider the speech of Shakespeare's characters removed from social practice and cultural signification, as Goldberg seems to. Shakespeare's text, I believe, is not a "mystic writing pad" from which male and female voices, untouched by constructions of gender outside the text, emerge and into which they also disappear (Goldberg 1985: 130). Rather, the text exists interactively, reciprocally, with the social world in which the poet lived. It is no feminist catchphrase but merely accurate to term that world patriarchal, because it was patrilinear and primogenitural in the means by which it deployed power and maintained degree as the basis of the social order.[3] There as in the Rome of the poem, it is men who rape women and patriarchal constructions of gender and power that enable rape. As one feminist historian remarks of rape in sixteenth-century England, "whether regarded as a crime against property or a crime against the person, rape was a crime by men against women, and the law as an intrinsic and powerful part of the patriarchy operated for men against women" (Bashar 1983: 28–42). Yet the poem fascinates and moves me precisely because Shakespeare, I believe, tries to fashion Lucrece as a subject not totally tuned to the key of Roman chastity and patriarchal marriage and to locate a position in which he as poet might stand apart from those values as well. He fails, but his attempt reveals how narrowly the rhetorical traditions within which he works are bounded by an ideology of gender in which women speak with the voices of men. Despite the "tongue" with which Shakespeare provides her and the understanding with which he represents her, ultimately he inscribes her within the same constructs of power and difference as Tarquin.

HEROIC DISCOURSE AND THE SCOPIC ECONOMY

Falling into two parts, the poem follows a structural pattern common in Shakespeare; in the portion preceding the rape, Tarquin's voice predominates as he struggles between conscience and desire; after the rape, we hear only Lucrece, who in a series of laments moves from grief to grievance and a determination to kill herself. In formal terms,

Lucrece's laments are the counterpart of Tarquin's debates, but the two linguistic occasions place them in radically different positions.[4] Whether figured as a thief stealing another man's treasure, a predator seizing his prey, or a warrior besieging a fortified city, Tarquin is an agonistic competitor and as such, whether his aims are noble or despicable, inscribed within a heroic discourse (which is one reason why critics like Prince find him more "interesting" than Lucrece). Lucrece, identified with the besieged city and not the besieger, takes her traditionally feminine position in the same discourse as victim of and also witness to the pathos and grandeur of its agons. And when she determines to take action herself, even as the victim of a deed that Shakespeare condemns as a crime in terms that clearly subvert its heroics, her action nonetheless remains inscribed within heroic discourse, creating a contradiction at the heart of the poem. By comparing the rhetorical strategies of Tarquin's debate with those of Lucrece's lament, we can realize the extent to which Shakespeare, despite efforts to challenge the patriarchal structures that authorize rape (however much they may also imply disapproval of it), is pulled back into them.

As Vickers so cogently argues, Shakespeare conceives the precipitating causes of the rape – Collatine's boast of his wife's chastity and Tarquin's reaction to her beauty – within the poetic tradition of the blazon, "shaped predominantly by the male imagination for the male imagination . . . in large part, the product of men talking to men about women" (Vickers 1986: 209–22). The term "blazon" means both a poetic description of an object and a heraldic description of a shield; when a woman is blazoned, then, she is incorporated into a certain heroic discourse. And when Lucrece greets Tarquin at Collatium, Shakespeare greatly intensifies this incorporation. Not only does he divide her body into parts in order to praise it, as blazon requires; he also employs heraldic terms to describe the parts as locked in chivalric combat. Virtue and beauty, liveried in the white and red of her complexion, create a "heraldry in Lucrece's face," "a silent war of lilies and roses" that extends over four stanzas (lines 50–77). This contest echoes the contest of description that took place in Tarquin's tent and impelled him to possess Lucrece; it also foreshadows the context that concludes the poem with the expulsion of the Tarquins from Rome by Collatine's party. All these rhetorical moves inscribe Lucrece several times over within the linguistic domain of heroism, as prize of rather than participant in its agons.

They also construct Tarquin as a knowing male viewer for whom seeing means desiring, and Lucrece as the innocent object of his gaze.

30

The insistently visual coding of Lucrece in the first 575 lines as one who is seen but does not see, who is seen but not heard, can hardly be overemphasized. In the Argument, Collatine praises his wife only for her chastity; it is after Tarquin actually sees her that he becomes "inflamed with Lucrece's beauty," and from that moment on, to see her is to want her. In contrast to the possessive, dominating gaze of Tarquin, Lucrece's innocence is figured as a passive, superficial looking:

> . . . she that never cop'd with stranger eyes,
> Could pick no meaning from their parling looks,
> Nor read the subtle shining secrecies
> Writ in the glassy margents of such books . . .
> (Shakespeare 1969a: lines 99–102)

The contrast is intensified when, having secretly entered her chamber, he draws back the bed-curtain and peers at her (lines 365–78), while her eyes "keep themselves enclosed." At this point, Shakespeare proceeds with a conventional blazon. The narrator names, describes, and praises parts of Lucrece's body: her cheek as it rests on her hand, her head, eyes ("canopied in darkness"), hair, and breasts. Finally he summarizes the whole, from Tarquin's point of view:

> What could he see but mightily he noted?
> What did he note but strongly he desired?
> What he beheld, on that he firmly doted,
> And in his will his wilful eye he tired,
> With more than admiration he admired
>   Her azure veins, her alabaster skin,
>   Her coral lips, her snow-white dimpled chin.
> (414–20)

The sleeping Lucrece is both figuratively and literally unconscious of Tarquin's gaze "mightily" taking possession of her. Laura Mulvey's analysis of the male gaze in Hollywood films illuminates a connection between his gaze and his power over her:

> According to the principle of the ruling ideology and the psychical structures that back it up, the male figure cannot bear the burden of sexual objectification . . . Hence the split between spectacle and narrative supports the man's role as the active one of forwarding the story, making things happen . . . The power of the male protagonist as he controls events coincides

with the active power of the erotic look, both giving a satisfying
sense of omnipotence.

(1988: 63)

No female character in Shakespeare is more decisively inscribed than
Lucrece in a scopic economy that makes her an object for the purpose
of control and domination. At this point, the rape seems inevitable
and the story is Tarquin's, not Lucrece's, because he controls not only
the gaze but also the story.

TRANSGRESSION

Of course, it is true that according to the Roman reverence for family
lineage and the sacred principle of the *domus*, Tarquin is breaking a
profound taboo. Nowhere in the poem is this sense of transgression
voiced more poignantly than by Tarquin himself as he struggles with
his desire:

> Fair torch, burn out thy light, and lend it not
> To darken her whose light excelleth thine;
> And die, unhallow'd thoughts, before you blot
> With your uncleanness that which is divine;
> Offer pure incense to so pure a shrine.

(190–4)

The imagery of shrine and holy fire is indebted to the cult of Vesta,
which replicated ancient Roman family rituals on a national scale
and centered on the maintenance of the sacred altar fire by the vestal
virgins. It was believed that catastrophe would befall Rome if this fire
were ever extinguished; thus the very existence of the state was made
symbolically dependent on the confinement of women's bodies within
the institutional boundaries of marriage, family, and *domus* (Kahn
1976: 50–1). Lucrece, described throughout the poem in the imagery
of Vesta, is established as the very embodiment of the goddess even
in the Argument. When Collatine, Tarquin, and their comrades post
back to Rome to verify the claims they have made for their wives,
only Lucrece is found at home, spinning with her maids, chastely
guarding the hearth.

Shakespeare would have known about Vesta from the same book
in which he read the story of Lucrece: Ovid's *Fasti*. The cult of Vesta,
as Ovid conveys it (and his account is paralleled by that of Cicero in
De Natura Deorum), is curious in two ways.[5] First, it is a virgin who is

identified with the hearth fire, prime symbol of family life, rather than a mother; second, of all the Roman pantheon, Vesta alone is unrepresented: no images of her are permitted. Jean-Joseph Goux remarks on the connection between these two elements of the cult:

> Vesta's virginity and her unrepresentability are both protected at once. A man (*vir*) should neither penetrate, nor see, nor imagine. The violable virginity and the strict unrepresentability are identical, as if there were a complicity, on some opposing plane, between "rape" by merely sensual desire (the Priapic appetite) and visualization which would be a phantasm and an impious fraud.
>
> (1983: 94)

Even before the rape, then, when Tarquin penetrates Lucrece's chamber and merely gazes upon her chaste and alluring body with "manly sensual desire," he is symbolically raping her – and also breaking what we might call the quintessential Roman taboo against Vesta as goddess not only of *domus* but of *civitas*, in whose cult the permanence and the sacredness of both are represented.

That Vesta is a virgin, that she guards a hearth fire, located at the physical center of the *domus*, signifying the sacredness and permanence of home and state, that she must be unseen: all these motifs combine to suggest that "she is the guardian of the innermost things (*rerum intumarum*)," as Cicero says (1951, 2: xxvvi). Goux links this inwardness with "the idea of a *self* which is not identical to the ego" and which he distinguishes from "the heroic will, the executive power of the heroic ego (which turns outward)" (1983: 100).

What does it mean, then, for Tarquin's heroic will, turning outward toward Lucrece as a Vesta figure, a figure of the self, to rape her? I suggest that it is precisely this transgression that allows Shakespeare to create a heroic male subject in whom the contradictions of the dominant ideology are internalized and set at war. Even as Tarquin reverences the sacredness of the Roman community, the Vesta principle, he is driven to desecrate it in obedience to a principle equally strong and just as central, though not symbolized so coherently in a single deity – the principle of *virtus*, which depends on rivalry, agon, and conquest. His dividedness as a subject makes him heroic in the tragic terms that Shakespeare, of all English poets, has decisively established for our culture.

In contrast to Tarquin, Lucrece, because she is modeled on the Vesta principle, is superbly unified; all that she says and does coheres around her chastity, and she dies in order to purify and reassert it. It is also this unity, however, that keeps Lucrece from attaining (as it were) the subjectivity that is Tarquin's. On the other hand, unlike Vesta, Lucrece can be *seen* – she is not sequestered from the agonistic rivalry just as important to Roman culture as its inviolable unity. She is a woman, not a goddess, and her body is the site – and sight – at which Shakespeare sets against each other these two contending aspects of the Roman ethos. Thus she divides the masculine Roman self, yet in dividing it confers on it a dimension of subjectivity and a tragic potential which we have learned to honor. Insofar as we can identify Lucrece with "the ideal of a *self*" associated, as Goux argues, with "the innermost things," that "self" isn't hers. Rather, it is Tarquin's – but her capacity to stand for and set into play the ideological contradictions of Roman culture allows Shakespeare to create Tarquin as an inwardly divided, heroically torn subject.

Besieging Ardea, capital of the Rutuli, is considered a legitimate exercise of Roman military power; besieging Lucrece is not, and in punishment Tarquin and his family are stripped of power. But the same metaphors that validate the conquest of a neighboring people frame the conquest of Lucrece by Tarquin:

> Affection is my captain, and he leadeth;
>   And when his gaudy banner is display'd,
>   The coward fights, and will not be dismay'd.
>
> (271–3)

> His drumming heart cheers up his burning eye,
> His eye commends the leading to his hand;
> His hand, as proud of such a dignity,
> Smoking with pride, march'd on to make his stand
> On her bare breast, the heart of all her land. . .
>
> (435–9)

> His hand that yet remains upon her breast,
> Rude ram, to batter such an ivory wall!
> May feel her heart, poor citizen! distress'd,
> Wounding itself to death, rise up and fall,
> Beating her bulk, that his hand shakes withal:
>   This moves in him more rage and lesser pity,
>   To make the breach and enter this sweet city.
>
> (463–9)

Does the metaphor of city and siege in these passages eroticize violence or militarize eros? One might argue that the difference of context – bedchamber, not battlefield – renders this heroic language ironic and suggests a critique of the rape, but the same sexual politics underlies both contexts. In the Rome of the poem, whether in bed or in battle, men are in command of physical force, political power, and the language that authorizes them; to none of these do women have free access. The transfer of language from one domain to the other does not challenge the structures of power that enable men to keep women hidden and mute. Shakespeare's language, at bottom, identifies rather than distinguishes erotic and military domination. Thus it elides and conceals that division within the Roman ethos of which Lucrece, as both incarnation of Vesta and object of masculine rivalry, is the metaphor, the trace.

The narrative moment in which the rape occurs specifically associates linguistic domination with the sexual domination of women by men through force. Tarquin interrupts Lucrece's pleas in mid-sentence (line 666) and in five compact lines reiterates his threat. With the ellipsis conventional in representations of rape, these lines narrate the act:

> This said, he sets his foot upon the light,
> For light and lust are deadly enemies:
> Shame folded up in blind concealing night,
> When most unseen, then most doth tyrannize.
> The wolf hath seiz'd his prey, the poor lamb cries,
>   Till with her own white fleece her voice controll'd
>   Entombs her outcry in her lips' sweet fold.
>
> (673–9)

Like a warrior marking his victory over an enemy, Tarquin stamps out his torch. The "shame" of line 675 is Tarquin's in that, like him, it "doth tyrannize" – but it is also Lucrece's, given her belief that she as much as Tarquin has "stained" Collatine, and this shame drives her to kill herself. The metaphorical design of lines 675–9 naturalizes that shame and along with it, the muffling of her voice.

The word Shakespeare's contemporaries often used for woman's sexual parts, *pudenda*, derives from *pudere*, to be ashamed. According to the standard of chastity to which she adheres, Lucrece's sexuality is held to be her shame and must be modestly concealed. Even when the shame of the rape is concealed by darkness, this shame "most doth tyrannize," because for Lucrece it resides not in what can be seen of her but in what is being done to her. When Tarquin seizes her and "entombs her outcry in her lips' sweet fold," in a single gesture he strips her of that modest concealment and robs her of language by using her nightgown to stifle her voice. In the phrase "her lips' sweet fold," we can discern an upward displacement of that "sweet fold" below, which when unmolested reflects – naturally as it were – the concealment dictated by Roman chastity. As Peter Stallybrass has argued, the chastity, silence, and confinement to the domestic realm urged on women in the Renaissance are parallel boundaries of containment: "the closed body, the closed mouth, the closed house."[6] In the patriarchal metaphors of this stanza, woman's shamefast body is folded back on itself, concealing her desire and her speech in its folds. When Tarquin muffles Lucrece's cries with the folds of her nightgown as he rapes her, though his act is brutal and unlawful, though he penetrates what ought to remain closed, at the same time he but repeats and reinforces the dominant tendency of the culture in concealing, sealing off, muffling women's desire and women's speech.[7]

RESISTANCE

When Tarquin "shakes aloft his Roman blade" (line 505) before raping Lucrece, he performs a gratuitous but potently symbolic gesture.[8] The rape violates Roman law, yet the physical force implied in the sword is fully congruent with the Roman martial ethos. That force is truly exemplified not in his sword, however, but in the cunning threat that he then proceeds to utter. He makes it clear (in lines 512–39) to begin with that he will take her, no matter what her resistance. And if she resists, he says, he will kill her after he takes her. He adds a final element of coercion to this, however. After doing away with Lucrece, he promises to kill "some worthless slave" in her household, place him with her, and claim he slew them both because he found them together. This threat takes its force from the entire Roman ideology of male honor and female chastity. Tarquin is spurred to possess Lucrece by his competitive, agonistic Roman mentality even more than by her beauty *per se*. He wants her because she is Collatine's, and therefore every indication of her chastity – that is, her husband's rights over her body, which she affirms – paradoxically increases his desire. Nonetheless, to judge from this threat (which Shakespeare takes from Livy and Ovid), he appears to understand her chastity from her point of view as well as from his. He sees that she has perfectly identified herself with her husband, as the seal of his honor, and therefore will not risk resisting Tarquin because it would dishonor Collatine. To save her husband, Tarquin guesses, she is sure to yield herself.

Whatever she does, Lucrece can't avoid being raped. Moreover, it is only by not *resisting* Tarquin that she can avoid disgracing her husband and herself, and Tarquin doesn't specify what he means by resistance. ("If thou deny, then force must work my way," he says in line 513). Actually, Lucrece *does* resist Tarquin, in twelve stanzas of passionate argument terminated by the rape, which also silences Tarquin; he then simply vanishes from the poem, vanquished by guilt. The inner consistency and dramatic intensity of Lucrece's verbal struggle against her assailant arises from its anatomy of marriage as the institution that effects male control of women's sexuality and thus determines the sexual politics of Roman (and English) society. It is only in terms of that politics that Lucrece can construct her protests, however, by invoking the very principles and institutions which also underlie Tarquin's threat:

> She conjures him by high almighty Jove,
> By knighthood, gentry, and sweet friendship's oath,
> By her untimely tears, her husband's love,
> By holy human law and common troth . . .
>
> (568–71)

> My husband is thy friend; for his sake spare me.
> Thyself art mighty; for thine own sake leave me.
> Myself a weakling; do not then ensnare me.
>
> (582–4)

Her appeals to religion, the social hierarchy, friendship between men, marriage, law, etc., simply reinscribe Collatine's claim to her body and reinvoke the conflict between it and the Vesta principle of Rome as a unified body politic, the conflict in which Tarquin as a subject has been defined. Whenever Lucrece does not figure herself as belonging to Collatine, she uses metaphors that picture her as a typically weak and suppliant woman, the subject if not the victim of power held by men: "a poor unseasonable doe"(line 581); "a weakling" (line 584) capable only of sighs, moans, tears, groans (lines 586–8).

Lucrece's resistance, then, in effect cancels itself out, because it is inscribed within the same structures of power as the rape is. Such resistance can be contrasted to Kate's outspokenness in *The Taming of the Shrew*. In her interpretation of the play Karen Newman reads Kate's speech as a version of Luce Irigaray's "mimeticism," a self-conscious strategy of subverting the dominant discourse "so that metaphors, puns, and other forms of wordplay manifest their veiled equivalences: the meaning of women as treasure, of wooing as a civilized and acceptable disguise for sexual exploitation, of the objectification and exchange of women" (Newman 1986: 86–100). Unlike Kate swearing to Petruchio that the moon is the sun if he will have it so, Lucrece doesn't mime the terms of her place in the Roman gender system; she reiterates them with passionate sincerity. And unlike *Taming*, Lucrece lacks a dramatic frame (the Induction), which, as Newman says, "[calls] attention to the constructed character of the representation rather than veiling it through mimesis." Furthermore, as narrative poem rather than stage play, it lacks the subversive effect of transvestite boy actors. Whether Tarquin uses power rightly or wrongly, it is his power to use, and Lucrece does not question that; she only invokes the same structures of male authority and force that Tarquin will call upon to justify – however reprehensibly – the rape.

THE VOICE OF LUCRECE

Being raped does grant Lucrece a voice – the voice of the victim. But the terms of her victimage do not constitute a vantage point distinct from the patriarchal ideology that generated Tarquin's act. They merely emanate from another region of that ideology. Like Andromache and the other Trojan women, she laments the consequences of men's power, yet remains helpless to challenge it – even, I shall argue, in inciting revenge against Tarquin. Significantly, in an image that clearly foreshadows her suicide, Lucrece identifies herself with Philomel:

> Come Philomel, that sing'st of ravishment,
> Make thy sad grove in my dishevel'd hair . . .
> And whiles against a thorn thou bear'st thy part
> To keep thy sharp woes waking, wretched I
> To imitate thee well, against my heart
> Will fix a sharp knife to affright mine eye,
> Who if it wink shall thereon fall and die . . .
>   (1128–9, 1136–9)

As Patricia Klindienst Joplin suggests, in Ovid's story Philomel is robbed of her speech because she threatens to expose her male oppressors by speaking out. But by weaving her story, through "the voice of the shuttle," she fashions revenge and resistance (Joplin 1984: 25–53). Lucrece identifies herself not with this weaving woman, but with the Philomel who is metamorphosed into the nightingale, the Philomel who vainly laments her shame, under cover of night – wounding not her oppressor, but herself.[9] Her laments begin with the prayer that night may cover what she describes as disgrace, sin, guilt, and finally "helpless shame" (lines 750–6). This extended plea for concealment may be seen as the opposite and counterpart of the visual troping of Lucrece that prevailed before the rape; now, as a raped woman, she suffers to the fullest the penalty of being seen and wishes only to be hidden.

As the prayer settles into an apostrophe to night, Lucrece begins to articulate her understanding of the rape. In doing so, she reworks exactly the metaphors in which Tarquin himself constructed the crime as he contemplated it. He envisioned the dishonor of rape as an "eye-sore" or "loathsome dash" placed on his escutcheon by the herald (lines 204–10) to shame his posterity; she now sees it in the same heraldic terms, precisely and profoundly symbolic of the patriarchal family, as an "attaint" and "crest-wounding . . . mot," motto or device (lines 825, 827–31), which will blazon her now private shame to the world. The "ever-during blame," the "shame and fault" over which Tarquin agonized before the rape as his, are now hers (cf. lines 223–4, 238–9 with 750–6).

But even before the apostrophe to night gives way to an apostrophe to opportunity (at line 876), Shakespeare seems to shy away from the implications of Lucrece's language. The verse slides into sententiae implying that the rape isn't a crime committed within a certain structure of power, but the result of a universal tendency:

> But no perfection is so absolute
> That some impurity doth not pollute.
>
> (853–4)

> The sweets we wish for turn to loathed sours
> Even in the moment that we call them ours.
>
> (867–8)

Specific references to Tarquin and Collatine are sparse; implicit connections are fitful. For more than a hundred lines (between, roughly, lines 848 and 967), the poem sinks into a bog of platitudes, as though Shakespeare can't allow Lucrece to mourn her injury in terms that would link it to patriarchal power and turn mourning into subversion. She blames night ("blind muffled bawd"), opportunity ("thy guilt is great"), and time ("be guilty of my death since of my crime") before she curses Tarquin and abandons "this helpless smoke of words" to form a plan of action.

That plan as first presented, however, does not entail action against Tarquin but solely against herself. Resolving to "let forth [her] foul defiled blood" (line 1029), she implies a symbolic *quid pro quo*, an exchange of her life for her shame. But as she explicates this symbolic act, an additional meaning emerges. According to Lucrece's thinking, suicide will substitute for the resistance that betokens perfect chastity – resistance she blames herself for not showing before:

> Poor hand, why quiver'st thou at this decree?
> Honour thyself to rid me of this shame:
> For if I die, my honour lives in thee,
> But if I live, thou liv'st in my defame.
> Since thou could'st not defend thy loyal dame,
>   And wast afeard to scratch her wicked foe,
>   Kill both thyself and her for *yielding* so.
>   (1030–6, my emphasis)

But Lucrece *did* resist; as we saw, she argued against Tarquin at some length and when he seized her cried like a "poor lamb" until he smothered "her piteous clamours" with her nightgown (673–86). In Lucrece's eyes, though, what *counts* as resistance? Evidently, not verbal protests or "piteous clamours," only physical action such as scratching her attacker, however futile it might be. But what about Tarquin's additional, more powerful and deadly threat, to kill her if she should resist and then implicate her in adultery with a slave, thereby irrevocably besmirching her and, more important, Collatine? In the light of this threat, *not* to resist physically really means to defend Collatine's honor; apparent passivity, in this peculiar case, must be read as covert resistance. Shakespeare, however, seems to have forgotten the alternatives Tarquin allowed Lucrece and makes her conceive her suicide as though she had had only the choice of physical resistance, however futile, or submission to Tarquin's superior force, which would have compromised her integrity.

In dissecting the critical procedures commonly employed in the reading of sexual violence, Ellen Rooney argues:

the *absence of feminine desire* in rape is read as simple (unequiv-
ocal) *passivity*. This maintains the valorization of the dichotomy
of the rapist, the subject of the discourse of desire in rape.
Because the "object" of rape is finally helpless, her defeat is
read as passivity, and her passivity is totalized. As a consequence,
her *resistance* (her *activity*) *goes unread*. Ironically, it is this activity
– the resistance of the victim – that makes rape rape.

(Rooney 1983: 1269–77)

Shakespeare makes Lucrece valorize the rapist's dichotomy between
active resistance and passive submission, read her resistance as
passivity, and totalize that passivity into "yielding." Thus it cannot be
maintained, as some recent critics do, that even when she leaves off
lamentation and takes action, she does so in a way that ceases to
affirm her inscription into patriarchy, that establishes a "self" for her
or gives that self a voice of its own.[10]

But let us turn, then, to that action as she finally orchestrates and
accomplishes it. Summoning her husband and father to Rome by a
letter that does not reveal the rape, when they are present she narrates
the event, but before naming the rapist requires them to take an oath
of vengeance. Only then does she sheathe the knife in her breast. In
the narration preceding her suicide, she mentions Tarquin's sword,
her cries, and his threat entailing "th'adulterate death of Lucrece and
her groom" (lines 1625–45). But in the final stanza of this account,
she explicitly states that she didn't even resist verbally:

> Mine enemy was strong, my poor self weak,
> And far the weaker with so strong a fear.
> My bloody judge forbod my tongue to speak;
> No rightful plea might plead for justice there . . .
>
> (1646–9)

Again the text "folds up" Lucrece's voice and "in her lips' sweet fold"
too; she herself reads her resistance right out of the story. Furthermore, she affirms Tarquin's claim that her beauty, not his lust, caused
her to rape her:

> His scarlet lust came evidence to swear
>   That my poor beauty had purloined his eyes;
>   And when the judge is robb'd, the prisoner dies.
>
> (1650–2)

As the Arden editor F. T. Prince notes, in this metaphor lust is no
longer the criminal; rather, it wears the scarlet robe of a judge and

is a witness to boot. Though Lucrece believes her plea is "rightful," she accepts the verdict of the rigged trial she portrays and seeks only to make her "excuse":

> Though my gross blood be stain'd with this abuse,
> Immaculate and spotless is my mind;
> That was not forc'd, that never was inclin'd
>   To accessory yieldings, but still pure
>   Doth in her poison'd closet yet endure.
>
> (1655–8)

Any such "accessory yieldings" would have been accessory only in the sense of protecting Collatine from the "blots" on his honor caused by the rape.

When I wrote about this poem twenty years ago, I cited three stanzas of authorial comment in the narrator's voice, lines 1240–60, as evidence of what I called "Shakespeare's sensitive understanding of the social constraints which force Lucrece into a tragic role" (Kahn 1976: 67–8). It now seems to me that his understanding of such constraints is itself constrained by the basic assumption underlying the entire passage – the assumption that women are "naturally" the weaker of the species. With their impressionable "waxen minds," their innocent "smoothness," their flowerlike beauty, they are more sinned against than sinning, not culprits themselves but "tenants" to the "shame" of men. In the comparison between male and female that structures the passage, women are always the subordinate term, creatures to be pitied rather than praised. Yet Shakespeare seems to want it both ways. He pities Lucrece for the (feminine) weakness that allows her waxen mind to be stamped with Tarquin's crime, yet also, and in equal measure, praises her for a (quasi-masculine) strength that empowers her to die like a later Shakespearean hero, "a Roman by a Roman valiantly vanquished."[11]

The poem ends with the rout of the Tarquins, carried out by Collatine and his kinsmen but authorized by Lucrece's account of the rape and her suicide. Thus she as a woman plays a peculiarly heroic role in the foundation of the Roman republic. As Michael Platt points out, Lucrece can be seen as "brief epic" resembling the *Iliad* or the *Aeneid* in centering on "the destruction and foundation of cities." Lucrece's body stands in the place of Troy; on its ruins is the new republic Rome built. As she gazes at the tapestry depicting the fall of Troy (lines 1541–7), she realizes that "she is a city and her rape a tyranny" (Platt 1975: 60, 65). In such a reading, the rape of Lucrece is seen as an aspect of Tarquin's overweening pride, associated with the tyranny of his house. The poem offers this view of the rape many times. But in another sense, given the metonymy of woman for city, the rape is, culturally speaking, inevitable; a continuation rather than a violation of the power held by men. The famous ekphrasis in which Shakespeare describes a tapestry depicting the furthest extent and final act of the siege of Troy suggests this sense.

In book 2 of the *Aeneid*, long recognized as the source of this episode, when the Greeks swarm into the inmost chambers of Priam's palace, their penetration is clearly imaged as rape. They tear off the portals leading to "the inner house," which creates "a gaping mouth" and leaves the long halls and private rooms "open, naked," as vulnerable to violation as the women, now wandering terrified amid the bridal chambers "that had such hopes of sons," will shortly be (Virgil 1971, 2: 634–79).

Neatly linking the end of the war to its begining, Lucrece comments:

Had doting Priam check'd his son's desire,
Troy had been bright with fame and not with fire.

(1490–1)

Given the continuity between Homer's Vergil's, and Shakespeare's epic poems, it is difficult to regard Tarquin's violation of Lucrece as a departure from the heroic norm.[12] In the transformation of Rome from monarchy to republic men retain their exclusive command over force and over women. The "Roman blade" that Tarquin flourishes over Lucrece is the same one that she turns against herself, and her death sanctions the continuation of the same force.

NOTES

1 For an interesting treatment of Lucrece's "secret and powerful feminine eloquence" in her apostrophes to Night, Time, and Opportunity, see Berry (1992: 33–40). She argues that Lucrece draws on Machiavellian motifs of "politic dissembling" associated with masculine *virtù*, but then concedes that Lucrece is "profoundly implicated in the hierarchical system of values and government which her appeal for revenge will eradicate" (35, 39).

2 See Froula for a similar argument concerning the silencing of women in the *Iliad* (1986: 621–44), and Jane O. Newman, for a valuable account of the traditions of women's political agency and women's violence embedded in the sources Shakespeare used, and recognized by his contemporaries. She argues that "This tradition is . . . pointedly invoked

– but then just as pointedly excised – in and by Shakespeare's *Lucrece*. It nevertheless haunts the margins (both literally and figuratively) of the sources of *Lucrece*, of the poem itself, and of its critical reception" (1994: 305).

3 See Stone (1971: 271) for a summary of the social practices, stressing patrilinear, primogenitural inheritance, by which patriarchy maintained itself in early modern England.

4 I completed an earlier draft of this essay before Joel Fineman's "Shakespeare's Will: The Temporality of Rape" appeared (Fineman 1987: 25–76). In arguing that rape, *Lucrece*, and "heterosexual desire *per se*" are modeled on the figure of chiasmus, Fineman also notes that "Tarquin and Lucrece both speak the *same* language" (43), and claims further that they are "inverse versions of each other, and for this reason *together* make the rape of Lucrece" (44). While I hold that patriarchy puts them in crucially different *political* positions, he sees them in terms of chiasmus as characters who occupy opposing but equal rhetorical positions.

5 Ovid, *Fasti*, 2: 721–852, and Livy, *The History of Rome*, 1: 57–60, are Shakespeare's two main sources for the story of Lucrece. I believe that he also drew upon Ovid's descriptions of the observances connected with Vesta: 3: 141–4; 4: 949–54; 6: 249–348. Cicero discusses Vesta in *De Natura Deorum*, 2: xvii.

6 In his essay "Patriarchal Territories: The Body Enclosed," Peter Stallybrass observes that in Renaissance England "the surveillance of women concentrated upon three specific areas: the mouth, chastity, the threshold of the house . . . Silence, the closed mouth, is made a sign of chastity. And silence and chastity are, in turn, homologous to woman's enclosure within the house" (1986: 126–7).

7 Fineman also notes the allusion to pudenda in "shame" but sees it as part of the same purely rhetorical chiasmic pattern that, he argues, informs the poem: "It is fitting that the rape, when it finally occurs, is figured in and as a simultaneously emergent and recessive in-between-ness forming and informing the fold of Lucrece's lips, for the smirky collocation of Lucrece's mouth with her vagina supports the formal implication that Lucrece is asking for her rape because her 'no,' as 'no,' means 'yes'" (Fineman 1987: 43). Thus his scrupulously formal, often fascinating interpretation of the poem arrives at the same reading of the rape as that dictated by a common misogyny: it's the victim's fault – she was asking for it.

8 See A. Robin Bowers's "Iconography and Rhetoric in *Lucrece*" (Bowers 1981: 1–21). He notes that in Titian's painting of the rape, completed c.1570, a visual parallel between Tarquin's "phallic knee" thrust between Lucrece's thighs and the blade held high in his right hand emphasizes the violence of the rape (7); I would read this parallel as a statement of the sexual politics of the poem. (This pose is repeated in five other versions of the scene attributed to Titian or his school.) Shakespeare achieves a somewhat similar effect in punning on Tarquin's "falchion" and "falcon" (lines 505–11).

9 For different readings of Philomel as a figure for Lucrece, see Bromley (1983), Maus (1986), and Newman (1994), who notes that "it is at the

44

level of plot that the story of Philomela most clearly diverges from that of Lucrece," in two ways. First, Philomela colludes with her sister Procne to "turn the sword against the victimizer rather than the victim." Second, the sisters' mode of revenge carries traces of the Dionysian rites practiced by women, in which they seize "political agency and responsibility heretofore reserved for [men]" (309, 311) – unlike Lucrece, who delegates revenge to her husband and male kinsmen.

10 For this view, see Bromley (1983). Dubrow (1987) also thinks Lucrece has a "self" and holds that her passivity, innocence, emotionality, and belief in absolutes makes her complicit, at least, in the rape.

11 Commenting on this passage, Ann Thompson and John O. Thompson (1987) call attention to the contradiction between the metaphor of women's minds as wax, which implies that "women are too weak to be held accountable for anything at all," and the fact that Lucrece can't be held accountable for the forcible rape committed by Tarquin (189).

12 See Helms on continuities between the *Iliad*, Euripides's *The Trojan Women*, and the *Aeneid*: she holds that all three works "[identify] military and erotic domination," creating "analogies between the rape of women's bodies and the conquest of walled cities" (1989: 28). See also Arthur (1981) on women in the *Iliad*.

3

THE DAUGHTER'S SEDUCTION IN *TITUS ANDRONICUS*, OR, WRITING IS THE BEST REVENGE

> The female must never control
> reproduction for herself . . .
> She must also never see, and
> certainly never speak about what
> she learns from her position.
>
> (Joplin 1990: 21)

Shakespeare was about thirty in 1594 when *Titus Andronicus* was published, but this sensational revenge tragedy is marked by the brashness and bravura of a younger poet, showing off both his knowledge of classical authors and his mastery of a crowd-pleasing popular genre. Weaving an Ovidian tale into a Senecan revenge tragedy, seeding allusions to the *Aeneid* in nearly every scene, Shakespeare revels in the *imitatio* that structured the transmission of Latin literature to the Elizabethan elite and those aspiring to join it Leonard Barkan notes "the competitive mode" in which Shakespeare appropriates Ovid:

> What is horrible in Ovid's Tereus story Shakespeare makes twice as horrible in *Titus Andronicus*. Not one rapist but two, not one murdered child but five, not one or two mutilated organs but six, not a one-course meal but a two.
>
> (1986: 244)

Furthermore, as T. J. B. Spencer remarked of Shakespeare's appropriation of Roman history in *Titus*,

> It is not so much that any particular set of political institutions is assumed in *Titus*, but rather that it includes *all* the political institutions that Rome ever had. The author seems anxious, not to get it all right, but to get it all in.
>
> (Spencer 1957: 32)

Yet this most self-consciously textual of all Shakespearean plays doesn't appropriate, imitate, allude to, and parody a host of classical authors merely to elicit plaudits for its author's learning and virtuosity.[1]

Even while he travesties Romanness, Shakespeare generates his main action from versions of Roman *pietas* and *virtus* – making this play a serious critique of Roman ideology, institutions, and mores. In the hero's character, G. K. Hunter notes, Shakespeare draws on the standard motifs of austere republican virtue that typify Rome's "great ethical heroes, Scipio, Regulus, Brutus" as chronicled by Livy, while placing him in an ambience of imperial decadence like that portrayed by Tacitus, Suetonius, and Herodian (1984: 182, 187). Republican virtue, though, perpetrates as much (if not more) horror than imperial decadence. The play insists on an antithesis between civilized Rome and the barbaric Goths only to break it down: the real enemy lies within.

Moreover, it can be argued, it isn't only Rome as Elizabethan culture knew it that the play attacks, but also the humanistic appropriation of Rome's textual legacy from grammar school through university in Shakespeare's England. As one critic notes,

> Rome is a tradition in which [the characters] have been schooled through school books: the works of Horace, Virgil, Ovid, and Seneca . . . Roman education, which seems to stand for Roman tradition in general, has been twisted to become the teacher and rationalizer of heinous deeds.
>
> (West 1982: 65)

In the late empire ambience of this play, even non-Romans can recognize a verse from Horace – but they don't understand what it means. And not only Titus writes copiously, but also Aaron the Moor (sometimes carving his messages on corpses); even Lavinia, though she lacks hands, scratches letters in the earth. In one of the play's eeriest moments, when the revenger-hero is finally empowered by learning the identity of his enemies, the revelation is accomplished through the material presence of a text, significantly a schoolboy's copy of Ovid's *Metamorphoses*.

This sophisticated awareness of the politics of textuality is interwoven with the play's central concern: the politics of sexuality. And in the schematically patriarchal world of *Titus*, sexuality is a family matter that only the father can deal with.[2] Of the several crimes against Titus, it is the rape and mutilation of his daughter Lavinia that establishes him in the central position of revenger. He proves his title of *paterfamilias*, one might say, with a vengeance – not only on those who violated and injured her so brutally but on the girl herself, when he murders her. *Titus* configures the father's investment in the daughter, relentlessly carrying out that "symbolics of blood" according to which, Lynda Boose argues, "A daughter's virginity is perceived to 'belong to' the blood of – and therefore to – the father".[3] Yet Shakespeare makes the hauntingly mute, hideously disfigured Lavinia much more than a patriarchal icon of the dutiful daughter. Deprived of speech and the usual means of writing, Lavinia herself becomes a signifier; as such, Douglas Green asserts, she is "polysemic and disruptive . . . beyond complete containment by the patriarchal assumptions of Shakespeare's time – and in some ways our own" (1989: 325). As Lavinia's male kin struggle to understand her grotesque body language, the cultural logic of the Roman father–daughter complex works itself out in a compelling series of scenes (2.4–4.1). They come to a climax in Lavinia's revelation of her rape and identification of the rapists – whereupon she disappears for four scenes (4.2, 3, 4; 5.1), to return not only mute but veiled, assisting in the revenge that now belongs to her father. Titus's subjectivity as a tragic hero is generated from his daughter's pain inscribed as his own.[4] Moving from sorrow to anger, finding his tortuous way to "revenge's cave," Titus carries out the father's role according to the "exchange model" of father–daughter sacrifice that Boose delineates: he sacrifices his daughter "to the perceived demands of the patriarchy and thus affirms his membership in it" (1989: 40).

THE FATHER'S TREASURE

Titus Andronicus opens in high Roman fashion by staging two public ceremonies, an election and a funeral. "With drums and trumpets," Titus is declared the new emperor of Rome. He makes his first entrance, though, not as successful *candidatus* but as grieving father, at the head of a funeral procession. Having lost twenty-one of his twenty-five sons in battle, he brings the last two of the slain home for burial in the monument of the Andronici. His surname "Pius" recalls the epithet that characterizes the first Roman hero, Aeneas, and his sons total in number half those of Priam, in whose defense Aeneas fought.[5] Clearly he embodies paternal authority and the historical tradition of *pietas* that supports it, as well as the gendered ideals of character typical of early republican *virtus*: "severity, self-

48

conscious masculinity, stoical self-denial" (Hunter 1984: 4). Finally, to complete this composite of typical Roman traits and values, he is a victorious general, returning from a ten-year campaign against the Goths with captives in tow.

As he prepares to sacrifice *ad manes fratrum* – to the spirits of his dead sons – the oldest son of his prisoner Tamora, Queen of the Goths, she pleads with him to spare the boy. She appeals to his love as a father, and to "the mercy of the gods," but Titus is adamant: the honor of the Andronici demands this tribute, which he has exacted five times before.[6] The victim is taken off, his limbs to be "lopp'd." Ironically alluding to Titus's surname, Tamora brands his action "cruel irreligious piety" (1.1.133). A few moments later, Titus's inflexible adherence to primogeniture in backing the elder of two brothers to take his place as emperor leads him, in a sudden eruption of fury, to kill his own son. The two filicides are paralleled: both sons are sacrificed in the name of the fathers, according to a piety that seems not only cruel and irreligious but also a perversion of *virtus*.

Titus's sacrifice of Tamora's son trips off the revenge mechanism that drives the play toward its savage denouement. The *quid pro quo* that Tamora extracts for her murdered son isn't the murder of Titus's son, though she does abet Aaron in murdering two of them, nor even that of a daughter, but rather a daughter's rape and mutilation. Lavinia then becomes the focus of action in the middle part of the play and the most shocking and memorable of its many images of bodily violation. In thus placing dramatic emphasis on her injuries, rather than on the murder of her brothers, Shakespeare calls attention to the role of women in Rome's sexual politics – a role that, overshadowed by the strident patriarchal motif of the opening scene, is nonetheless central. For Titus, Lavinia's worth resides in her exchange value as a virgin daughter. In a larger sense, she is symbolically important to Roman patriarchy: as an emblem of what Joplin calls "sacralized chastity," she is "the sign of her father's or husband's political power" – the power of male kin to control women's sexual desire and reproductive power (Joplin 1990: 53). Both her exchange value and her symbolic value are nullified several times over by what is done to her at Tamora's behest. Not only is she violated by the queen's two sons: her tongue is cut out and her hands are cut off. Thus Tamora gets back at Titus through his daughter by mocking and despoiling his investment in her.

According to Lévi-Strauss, the structure of the patriarchal family derives from the interlocking operation of two cultural imperatives: the incest taboo and exogamy.[7] Forbidden to marry within the family, its sons and daughters must be married out. The sons, however, remain identified with the paternal family, carrying on its name into posterity and inheriting the father's prerogatives, while the daughters pass from their paternal households to those of their husbands, to mediate the continuation of another patriarchal lineage. The only members of the family whose destiny is to leave it, they are thus made liminal, and turned into creatures of passage. Moreover, they are distinguished from sons in another important way. As Boose points out, appropriating Lacan's family script,

> [The mother] is the necessary mediator between [father and son], the empty vessel through whom, in psychoanalytic terms, the father's phallus and sign of the father's authority is passed to the son . . . The son receives the externally evident sign of the father and becomes synonymous with him at birth. By parallel, what the daughter receives from the mother is not the sign *of* maternity but the hidden receptacle *for* it, the so-called empty space . . . a signal passed on to her not *from* the mother but from the phallus that is the sign of the father.
>
> (Boose 1989: 21)

The virgin daughter's womb is the hidden, prized treasure of her father, to be guarded, given or exchanged as he determines. What Page DuBois calls "thesaurization," the representation of the female body in Greek culture as vase, oven, and temple – enclosures "for keeping safe, for entreasuring" – is further elaborated in the woman's role in Greco-Roman culture generally: "women preserve and maintain the goods brought to them by the men of their households . . . the wife as treasure ensures the prosperity and endurance of the house" (1988: 97, 103). The Roman worship of Vesta, virgin goddess of the hearth (described in chapter 2), places thesaurization at the center of the state religion, inscribing both the centrality and the hiddenness of women and their sexualized bodies.[8] The image of the chaste woman as impermeable container was also highly visible in the Renaissance through the legend of Tuccia, first recounted by St Augustine in *The City of God*. This vestal virgin proved her chastity by carrying water from the Tiber in a sieve, a "miraculous inversion of the vessel's ordinary function [that] replicates the prodigy of virginity itself" (Warner 1985: 242). Tuccia reappears notably in the *Trionfi*, Petrarch's sequence of allegorical poems, heading a host of

50

virtues represented by female figures. For Shakespeare's England, she was familiar in portraits of Elizabeth, several times portrayed as Tuccia with a sieve in her hand.

In *Titus*, the problematics of liminality and thesaurization are dramatized in Lavinia's troubled passage from father to husband to violators and back to father. Conspicuous as the only daughter among twenty-five sons, she enters the play after her father completes the solemn sacrificial ritual of burial by placing the last of his slain sons in the family tomb. Greeting her father by repeating his words of farewell to her brothers, offering "tributary tears" for them, and kneeling at his feet, she asks for the blessing of his "victorious hand" (1.1.162–6). Despite these indications of her complete subjection as a model patriarchal daughter, Titus seems curiously negligent in supervising her betrothal – the crucial transmission of his treasure to another male guardian. When Bassianus suddenly declares that Lavinia is his, Titus exclaims, "Lavinia is surpris'd" (288); in the context, surprise seems a delicate euphemism for what is later called "this rape" (409). But it also marks one of the many oddly comic moments in this play, for it is he, not his daughter, who is surprised that she has evidently been party to a previous betrothal.[9] Further, in offering to make Lavinia his empress, Saturninus tells Titus he will "advance / Thy name and honorable family" (242–3) – as though paying him back for supporting his bid for emperor over that of his younger brother. Titus responds to this proposal by offering his sword, chariot, and prisoners – rather than Lavinia herself – as "tribute that I owe" (255) to his prospective son-in-law. Lavinia's betrothal thus takes its place in a sequence of exchanges between her father and the newly elevated emperor that stress Titus's reverence for tradition and authority and his eagerness to garner imperial favor, while effacing or even exploiting her.

Titus's delinquency as a father derives from his over-zealous (and in the killing of his son Mutius, self-contradictory) commitment to those forms of *pietas* specifically involving men: dedicating all his many sons to the service of the state, insisting on the strict observance of blood sacrifice to their spirits despite a mother's plea for mercy, opting for primogeniture without considering a rival claim, and defending imperial power even to the point of slaying his own son. When his brother Marcus asks Titus, "How comes it that the subtle Queen of Goths / Is of a sudden thus advanc'd in Rome?" (397–8), the obvious answer is that it happened because Titus failed to oversee properly both the transmission of political power and the exchange of a

51

daughter. The sequence of events in the first scene that connects the election of the emperor with the betrothal and "rape" of Lavinia, and with the double wedding of the emperor and his brother-rival, demonstrates the tight-woven interrelation of the two kinds of passage. Similarly, in the *Aeneid*, the hero's betrothal to Lavinia represents both a vital political alliance between the Trojans and the stable native kingdom of Latium and the acquisition of the female reproductive power that is crucial to the continuity of the state they seek to found. Similarly also, the Virgilian Lavinia's passage from her father to her husband is troubled by a rival suitor (Turnus), and like Lavinia's marriage in *Titus*, gives rise to carnage and civil war (Miola 1983: 55, 45).

The father's exaggerated investment in the patriarchal order is commandingly represented onstage by the tomb of the Andronici, five hundred years old and "sumptuously re-edified" by Titus (1.1.356). It is the site of two separate funerals in the play's first scene, each of them interrupted and troubled: the first by Tamora's pleas that Alarbus be spared, the second by Titus's refusal to bury with his brothers the son whom he has just killed, on the grounds that "Here none but soldiers and Rome's servitors / Repose in fame; none basely slain in brawls" (357–8). The tomb thus represents not simply the continuity of the family so much as the subordination of the family to the military needs of the state – the original and hallowed medium of *virtus*.

The terms of the hero's apostrophe to the tomb, however, also suggest its feminine counterpart:

> O sacred receptacle of my joys,
> Sweet cell of virtue and nobility,
> How many sons of mine hast thou in store,
> That thou wilt never render to me more!
>
> (1.1.95–8)

Like the daughter's virginal womb, it is a receptacle, an enclosed cell, that stores up the joy and sweetness of successive generations, specifically through commemorating for posterity the fame gained by male ancestors through death in battle. The daughter's womb is intended to produce sons for the state; the fathers' tomb keeps them "in store," to generate ideological as distinct from biological *virtus*.

When Aaron incites Chiron and Demetrius to rape Lavinia in the forest, his language evokes the thesaurization that the rape is intended to undo:

There speak, and strike, brave boys, and take your turns;
There serve your lust, shadowed from heaven's eye,
And revel in Lavinia's treasury.

(1.1.629–31)

Demetrius perpetuates the image when he jeers at Lavinia as "corn" to be harvested; Chiron refers to her "nice-preserved" honesty: and Tamora calls her "the honey we desire" (2.2.123, 135, 131). Lavinia is both the container they would break open and the valued nourishment it stores. Lavinia, totally subjected to this construction of herself, supplies a precipitating cause for the rape when she taunts Tamora for her "goodly gift in horning" (2.2.67), by which Lavinia implies her own unspotted chastity. This slur functions somewhat like Collatine's boast of Lucrece's chastity in *Lucrece*, in that it implicitly sets up a competition centering on a man's possession of his wife's body (see chapter 2). Here, however, it is the women who compete. Preening herself as properly "contained" by her husband, Lavinia scorns Tamora's freedom from sexual constraint, thus giving Demetrius a pretext for defending his mother's honor by violating Lavinia's:

This minion stood upon her chastity,
Upon her nuptial vow, her loyalty . . .
And shall she carry this unto her grave?

(2.2.124–5, 127)

The brothers' plan to drag Bassianus "to some secret hole / And make his dead trunk pillow to our lust" travesties the marital chastity of which Lavinia boasts (2.2.129–30) by fusing the scene of marital consummation with the scene of rape, making it obscene. The travesty is furthered when the Andronicus brothers, having fallen into the same pit, remark on the "precious ring" that Lavinia's dead husband wears on his "bloody finger," likening it to "a taper in some monument" (2.2.226–8). This image alludes, again obscenely, to Bassianus's sexual guardianship of his wife, brutally mocked by both his murder and her rape (compare the similar implications of "Nerissa's ring" in *The Merchant of Venice* (Kahn 1985). It also connects and contrasts Lavinia's "treasury," her precious but violated womb, with the monument of the Andronici that Titus obsequiously honored as the "sweet cell" of sons who died for Rome. He venerated one pious place while neglecting another, which will prove to be his undoing as well as his daughter's.

53

Lavinia's "treasury" and the monument of the Andronici also stand in close, overdetermined relationship to another site already mentioned: the "abhorred pit" that is the scene of the murders, rape, and mutilations committed by Chiron and Demetrius.[10] This pit is first rhetorically conjured into existence by Tamora, who locates it in "A barren detested vale" where "nothing breeds," then associates it with "A thousand fiends, a thousand hissing snakes, / Ten thousand swelling toads, as many urchins" (2.3.93–101). The unwitting Lavinia then connects this locale of nightmarish fecundity to the scene of her own rape when, using the euphemistic language that befits her chastity, she pleads with Tamora,

> 'Tis present death I beg; and one thing more
> That womanhood denies my tongue to tell.
> O, keep me from their worse than killing lust,
> And tumble me into some loathsome pit,
> Where never man's eye may behold my body . . .
> (2.2.173–7)

When Titus's sons further elaborate the pit as an image of female genitalia, their metaphors evoke virginity and defloration:

> What subtle hole is this,
> Whose mouth is covered with rude-growing briers,
> Upon whose leaves are drops of new-shed blood
> As fresh as morning dew distilled on flowers?
> (2.2.198–201)

Though Lavinia is "a new-married lady" (2.1.15) when she is raped, Tamora uses the term "deflower" (2.2.191) to describe what is done to her, thus representing her as virginal daughter rather than chaste wife, even before her husband is murdered and she returns to her father in the daughter's position (2.2.191). The spoliation of her virginal fertility by rape contrasts with Tamora's wanton fecundity; already the mother of two grown sons, she soon will bear a bastard child by a Moor. To sum up the relationship between chaste daughter and whorish mother implied by the burgeoning metaphoricity of the pit: the virginal daughter's fertility is cut off at a womb-like place that associates rape and murder with the maternal. The father's treasure is stolen and destroyed by the mother.

As several critics have demonstrated, the imagery of the pit prolif-erates meaning in a way that suggests what I would call the *ur*-meaning of that imagery: maternal fecundity that, eluding patriarchal

54

control, becomes excessive, destructive, and malignant, breeding further evils. The extremely fecund mother of the twenty-six Andronici – never mentioned in the play, and conspicuously absent from the funeral rites of the first scene – has been excised from Rome, displaced onto Tamora, the Gothic outsider, and demonized with a ferocious linguistic and theatrical inventiveness. When Titus offends Tamora's maternity by sacrificing her son and facilitates her incorporation into Rome by mishandling his political and filial responsibilities, she becomes the breeding-ground of outrages, as much a spur to others' wickedness as a source of it herself. Aaron sets on her sons as a way of obscurely realizing his own ambitions to "mount her pitch"; those sons kill, rape, and mutilate to satisfy their mutual rivalry, and assist her in revenge. One crime spawns another, and the ultimate source of all is the offended, alientated mother.[11]

In the composite Romanness of the first scene, maternal presence is entirely excluded, but alienated and given compelling voice in Tamora, while the father's power is foregrounded as rashly, cruelly, and hubristically dominant. As Marion Wynne-Davies notes, however, "The womb is not only the centre of female sexuality, but the repository of familial descent . . . Control of the womb was paramount to determining a direct patrilineal descent" (1991: 136). Under proper patriarchal control, the womb is subordinated to the tomb, to the patriarchal family as configured by the Roman state, its military aims, and the dictates of *virtus*. Eluding that control, the maternal womb burgeons aggressively, pollutes patrilineal descent, and destroys civil order, whereas the daughter's womb, first virginal and then violated, serves as the focal point whereby the father defends patriarchy against the mother's attack and ultimately regains control. *Titus* positions its hero between a rampaging mother and a dutiful daughter.

The play's first scene locates the initiating mechanism of the revenge play not in an injury done to the hero through his kin as in *The Spanish Tragedy* or *Hamlet*, but in the hero's injury to a mother.[12] Once Alarbus's limbs are lopped, Tamora becomes Titus's enemy, and once she conspires against his children – notably, his daughter – he becomes the offended party, the injured father, the avenging hero. The play can be seen as the story of Titus's transformation from Roman hero to revenge hero, which he accomplishes by hacking and hewing his way through the tangled matrix of outrages and injuries that Tamora spawns.

Titus thus bears a strong resemblance to Shakespeare's Richard III who, as Janet Adelman argues, imagines and enacts his masculinity

Plate 1 "Enter Tamora pleadinge for her sons going to execution," ink drawing by Henry Peacham, ?1604–14. The drawing distills the play's action into a confrontation between father and mother, Romans and Goths. Headed by Titus in toga and laurels, the Romans on the left are divided from the Goths – Tamora kneeling, her two sons, and Aaron the Moor on the right – by Titus's spear. Reproduced by permission of the Marquess of Bath, Longleat House, Warminster, Wiltshire, Great Britain

as a response to his mother's depriving, malignant womb, where love "forswore" him. Deformed and unloved, he seeks compensation in the crown. Fantasizing the obstacles to it as "a thorny wood," a suffocating matrix that replicates the hostile womb, he determines to "hew [his] way out with a bloody axe" (*3 Henry VI*, 3.2.153–81). Richard's character localizes what Adelman calls "a whole range of anxieties about masculinity and female power . . . diffused over the whole surface of the text" (1992: 3). Similarly, in Titus's tragic plight Shakespeare tries to focus the anxieties that are diffused (to say the least) in the crimes Tamora sponsors and in the over-elaborated pit metaphorically equated with vagina ("secret hole"), "swallowing womb," tomb ("this deep pit, poor Bassianus' grave"), mouth and hell itself ("this fell devouring receptacle, / As hateful as Cocytus' misty mouth") (2.3.129, 192–240).

As Douglas Green remarks, "It is largely on and through the female characters that Titus is constructed and his tragedy inscribed" (1989: 319). By pitting Gothic mother against Roman daughter, the angry, aggressive maternal womb against the subjected, violated daughterly womb, Shakespeare configures Titus's passage from *pietas* to revenge.

THE HANDMAIDEN

In conformity with the usual decorum, the rape of Lavinia is not enacted onstage. She is taken off by her assailants in one scene (2.2) and returns in the next according to the following stage direction: *"Enter the empress' sons, with Lavinia, her hands cut off, and her tongue cut out, and ravish'd"* (2.3.S.D.). Ravishment leaves no outward mark, no visible sign save those contrived by convention: dishevelled dress, unbound hair.[13] From this point on, Lavinia's rape is signified to us as audience or readers by her mutilations, but her male kin take those signs for the thing itself. Until she writes "Stuprum" in the dust, they remain transfixed by her external wounds and ignorant of the internal one, which has the greater symbolic significance. The mutilations are an afterthought, a corollary to the main crime, presumably necessitated by the brothers' desire to conceal the crime and avoid punishment (also, perhaps, marked by Shakespeare's desire to emulate Ovid and Seneca). While the rape was planned and discussed extensively (1.1.599ff., 2.2.122–86), the mutilations come as a surprise to us. Yet it is the mutilations that distract Lavinia's uncle, father, brother, and nephew and keep them from realizing that she has been raped as well.

Or rather, the text voices and then suppresses that realization. When Marcus first encounters his niece he describes the sight she presents in an often-quoted passage that imitates a typically Ovidian mingling of the erotic with the grotesque:

> Speak, gentle niece, what stern ungentle hands
> Hath lopp'd and hew'd and made thy body bare
> Of her two branches, those sweet ornaments,
> Whose circling shadows kings have sought to sleep in,
> And might not gain so great a happiness
> As half thy love? Why dost not speak to me?
> Alas, a crimson river of warm blood,
> Like to a bubbling fountain stirr'd with wind,
> Doth rise and fall between thy rosed lips,
> Coming and going with thy honey breath.
> But, sure, some Tereus hath deflower'd thee,
> And lest thou should'st detect him, cut thy tongue.
>
> (2.3.16–27)

Marcus easily and immediately connects Lavinia's bleeding mouth with Philomel's, the visible wound with the hidden fact of rape.[14] A few lines later, he elaborates the connection by noting that while Philomel only lost her tongue, "A craftier Tereus" has cut off Lavinia's "pretty fingers" to keep her from telling of her rape in needlework (38–43). Just after he mentions Tereus, Marcus says his niece turns away her face "for shame," as if "blushing to be encountered" (2.3.28–32) – her blush implicitly confirming his suspicions. But these moments of truth vanish, to be followed by three successive scenes in which Marcus seems to be just as much in the dark as his male kinsfolk. As Lyn Higgins and Brenda Silver point out, in many representations of rape in western literature, "Rape exists as an absence or gap that is both product and source of textual anxiety, contradiction and censorship . . . [a] constantly deferred origin of both plot and social relations" (Higgins and Silver, 1991: 3). In this play, like Chiron and Demetrius the text flaunts the rape, then conceals it; points it out, then censors it. Here as in other of Shakespeare's Roman works, a wound works like a fetish as a site of undecideability about inscriptions and relations of gender (see chapter 1, pp. 17–18).

Higgins and Silver also comment that "Who gets to tell the story and whose story counts as 'truth' determine the definition of what rape is" (1991: 1). The "absence or gap" that Marcus's amnesia creates is filled by a sequence of scenes in which he and other men try to interpret Lavinia, mistaking her meanings and appropriating her signs for their own. Because we know her hidden truth, however, these scenes ironically serve to dramatize and thematize the erasure of the feminine in patriarchy; to destabilize the language in which women are customarily figured as objects of exchange or vessels for reproduction; and to bring obliquely to light – for us – what has been censored.

In this part of the play, the polluted Lavinia, neither maid nor wife nor simply widow, passes from a state of liminality and passivity to an active role as communicator of her own meaning. When Marcus first glimpses her, she is evidently fleeing from him so that her injuries are hidden. He asks her, "Where is your husband?" (2.3.12), a normal response to the sight of a married woman wandering alone in the woods. Then he pours out the Petrarchan travesty quoted above that moves back and forth between hands and tongue, tongue and hands to blazon her ruination as both marriageable daughter and chaste wife. The shocking disparity between Marcus's rhetoric (he calls Lavinia's arms "circling shadows kings have sought to sleep in," 2.3.19) and the maimed body to which it pertains makes it clear that the Lavinia who existed before the rape as an object of desire and exchange was a construction of the language wielded by the men who exchanged and desired her. Marcus's recourse to that language when it can no longer function both highlights it and the places for women that it normally creates, and indicates that Lavinia can no longer occupy those linguistic or social sites.[15]

Throughout the next two scenes (3.1 and 3.2), Titus tries both to assimilate Lavinia into the losses he is already suffering (his two sons, framed as the murderers of Bassianus, are executed after Aaron tricks him into cutting off his hand to free them) and to project his own meanings onto her gestures. Even before he loses his hand, he takes her amputations as an emblem of Rome's ingratitude towards him, its chief warrior:

> Speak, Lavinia, what accursed hand
> Hath made thee handless in thy father's sight? . . .
> Give me a sword, I'll chop off my hands too;
> For they have fought for Rome, and all in vain . . .
> 'Tis well, Lavinia, that thou hast no hand,
> For hands to do Rome service is but vain.
>
> (3.1.67–8, 73–4, 80–1)

He places her at the top of his hierarchy of woes – two sons killed, one son banished, his brother weeping for him – as "dear Lavinia, dearer than my soul" (103). But as the scene progresses, his attempts and those of his kin to interpret her wounds and her gestures invariably point back from her to the men in her family:

Titus: Look, Marcus! ah, son Lucius, look on her!
       When I did name her brothers, then fresh tears
       Stood on her cheeks, as doth the honey-dew
       Upon a gath'red lily almost withered.
Marcus: Perchance she weeps because they kill'd her husband;
       Perchance because she knows them innocent.
       (3.1.111–16)

Lucius: Sweet father, cease your tears; for at your grief
       See how my wretched sister sobs and weeps
       (3.1.137–8)

Titus's suffering centers in himself, standing "as one upon a rock / Environ'd with a wilderness of sea" (94–5), while he interprets his daughter's anguish as reflexive and empathetic, responding to others. He claims, "I understand her signs" (144), but as he reads them, those signs have nothing to do with her, and in the rhetoric of his grief he eclipses both her and his other kin. He is no longer a rock surrounded by sea but the sea itself and the earth as well:

> I am the sea. Hark how her sighs doth blow;
> She is the weeping welkin, I the earth;
> Then must my sea be moved with her sighs;
> Then must my earth with her continual tears
> Become a deluge, overflow'd and drown'd . . .
>
> (3.1.226–30)

Lavinia does respond to her father's pain, to some extent bearing out his projections: she kneels with him (210). But his every reference to her wounds and her gestures is nonetheless both ambiguous and ironic, because the wounds are both metaphor and metonymy for the hidden, adjacent wound of rape, of which, in his egocentric grief, he remains ignorant. Furthermore, as responsive to Titus as Lavinia is, all her gestures may be construed as in some way self-referential, too. When she seeks to kneel with her father, for instance, her reasons for prayer can't be the same as his. She wears her rue with a difference.

When Titus finally turns from tears to mad laughter, and assembles his remaining family into a circle to swear revenge (267–88), it would seem that her part in this ritual signifies her return to the role of patriarchal daughter. "Bear thou my hand, sweet wench, between they teeth," he commands, making her the handmaid of his revenge, a metaphor gruesomely literalized both here and later (5.1) when with her stumps she holds a basin to catch the blood while he slits the throats of her attackers.[16] But there are other ways to read this image, as Mary Loughlin Fawcett suggests. The substitution of father's hand for daughter's tongue can indicate the patriarchal origin and status of language, for example; or as parody of the marriage ceremony in which the father gives away his daughter's hand, it can hint at the incestuous return of the daughter to the father (Fawcett 1983: 261–2). Meanings such as these call attention to the social and linguistic structures that *make* daughters into handmaidens.

When Lavinia sits down at the banquet table in the next scene (3.2), the emphasis shifts from the hero's grief to the problematics of Lavinia as signifier. Though Titus still professes, "I can interpret all her martyr'd signs" (36), it is more obvious than ever that he can't. Since neither he nor his daughter can eat normally, the scene offers further opportunities for wordplay about hands, and gestures complementing it. Marcus rebukes his brother for suggesting, in a grotesque conceit, that she in effect commit suicide: "Fie, brother, fie! teach her not thus to lay / Such violent hands upon her tender life." Reasonably enough, since she has indeed lost all manual dexterity, Titus replies, "What violent hands can she lay on her life?" (3.2.21–2, 25). Lavinia renders even commonplace metaphors dysfunctional. Futhermore, in the context of Titus's earlier reference to his hands that "fought for Rome and all in vain" (3.1.74), it is evident that the meaning of hands is gender-specific. Even when she still had her hands, Lavinia's use of them was limited to lute-playing and sewing "tedious samplers," the ornaments of her chastity; she had no access to agency.

After continuing, somewhat tediously, to "handle . . . the theme . . . of hands" (3.2.29), Titus now volunteers more modestly to "learn" what Lavinia means:

> Thou shalt not sigh, nor hold thy stumps to heaven,
> Nor wink, nor nod, nor kneel, nor make a sign,
> But I of these will wrest an alphabet . . .
>
> (3.2.42–4)

This list, which isn't comprehensive, indicates the scope of gestures available to the actor playing Lavinia, and the opportunity for possibly disruptive or subversive meanings in her "alphabet."[17] It is not simply through gestures, though, that she finally manages to identify her rapists. The scene closes as father, daughter, and nephew go off to read together – a touching family group – seemingly just for distraction from their overbearing griefs (3.2.82–6). This moment heralds the play's most interesting critique of the linguistic bases of patriarchy.

The next scene opens with a burst of activity emanating from a transformed Lavinia. No longer weeping or kneeling, she chases her nephew around the stage as though possessed by "some fit or frenzy" until she gets hold – in a fashion – of the book she seeks, Ovid's *Metamorphoses*, turns to the tale of Philomel, and finally gets her message across. No longer misled by her visible wounds, Titus now sees the hidden truth through the medium of a text: "And rape, I fear, was root of thy annoy" (4.1.49).

Previously, Lavinia unwittingly disrupted language by conveying meanings she didn't intend, and couldn't tell the story she wanted to tell. Now she tells it, but in the revealingly mediated form of a citation from one of the master texts of Latin culture. Thus she figures the cultural double bind of women, who must either speak in the language of the fathers or improvise some other means of communication in its interstices. When Chiron and Demetrius turned her loose in the woods after raping and maiming her, they jeered:

> So, now go tell, and if thy tongue can speak,
> Who 'twas that cut thy tongue and ravish'd thee.
> Write down thy mind, bewray thy meaning so
> And if thy stumps will let thee, play the scribe.
> See how with signs and tokens she can scrowl.
>
> (2.3.1–5)

The last word "scrowl" is a variant spelling of "scrawl," defined in the *OED* as "to spread the limbs abroad in a sprawling manner." The physical activity of writing that normally passes unremarked becomes in Lavinia's case grotesquely indecorous. To a modern reader it may also suggest other forms of signification such as "scrawl" and "scroll," referring to writing and written text (the *QED* offers no examples contemporary with the play), and "scowl," a facial expression as non-verbal signifier. Lavinia eventually does manage to "scrowl" the Latin word for rape, and the names of the rapists, in the earth; by following her uncle's example, she holds a staff between her teeth and guides it with her stumps. After the prolonged irony of the preceding textual aporia, during which Marcus's initial recognition of rape was effaced, this moment comes as Lavinia's peculiar, hard-won triumph. But it is also true that, as Fawcett argues, "When she takes her uncle's staff into her mouth, she uses the language of the fathers, the cultural dominators" (1983: 269), for she writes in Latin. What Shakespeare gives with one hand, one might say, he takes away with the other.[18]

Though the story of Philomel supplies the most fully elaborated paradigm of Lavinia's role in the revenge scenario, it is but one in a sequence of classical references in this scene – a sequence that as a whole suggests the complexity of women's relations to textuality in patriarchal culture. More specifically, it reveals Shakespeare's effacement of female agency in his selective retention and deletion of elements in the stories of women.[19] The sequence begins when Marcus, urging his nephew not to be frightened by the aunt who is furiously pursuing him, compares her to Cornelia, mother of the Gracchi, who read to her sons. Just as Cornelia prepared them for their political roles, he implies, so has Lavinia, by reading poetry and Cicero's *De Oratore* to the boy, performed the office of a mother by mediating literacy to the next generation of males (without seizing its power for herself). The boy then compares his aunt to a strikingly different kind of mother, "Hecuba of Troy" who, he has read, "Ran mad for sorrow" (4.1.20–1).[20]

Hecuba's sorrow, interestingly, motivates only the first part of the story Ovid tells in the *Metamorphoses*. After the defeat of Troy, when her only surviving daughter Polyxena is sacrificed to appease Achilles' shade, Hecuba beats her breast and grieves both for her daughter and her lost dignity as queen. But when she discovers that Polydorus, the last of her sons, has been treacherously murdered by Polymestor, to whom he was given to be kept safe from the war, she sets out to avenge him and herself. Ovid stresses the empowerment anger gives her: "In that rage / She towered, a queen again, whose whole employment / Spelled out the images of fitting vengeance" (*Met.* 13.545–7).[21] That vengeance is no less terrible than the one exacted by Titus. Hecuba lures Polymestor to an audience and with the aid of the other captured women, grabs him. Then she not only digs out his eyes from their sockets but keeps on, "In manic fury, with bloody fingers, scooping / The hollows where the eyes had been" (*Met.* 13.563–4). In suppressing the second part of Hecuba's story in the Boy's reference to Lavinia as Hecuba, Shakespeare excises a female agency that takes violent retribution against patriarchy, and retains as the woman's part the ineffectual empathetic sorrow – witness as opposed to agency – that Titus and the others ascribe to Lavinia.

The Philomel story offers a more complex array of parallels and differences. In both the Ovidian tale and the Shakespearean play, "the exchange of women articulates the culture's boundaries" and the woman's sexualized body serves as "the ground of the culture's system of differences" (Joplin 1984: 37, 38). Ovid's tale (*Met.*, 6. 419–672) begins with a father giving his daughter in marriage. Because Tereus, king of Thrace, came to his aid when Athens was threatened with invasion, Pandion gives him his daughter Procne. (Similarly, as noted above, Titus furthers Lavinia's betrothal within a sequence of exchanges between men.) In making this alliance, Pandion unwisely breaches the boundary between civilized Athens and wild Thrace. Similarly, in taking Tamora, the licentious and barbarous Goth, as wife, Saturninus opens Rome's gates to its cultural other, while his brother's marriage to Lavinia, the epitome of chaste Roman womanhood, marks the difference between Roman and barbarian. But that difference, already destabilized by the blurring of distinctions between rape and marriage in the passage of Lavinia from one brother to the other, is violently confounded when she is raped by two Gothic brothers. In Ovid's story, Tereus takes two daughters from the same man: he marries Procne, but he then rapes her sister Philomel, becoming the husband of two women and changing sisters to rivals (*Met.*, 6.536–9). Thus both the tale and the play point to exogamy as a perilous marker of cultural difference, and generate their plots from the disruption of the lawful exchange of women in marriage by the violent seizure of women in rape.

The tale and the play diverge importantly, however, in scripting women's responses to rape. Lavinia, complicit with her patriarchal role as daughter and wife, helped precipitate rape by boasting of her chastity, and loses her tongue simultaneously with her chastity. As I have just argued, the text registers anxiety about rape, rather than protest, by muting not only Lavinia but also Marcus, whose recognition of her rape as a version of Philomel's is dramatized, then effaced. Philomel, in contrast, speaks out against Tereus, boldly indicting him and threatening to reveal the rape:

> O wicked deed! O cruel monster,
> Barbarian, savage! . . .
> Now that I have no shame, I will proclaim it.
> Given the chance, I will go where people are,
> Tell everybody; if you shut me here,
> I will move the very woods and rocks to pity.
> The air of Heaven will hear, and any god,
> If there is any god in heaven, will hear me.
>
> (*Met.* 6.532–3, 545–50)

Moved equally by fear and anger, Tereus cuts off her tongue and hides her in the forest.

From this point, Ovid stresses the bonds among women by means of which a terrible revenge against Tereus is enacted (Joplin 1990). A silenced Philomel makes the traditionally feminine art of the loom a medium of communication with her sister. She weaves her story into a tapestry and gives it to an old woman, who brings it to Procne. Taking advantage of a women's rite, a festival of Bacchus attended by "all the Thracian mothers," dressed in vines and deerskin Procne joins the raging worshippers and finds her sister, hidden in the forest. Reunited with Philomel, she immediately begins to plot vengeance, telling her, "This is no time . . . / For tears, but for the sword, for something stronger / Than sword" (*Met.*, 6.613–15) – namely, murdering her son and serving him to his unwitting father as a ritual meal. Procne hesitates only when her son embraces her; at that moment, she explicitly weighs his claim on her, and her husband's,

64

against her ties to her sister: "Since he calls me mother, / Why does she not say Sister? Whose wife are you, / Daughter of Pandion?" She concludes, "But devotion to him [Tereus] is a worse crime," and together the sisters swiftly take their bloody retribution on the rapist – appropriately through his son, his stake in the continuity of patriarchal power (*Met.*, 6.634–8).

In contrast, Lavinia depends not on the feminine art of textiles, but, as I have argued, on the texts authored by men that authorize patriarchal culture. Shakespeare marks the moment in which dramatic focus shifts from Lavinia's communication of rape to Titus' enactment of revenge by making Titus, the avenging father, address the father of the gods in Latin: "*Magni dominator poli, / Tam lentus audis scelera? tam lentus vides?* (4.1.81–2) (Ruler of the great heavens, art thou so slow to hear and to see crimes?)[22] Titus is the offended party, and it will be Titus who initiates, supervises, and carries out revenge. Construing the injury done to Lavinia as an injury to himself, as he prepares to slaughter Chiron and Demetrius he tells them, "For worse than Philomel you used my daughter, / And worse than Progne I will be revenged" (5.2.194–5).

Wherever the story of Philomel is evoked in Shakespeare, the story of Lucrece is also brought in.[23] Celebrated on adjacent days in Ovid's *Fasti*, the two stories are parallel and complementary in their portrayals of rape and women enacting retribution. While Philomel and Procne act against the rapist only, in killing herself Lucrece also motivates her kinsmen to take retribution. Trying to learn who raped his daughter, Titus turns from Ovid's myth to Livy's history:

> Give signs, sweet girl, for here are not but friends,
> What Roman lord it was durst do the deed:
> Or slunk not Saturnine, as Tarquin erst,
> That left the camp to sin in Lucrece' bed?
>
> (4.1.61–4)

By citing the rape of Lucrece, Titus raises the possibility that Lavinia, like Lucrece, might represent herself, articulate the meaning of sexual violation, and lay the foundation for the revenge that follows. Summoning her husband, her father, and her other male kin, Livy's Lucrece reveals the crime and its perpetrator. She also affirms that "It is my bodye onely that is violated, my minde God knoweth is guiltles," but stresses what it means for the honor of her father and her husband rather than to herself. Most importantly, she declares that, despite her innocence, she nonetheless intends to commit suicide, and links this act to the action she expects them to take, saying:

> I praye you consider with your selves, what punishmente is due for the malefactour. As for my part, though I cleare my selfe of the offence, my body shall feele the punishment: for no unchast or ill women, shall hereafter impute no dishonest act to Lucrece.
>
> (Painter's *Pallace*, quoted in Prince 1961: 194–5)

This double move constitutes an exceptionally lucid representation of the role of sacralized chastity, incorporate in the female body, in Roman patriarchy. Lucrece takes it upon herself to maintain the ideological purity of chastity for future generations, by making her suicide a symbolic purification of the pollution of her chastity wrought by the rape.[24] Furthermore, by drawing a parallel between "what is due the malefactour" and "my parte," when she turns the knife against herself she makes it imperative for the men to turn it against the tyrant. Thus she establishes a narrative linkage between rape, revenge, and revolution that, as Stephanie Jed (1989) has argued, reaches back to Thucydides and Aristotle, and forward to Machiavelli and Salutati – and to Shakespeare.

This promise of empowerment for Lavinia, however circumscribed by patriarchal ideology, is not borne out. In the stage action so suggestive of woman's relation to patriarchal language and power, Lavinia follows her uncle's guidance, takes a staff in her mouth, and scratches in the earth the names of the crime and the criminals. Then, instead of inciting her kinsmen to revenge, she becomes part of the ritual her uncle leads, a ritual modeled on the oath-taking in Livy's narrative. Marcus commands:

> My lord, kneel down with me; Lavinia, kneel;
> And kneel, sweet boy, the Roman Hector's hope;
> And swear with me, as with the woeful fere
> And father of that chaste dishonoured dame,
> Lord Junius Brutus sware for Lucrece' rape,
> That we will prosecute by good advice
> Mortal revenge upon these traitorous Goths,
> And see their blood, or die with this reproach.
>
> (4.1.87–94)

Once Lavinia makes the rape known, the task of avenging it passes into male hands. For her, it remains only to assist her father in killing

66

the rapists, and according to the last of the many textural precedents and parallels cited, not to kill herself but to be killed by her father. If, in Joplin's interpretation, the chaste woman is the sign of her father's or husband's power, when that woman is raped, such power is mocked, challenged, diminished (1984: 33–4). Through revenge, it can be restored.

THE REVENGER

Curiously, however, once Titus finally has his mandate for revenge, he doesn't seize it. Not he but his brother Marcus leads the Andronici in swearing revenge, and in the next three scenes, Titus repeatedly seeks recourse to actions that, though symbolically potent, don't effect revenge. He sends to the rapist a bundle of weapons wrapped in a scroll on which a famous verse from Horace is written (4.2); together with the weapons, it constitutes an ironic comment on their guilt, but its meaning eludes them. Next he organizes a group of Romans to shoot arrows addressed to various gods toward the court, an elaborate dramatic conceit signifying – again, through a well-known Latin tag – that he can find no justice here on earth (*"Terras Astraea reliquit"* [Ovid, *Met.*, 150], 4.3.4). Finally, he sends Saturninus an oration wrapped around a knife. All these gestures combine texts with weapons to signify ambivalently that while words can work like weapons, they aren't weapons, and weapons, in this case, work like words, signifying but not committing aggression.

This recoil from revenge could be explained generically, for Titus now finds himself in the same position as the revenge tragedy heroes Hieronimo or Hamlet: he knows the identity of his enemies, and they are the ones in power. In acting against them he would commit treason and risk his own destruction. Furthermore, revenge heroes are inherently decent men reluctant to act outside the law. This kind of impasse necessitates the delay standard to the revenge play, delay that creates an ethical and dramatic tension released in the final outburst of bloody retaliations. Titus's reluctance to act, however, is based on more than revenge convention; it fits into the pattern informing the whole play that positions him between the daughter and the mother. Empowered by his daughter's words, Titus must now face Tamora, the evil mother – and here he pauses:

> But if you hunt these bear-whelps, then beware:
> The dam will wake, and if she wind ye once

67

She's with the lion deeply still in league,
And lulls him whilst she playeth on her back,
And when he sleeps will she do what she list.
(4.1.96–100)

Tamora (and unknown to Titus, her paramour Aaron) have made
Rome "a wilderness of tigers." This feral mother, Titus argues, fiercely
guards her bearish sons, "lulls" the emperor her husband while she
cuckolds him, and can have her way against any who challenge her.
Though Marcus thinks his brother won't act because he is "yet so
just that he will not revenge" (4.1.128), it is specifically Tamora from
whom Titus recoils.

At this point, the half-mad Titus fantasizes making the most futile
of textual gestures: writing a version of the Sibyl's prophecies (presumably indicting Tamora), to be blown away "like leaves before the
wind" (4.1.102–6). This impotence is contrasted to the Boy's boast:
"if I were a man / Their mother's bedchamber should not be safe"
(4.1.107–8). He would revenge rape by rape, and, his uncle assures
him, "thy father hath full oft / For his ungrateful country done the
like" (4.1.110–11). In other words, rape is manly, Roman, and in
warfare, surely, a component of *virtus*. This fleeting fantasy of raping
a mother as revenge hardly models the action that an upright Roman
like Titus would pursue. But it recalls the sexually overdetermined
image of the pit as vagina, womb, tomb, and hell, an image that
represented a complex of male anxieties primarily surrounding the
maternal feminine, unleashed when Tamora became Titus's enemy.
It is those fears that Titus must confront in avenging his daughter's
rape.

Tamora, absent from the stage since the scene in which the pit
figured, the scene of the rape, returns as an offstage presence in the
next scene. A trumpet flourish announces that she has given birth to
a child, and the Nurse brings the baby onstage. The scene then
centers on whether this black baby shall live or die. Tamora and her
sons want to do away with it, because the child's skin color proves
her mother's adultery; as the Nurse says, the baby is "Our empress'
shame, and stately Rome's disgrace" (4.2.60), while Aaron proudly
claims it as his own. In ideological terms, what is at stake is the
preservation of sacralized chastity in Rome, either through deception
by means of infanticide, or through the revelation of Tamora's
breach of chastity and the restoration of the real thing. Constant reference to the baby's blackness and many physical threats to its life ("I'll

broach the tadpole on my rapier's point," says Demetrius, 4.2.87),
make it very much a creature of the flesh and emphasize its fleshly
connection to Tamora. Her labor pains are mentioned (4.2.46–7),
and Aaron rebukes Chiron and Demetrius by saying,

> He is your brother, lords, sensibly fed
> Of that self blood that first gave life to you;
> And from that womb where you imprisoned were
> He is enfranchised and come to light . . .
>
> (4.2.124–7)

With every reference to Tamora's maternity, we are also reminded of
her lasciviousness. She flaunts sacralized chastity and also the Roman
ethnic purity it protects, her bastard child being by blood half-Goth,
half-Moor. This nameless infant embodies the anxieties about the
unconstrained maternal womb represented by the pit in act two –
anxieties that Titus must confront and recontain.

While his last remaining son, Lucius, the representative of unblem-
ished *virtus*, leads an army of Goths against Rome to rid it of the
demonized mother, Tamora plans to set father against son by
persuading Titus to make his son relent. In the play's cleverest scene,
she finds him in contemplative retreat in his study, "ruminat[ing] plots
of dire revenge" (5.2.6); that is, he is writing. "What I mean to do /
See here in bloody lines I have set down," he says, "And what is
written shall be executed" (5.2.13–15). But, he adds sardonically, he
lacks "a hand to give it action" (5.2.18). Tamora has disguised herself
as Revenge, and her two sons as Rape and Murder; because Titus
is mad, she thinks, he won't recognize them. Serving as a sort of anti-
muse, she tells him she is "sent from th'infernal kingdom / To ease
the gnawing vulture of thy mind" (5.2.30–1) by working vengeance
on his enemies. In this scene, as Willbern suggests, Tamora's self-
association with hell is more than conventional, given the imagery of
the pit that connects hell not only with female sexuality (a connection ubiquitous in the Shakespearean canon as well) but more specifically, as I have argued, with the malign fecundity of the maternal
womb. Ascending, perhaps, from the trapdoor that localizes hell
onstage, she "stands within the symbol of her dreadful power" and
accosts the reclusive Titus (Willbern 1978: 177–8). She would entice
him "down" – into the damnable evil of revenge – by offering to put
into action for him the plots he has put into writing. Titus first resists
her, claiming that he's not mad and that he recognizes her, joking
with bitter irony, "Is not thy coming for my other hand?" (5.2.27).

Finally, pretending to be taken in by her transparent ruse, he descends, and meets her on her own ground, materially and morally: he is now ready to act, to perform by his own agency, not hers, the plot that he (with the aid of Ovid and Seneca) has written. In terms of the play's gender politics, he confronts the mother and repossesses the initiative that she had illicitly seized; he reestablishes patriarchal control over a matrix made evil when he lost control. The banquet that she suggests to him as her device he appropriates for his own purposes as a Thyestean banquet of her own flesh, a supremely fitting revenge. She attacked his progeny by supervising the murder of his sons and, more cruelly, the rape of his daughter; she raided his treasury and mocked the sign of his power, his chaste daughter. Now he insults her womb (the word also means stomach), the site of her power, by making her "swallow her own increase" (5.2.191).

Of equal ideological significance in the gender politics of *Titus*, though, is the action that precedes the eating of the forbidden food – the murder of Lavinia. Here we confront the last of the several textual precedents by which Lavinia is represented. She has been compared to Cornelia, Hecuba, Philomel, and Lucrece; in her final moments she is a Verginia, not mother, sister, or wife but definitively daughter, at last restored to Titus, though only by the knife. In Livy, the long and complex story that reaches its climax with the murder of Verginia is explicitly paralleled with that of Lucrece. Like the Tarquins, the decemvirs (a council of ten that seizes more power than it was originally granted, and, backed by force, refuses to surrender its office) are tyrants; as in the Lucrece narrative, their abuse of political power is figured in a sexual act, the culminating insult to the Roman social order.

The decemvir Appius Claudius conceives a passion for Verginia, daughter of the upright soldier Lucius Verginius; she is already betrothed to Icilius. Through a legal maneuver Appius seeks to claim her as his slave and subject her to his lust. In resisting him, the father and the intended husband function as a pair, occupying complementary positions as Verginia's present and future guardians. Verginia is helpless and unable to speak for herself; her father is away at the front, and in the buildup to confrontation between him and Appius, "the maiden's safety turn[s] on her protector's being at hand in time" (III.xvi.6). So Icilius steps in to act as her protector, articulating precisely his and her father's interest in her chastity:

70

This maiden I am going to wed, and I intend that my bride shall be chaste . . . If Verginius yields to this man's claim, he will have to seek a husband for her.

(III.xlv.6–7, 11)

When her father arrives, he makes a pubic appeal that contrasts the father's legitimate control over his daughter's body in marital exchange to the rape of daughters and wives in war:

He then began to go about and canvass people . . . saying that he stood daily in the battle-line in defence of their children and their wives . . . to what end, if despite the safety of the City those outrages which were dreaded as the worst that could follow a city's capture must be suffered by their children?

(III.xlvii.2)

Just as importantly, Verginius parallels the male role as warrior-protector of Rome with that of *paterfamilias*. The internal order of the city and its safety from external threat both depend, he argues, on the father's guardianship of the daughter.

The crowd to which Verginius appeals is cowed by the decemvir's authority, and Appius prepares to seize Verginia. To prevent him, the father stabs his daughter to the heart, saying "'Tis you, Appius, and your life I devote to destruction with this blood!" (III.xlviii.5). Only then does popular resistance begin to take hold, and Appius retreats; in the end, the decemvirs are forced to abdicate. Even more explicitly than in the story of Lucrece, patriarchal control over female sexuality is linked to the order and safety of the state. In both stories, the body of the slain woman, exhibited to the people, incites them to rise against tyrants.

In *Titus*, a political over-plot – the assault on Rome to unseat Saturninus, led by Titus's son Lucius – is paralleled and interwoven with the revenge plot against Tamora that Titus carries out. Titus doesn't seize political initiative as Verginius does; that falls to his son. But both stories represent filicide as an act that is both personal and political, an act based on a recognition of the social and ideological centrality of the father's control over the virgin daughter. Verginius kills his daughter so as to prevent the loss of her chastity, and makes her blood the sign and ground of resistance – his and that of the people – against the decemvir. When Titus kills Lavinia, he stresses his sorrow (in line with the play's earlier emphasis) and links it with her shame (5.3.45–6), as though only personal feelings matter. But in

71

citing Livy's story as "A reason mighty, strong, and effectual; / A pattern, president, and lively warrant" for the murder (5.3.42–3), Titus supplies a historical context in which chastity has a fully developed political significance.

In her last brief appearance onstage, Lavinia is veiled, so that Tamora and Saturninus won't recognize her and guess what Titus is up to. This veil can also be read to indicate her liminal status as neither maid nor wife, polluted by the stain of rape. When Titus kills her – as Verginius did, "with his own right hand" – he purges her of that pollution, as Lucrece purged herself of her "forced stain" (*Lucrece*, 1700–50), and restores her to the right hand of paternal blessing.[25] What Joplin says of Lucretia's death by her own hand in Livy is equally true of Lavinia's death by her father's hand:

> Lucretia, raped and alive, would be a sign of contradiction that cynical and less virtuous women might interpret to their own ends. Lucretia, raped and dead by her own hand, neatly circumscribes and seals off the potential pollution of her sexual violation.
>
> (1990: 63)

Now Lucius can restore her to the Andronici, giving orders that "My father and Lavinia shall forthwith / Be closed in our household's monument," while Tamora, "that ravenous tiger," that murderous mother, be left unburied, prey for beasts and birds (5.3.191–200).

NOTES

1 A number of critics have identified classical sources and analogues in *Titus* and interpreted their function in the play. Law (1943) added the *Aeneid* and Plutarch's "Life of Scipio" to Kittredge's list of sources (Seneca's *Thyestes* and *Troades*, Ovid's tale of Philomel in the *Metamorphoses*, Plutarch's "Life of Coriolanus," and the story of Verginius and Verginia in Livy). Mowat (1981) suggests that the "larger shaping myth [in addition to that of Philomel] is actually . . . Hecuba's revenge, into which the Philomel myth and others are embedded" (59). See also G. K. Hunter (1984) for an important contribution to theories of source material and their meaning, and West (1982) for an interpretation of Latin texts in the play's action, both noted below. James Galderwood (1971) discovers in the transformation of Rome from civilization to barbarism an overarching allegory of Shakespeare's sense of his own descent from the purity of his literary models to "theatrical sensationalism" (41). Richard T. Brucher (1979) argues that by surpassing the violence in his classical sources, Shakespeare "push[es] the audience into an unfamiliar realm of

experience where conventionally serious responses are disallowed" (87). Mary Loughlin Fawcett (1983) uses *Titus* "as a primary text to evolve a theoretical account of the relationship between the body, signs, speech, and writing," and comments interestingly on its use of Latin (262–3)

2 Miola, astutely noting Shakespeare's many appropriations of the *Aeneid* and the *Metamorphoses*, reads *Titus* as dramatizing the decline of Roman values from their original *pietas*, and stresses "the importance of familial unity" to those values (1983: 59, 66–7 *et passim*). He does not criticize, as I do, the patriarchal terms of that unity.

3 See Boose (1989) (to which I am much indebted in this chapter) for a cogent analysis of the daughter's position in the patriarchal family, in structural and historical terms.

4 Green's insightful essay, originally prepared for a seminar at the Shakespeare Association of America in 1986, first spurred me to think about Lavinia's role in the construction of her father as hero. Here I have tried to extend Green's argument that "[Lavinia's] mutilated body' articulates Titus's own suffering and victimization" (1989: 322).

5 Tracing Virgilian parallels, Jonathan Bate points out that "as in the *Aeneid*, the main threat to [Titus] is an exotic woman from a rival empire," and that "Virgil's Lavinia, the mother of early Rome, becomes the mutilated daughter of late Rome" (1995: 18). In a richly detailed and suggestive intertextual reading, Heather James interprets the entire play in terms of "a discourse of cultural disintegration" in which "Shakespeare first invokes the *Aeneid* as the epic of empire-building, order, and *pietas*, and then allows Ovid's *Metamorphoses* to invade, interpreting the fundamental impulses of Vergil's poem as chaotic, even apocalyptic" (1991: 123).

6 This and all further quotations from *Titus Andronicus* are taken from the Arden Shakespeare, third series, edited by Jonathan Bate (London and New York: Routledge, 1995).

7 Lévi-Strauss's theory of kinship, exchange and culture has been appropriated, revised, and criticized by feminists. For an influential critique of it, see Rubin (1975); also see Greene and Kahn (1985).

8 Lynda Boose's discussion of the daughter's meaning in *Beowulf* suggests the dimensions of thesaurization in *Titus*: "As the means of production for all the bonds within either her father's or the enemy's group, the daughter is every tribe's central treasure . . . As potentially multiple mediator of bonds inside, outside, or between oppositions, she defines the poem's emblematic nexus of conflicting desires" (29). See also the essays by Traub (1992) and Ziegler (1990).

9 What might seem merely clumsiness in dramatizing the conflict over Lavinia in the play's first scene can be interpreted, in several ways, as implying a comment on the patriarchal exchange of women. David Willbern states that Lavinia's first "rape . . . suggests the unconscious equation of marriage and rape, sexuality and violence, which permeates the play" (1978: 163). On a theoretical level, Patricia Klindienst Joplin's claim that rape, as a failed exchange, is homologous with marriage, can be applied to the rape / marriage of Lavinia. In rape, the woman is taken, not given, but she signifies the same thing: "In truth, they are one: prohibition (sacralized chastity) and transgression (rape by the

sacred) are two sides of one coin . . . [in that the] object of desire the female body represents is supreme authority" (1990: 59). Similarly, John Winkler interprets the episodes of sexual violence in Longus's story of Daphnis and Chloe as revealing "the inherent violence of the cultural system . . . in the integration of males and females into the competitive and hostile economy of Greek culture" (1991: 17, 21).

10 In Peter Brook's acclaimed 1955 production of the play (in which Lawrence Olivier played Titus), the set was dominated by large pillars; when moved aside, they revealed an inner recess that first served as the tomb of the Andronici, then as the pit, and finally, as Titus's study or "Revenge's cave" – thus linking the three sites.

11 David Willbern's fascinating psychoanalytic interpretation places the pit, representing the mother's body, at the symbolic core of the play. He views rape and revenge as interlocking parts of a basically oedipal fantasy of attack on and defense of the mother's body: "revenge is both a substitute for sex and a defense against it." In social terms, a maternal Rome (represented by Lavinia) is raped by the Goths, and must be defended by revenge against them. He equates Tamora with a different aspect of the maternal – "the dreaded devouring mother" (1978: 166). In his view, Lavinia and Tamora are in a sense interchangeable representatons of the maternal, reflecting the desire and dread of the oedipal subject. In mine, as alienated mother and violated daughter, they enact opposing feminine positions in the patriarchal family. Albert Tricomi notes that Tamora's description of the pit (2.2.94–104) links it to the underworld, as would the use of a trapdoor, "not only a symbol of the demonic power but a theatrical embodiment of it," in the staging of 2.2 (1974: 18).

12 The Longleat manuscript, which may be dated as early as 1595 or later than the Folio of 1633, emphasizes Tamora's importance and, as Alan Dessen points out, portrays her rejected plea as a key moment in the play (1989: 6). Strikingly, in its drawing of Tamora kneeling with her sons before a standing Titus, she is as tall as he is. Transcripts of her plea for Alarbus and Aaron's boastful list of his many crimes are linked by lines from Titus's speech justifying the sacrifice, implying that his action provokes the network of vengeance that Aaron plots. Jonathan Bate comments that the drawing "demonstrates how a contemporary of Shakespeare's visualized the play," and further interprets Peacham's scene as "an emblematic reading of the whole play" representing Titus and Tamora as opposites, their gestures "the central gestures of the play: authoritative command against supplication on knees" (1995: 41–2).

13 For a different view of Lavinia's mutilation, see Leonard Tennenhouse (1986b: 107–8), who regards it as Shakespeare's "highly self-conscious revision of his classical materials," intended to displace rape so as to make Lavinia's body a symbol of the state.

14 Gail Kern Paster remarks on the "conventional metonymic replacement of mouth for vagina" in this speech, in which "the blood flowing from Lavinia's mutilated mouth stands for the vaginal wound that cannot be staged or represented . . . the sign of an immutable condition – the condition of womanhood . . . ultimately inseparable from the more

conventional meaning of vaginal blood as a sign of male mastery over the body of woman, or (as here) of male sexual violence" (1993: 98–9).

15 This speech, to be sure, possesses other dimensions as well. In Deborah Warner's landmark 1987 production, Donald Sumpter as Marcus delivered it uncut and produced the effect described by Stanley Wells: "it became a deeply moving attempt to master the facts, and thus to overcome the emotional shock, of a previously unimagined horror . . . an articulation, necessarily extended in expression, of a sequence of thoughts and emotions that might have taken no more than a second or two to flash through the character's mind, like a bad dream" (Wells quoted in Bate 1995: 62). Jonathan Bate remarks that "a lyrical speech is needed because it is only when an appropriately inappropriate language has been found that the sheer force of contrast between its beauty and Lavinia's degradation begins to express what she has undergone and lost" (1995: 63).

16 Heather James credits me with spotting this visual joke, in a paper I gave in 1988 (1991: 133, 140); Jonathan Bate also remarks on it (1995: 11–12) in passing, without noting how it subsumes Lavinia's injury in her father's, and subordinates her to his heroic mission.

17 Alan Dessen (1989) surveys the range of modes in which the role of Lavinia has been performed and staged. In Peter Brook's 1955 production, crimson ribbons streamed from Lavinia's mouth and arms to signify mutilation, while in Trevor Nunn's (1972), Lavinia was "a pitiable, hunched grotesque crawling out of the darkness like a wounded animal." In her 1985 BBC production, Jane Howell's Lavinia displayed "verisimilar stumps and bloody mouth." Deborah Warner, directing *Titus* for the RSC in 1987, wrapped Lavinia's stumps, coated her with mud, and allowed "but a trickle" of blood to escape her mouth. Both stylized and naturalistic representations of the mutilation seem to have been effective.

18 For diverse readings of Lavinia's writing, along with essays by Green and Fawcett, see Hulse (1979) who views it as *fellatio* and a reenactment of her violation; Danson (1974), as figuring the frustrated human need to speak and be understood; Calderwood (1971), as part of Shakespeare's protest at being forced to abandon "the chaste poetic word" in his lyric and narrative poems and turn to the barbaric language of the popular theatre.

19 See chapter 1, pp. 20–1, on the work of Jed (1989), Joplin (1984, 1990), and Newman (1994) on gender bias in the appropriation of classical materials by Renaissance authors.

20 Barbara Mowat traces the suggestive parallels between Titus and Hecuba; her article (cited in note 1) first showed me the pertinence of that Ovidian story to the play.

21 This and other quotations from the *Metamorphoses* are taken from the translation by Rolfe Humphries (Bloomington: Indiana University Press, 1961).

22 Jonathan Bate astutely notes that this line conflates two Senecan passages, one from "a moment of appalling sexual knowledge in the *Hippolytus*" and one from the *Epistulae Morales* "on accepting death and enduring

75

whatever nature throws at you"; thus tragic recognition is combined with "the idea of submission to the will of the universe" (1995: 30). I would add that such a fusion serves the basically patriarchal structure of this revenge play by implying that a father has no choice but to revenge a daughter's defilement and die defending his investment in her chastity.

23 See for example *Lucrece* 1079–80, 1128–49; *Cymbeline* 2.2.12–14, 44–6.
24 For an extended argument on this point, see Kahn (1976).
25 Titus still has, significantly, his right hand, for at 3.2.7–8 he comments, "This poor right hand of mine / Is left to tyrannize upon my breast."

4

METTLE AND MELTING SPIRITS IN *JULIUS CAESAR*

> My heart laments that virtue cannot live
> Out of the teeth of emulation.
>
> *Julius Caesar* 2.3.11–12[1]

In comparison to *Lucrece* and *Titus Andronicus*, Shakespeare's concern with sexual difference *per se* in *Julius Caesar* would seem minimal, peripheral, and obvious. It has only two female characters, Portia and Calphurnia, the wives of Brutus and Caesar, and each of them speaks in only two scenes. Portia worries aloud to her husband and Calphurnia warns hers about the same thing, which neither woman is in a position to name as such: the conspiracy. Both characters are observers at best, and surely not actors, in the self-evidently masculine world of Roman politics. But the sexual difference that really counts in *Julius Caesar* isn't framed simply as one between male and female and doesn't depend on the presence or absence of female characters.

Rather, the "Rome" so frequently invoked as touchstone of liberty and freedom (thirty-two times in some form, more than in any other Shakespeare play) is the signifier through which the male subject is constructed. This "Rome" is specifically the republic, created out of the uprising against the Tarquins led by Brutus' ancestor and namesake Lucius Junius Brutus. It is the *mythos* of the republic that impels Brutus to lead the conspiracy against Caesar, that compels the conspirators' belief in their cause, that generates a discourse instating them and Caesar as well with identity, agency, and masculinity. In this play more than any other, Shakespeare grounds *virtus* in a specific political ideology, one that both constitutes and fractures its male subjects. And that ideology is itself constituted by its opposition to the feminine: like the republic as conceived by Aristotle, the Roman republic is built on a profound distinction between *polis* and *oikos*, between politics as the freely willed action of rational men and household as the realm of mere physical necessity, of women, children, and slaves.[2] More subtly than in *Lucrece* or *Titus*, though the feminine is socially peripheral, it is nonetheless (to borrow Barbara Babcock's formulation), symbolically central to the world of *Julius Caesar* (Babcock 1978: 32).

Critics have often remarked on the "public" style of the play: major scenes take the form of oratorical persuasions or public debates, and even in private characters speak formally, in lofty abstractions (Greene 1980; Velz 1968a, 1982). Characters conceive themselves and others in terms of their national identity. Not only Julius Caesar, but Brutus and Cassius as well refer to themselves in the third person, as though they are spectators and audience of themselves as public figures. And at several strikingly metatheatrical moments, they present themselves as actors both histrionic and historical in the "lofty scene" of politics, performing their parts with the "formal constancy" of stage actors before an audience of posterity (Stirling 1958; Velz 1968a). This construction of the self as a public entity closely resembles the kind of class identity fostered by the patrician sense of history, ancestry, and public service that is richly evident in Roman social practice as well as Roman literary and historical texts. According to Leo Braudy's account,

> the political history of Rome was clearly written in the genealo-
> gies of its great families for all to see. *Nobilis* in Latin originally
> means someone who is *known*. The upper class, the political
> class, was therefore by definition a class whose families were
> known for their public adherence to the public good . . . a class
> history had made extremely sensible to their visibility in the
> state. In all Roman noble houses were displayed *imagines* (wax
> masks) – first idealized, later realistic – of ancestors who had
> held the chief offices in Rome reserved for those of aristocratic
> privilege.
>
> (Braudy 1986: 59)

The play's predominantly public mode, then, would seem an aspect of Shakespeare's fidelity to a certain verifiable image of historical Rome on which T. J. B. Spencer remarked (1957: 33). Nonetheless, the play has typically been interpreted within the liberal problematic of an opposition between private and public, or between the individual and his society, in which the private realm and the individual take precedence over or transcend the public realm of society. According to the editor of a widely used anthology of critical essays

on the play, it is often viewed "not so much as a play as a collection
of biographies" (Dean 1968: 1). T. S. Dorsch's introduction to the
new Arden edition, organized as a series of character portraits in
sections headed "Julius Caesar," "Brutus," and so forth, affirms this
conception (Dorsch 1955). Critics tend to pose political issues as an
ethical choice between Brutus and Caesar (Proser 1965; Smith 1959).
Though several distinguished essays in the past decade have shifted
the critical focus to explore how discourse and social process constitute
meaning in *Julius Caesar*, they haven't dislodged the liberal problematic
of character, as A. R. Humphreys' introduction to his Oxford edition
attests: "Always in Shakespeare political attitudes stem from personality" (Humphreys 1984: 36).[3]

Shakespeare is too responsive to his Roman source materials to
make politics merely a clash of egos. Yet neither is he so "Roman"
as to naturalize the priority of public over private. As Gary Miles
remarks, "It is . . . precisely the public dimension of his Romans' lives
that is most problematic for Shakespeare," because he also pursues
such "a distinctive interest in the interior life of his characters" (1989:
279)[4] It is the coexistence of these two dimensions of existence and
the dilemma of their interrelationship, not the priority of one over
the other, that drives and animates the action in *Julius Caesar*.
Shakespeare dramatizes the separation of the inner subjective realm
from the distinctively public world of *romanitas* in such a way that it
is readable as ideologically produced in that world by the ethos of
the republic. Even as this private subject is being constituted in and
by a social field, it is also being gendered masculine, through the
association of the public realm with Roman "firmness" and the private
realm with "the melting spirits of women." While this engendering
of republican virtue is centered in the character of Brutus, Brutus's
emergence into Roman virtue is itself staged as a social process: the
conception and formation of the conspiracy, the assassination, and
the shift of power to the triumvirate afterwards. That social process
is dramatized as the evolution of oppositions between private and
public, feminine and masculine; scripted in these oppositions, Brutus
becomes the supreme representative of republican *virtus* who slays his
best lover to restore "Rome".

"PASSIONS OF SOME DIFFERENCE"

In two significant encounters, one with Cassius and one with Portia,
we can chart the evolution of Brutus as exemplar of Roman *virtus*.

The first, an intensely personal conversation between Cassius and Brutus held within earshot of a huge crowd, preceded and followed by a public procession, is situated on the border between public and private (act 1, scene 2).[5] The second takes place between Brutus and Portia in the "orchard" or garden of their private home, penetrated by the conspirators as their secret meeting place, in pursuit of their public duty as they conceive it (act 2, scene 1). In both settings, Shakespeare ambiguates distinctions between private and public to suggest not their opposition but their mutually constitutive relationship. In both scenes, a realm apparently removed, hidden and personal is recuperated as a site of public action. In the first scene, masculine identity is confirmed; in the second, subverted. In the first, one man seduces another from passivity to political action (the metaphor is Cassius's); in the second (to be discussed in the last section of this chapter), a woman fails to draw a secret from her husband, but embodies the "feminine" Other within him.

In the first scene, Cassius offers to serve as a mirror for his troubled friend, a glass that will reveal to Brutus his "hidden worthiness." Pursuing an intricate (and highly conventional) series of optical images, Cassius asks Brutus to look into Cassius's eyes and see there what he cannot see with his own, "That of yourself which you yet know not of" (1.2.69). A similar moment occurs in *Troilus and Cressida* when Ulysses, trying to gain Achilles' confidence so as to lure him back to battle, tells him that no man "feels what he owes [owns, possesses], but by reflection" (3.3.99). In each scene, one man proposes in effect to deliver another into his full manhood, his true identity, in a counterpart of the originary mother–child dyad in which the mother's gaze confirms the child's existence.[6] Explicating the fashioning of male identity in *Troilus and Cressida*, Linda Charnes comments:

> The male fantasy in this play is to move freely between the symbolic (the realm of 'honor,' renown, reputation) and the imaginary (the realm of the confirming, immediate gaze) without any of the threats posed by the intrusion of women . . . precisely to *escape* the need for confirmation from the eyes of women.
>
> (1989: 27)

As long as Brutus sees himself in another man's eyes, he is a Roman, whole and coherent. But when (in act 2, scene 1) Portia reflects a different image of him as divided and troubled, that Roman identity is, however fleetingly, compromised. "Confirmation from the eyes of

80

women" can't be relied upon; other to the masculine world of *virtus*, they are easily (though not invariably) associated with weakness, the non-rational, and disorder.

This image of Brutus that Cassius proceeds to refract verbally echoes that with which Plutarch's *Life of Marcus Brutus* opens: "Marcus Brutus came of that Iunius Brutus, for whome the auncient Romanes made his statue of brasse to be set up in the Capitoll, with the images of the kings, holding a naked sword in his hand: bicause he had valiantly put downe the Tarquines from their kingdom of Rome" (*Life of Marcus Brutus* 6: 182). Cassius evokes an idealized Rome emerging into the dawn of the republic under the heroic leadership of Brutus's ancestor and namesake:

> O, you and I have heard our fathers say,
> There was a Brutus once that would have brook'd
> Th'eternal devil to keep his state in Rome
> As easily as a king.
>
> (2.1.165–8)

"There was a Brutus once" – Cassius stops short of directly urging the Brutus he addresses to strike at Caesar. Rather, as Gayle Greene notes, "Cassius's real appeal is made in veiled, allusive terms which communicate not through what they state but what they suggest" (1980: 75) – precisely because he can count on Brutus to catch his meaning and embrace his ancestral heritage as a mandate for present action.

A few scenes later, reading the messages Cassius has had thrown in at his window, wrestling with the question of whether Caesar intends to become king, Brutus himself evokes the same key moment:

> My ancestors did from the streets of Rome
> The Tarquin drive, when he was call'd a king.
>
> (2.1.53–4)

As many in Shakespeare's audience would have known, according to legend and history, Rome began as a kingship founded by the famous twin Romulus and continued as such for some 150 years until the revolution to which Cassius and Brutus refer abolished not only the reigning dynasty but kingship itself. Both men equate Rome, here and throughout the play, with the republic and the values it purports to embody. They see themselves as Romans because they believe in the republic and that means repudiating kingship to share power

81

among ruler, aristocracy, and people. Then, supposedly, no "one man" can dominate Rome; all men will be free and equal. Indeed, as I am arguing, all will be men *per se* only if this republican equality is preserved.

How did Shakespeare become acquainted with Roman republicanism? Though the Tudors had firmly established monarchy as a divinely ordained form of government, humanist veneration of Roman institutions made the republic a well-known and respected political form. Aristotle's *Politics*, which Deborah Shuger calls "a normative, central text for political theory" in the Renaissance, was crucial in disseminating that form (1993: 489). It had seventy-three Latin printings before 1600 and was translated into English in 1598, a year before *Julius Caesar* was performed. Sir Thomas More, John Ponet, and Sir Walter Raleigh drew on Aristotle for basic definitions of the republic as a mixed government compounded of three other kinds – monarchy, aristocracy, democracy. All these, it was held, tended to degenerate. Monarchy turned into tyranny and aristocracy into oligarchy, while democracy declined into mere mob rule. Republican government was designed to prevent this instability by combining the three forms and balancing them so that each would check the others (Fink 1962).

Historically speaking, the Roman republic was intended to redress years of humiliation under the Tarquins' tyranny; as a mixed government of powers held in mutual check, it offered equality in place of servitude. When Cassius harps on the idea that Caesar, Brutus and he are equals as Romans and republicans he doesn't merely voice his personal grudge at being dwarfed by Caesar's colossal power; he evokes a shared historical legacy. Hammering away at a rhetorical opposition between "Rome" and "one man," he portrays Caesar's preeminence as desecrating the very nature of the republic: When could they say, that talked of Rome,

> That her wide walks encompass'd but one man?
> Now is it Rome indeed, and room enough,
> When there is in it but one only man.
>
> (1.2.152–5)

If such sentiments reflected only Cassius's particular envy, his words might well go unheeded, not only by Brutus but by the other conspirators as well. It is his ability to articulate stirringly the key premises of a shared republican ethos that instigates the conspiracy which Brutus then molds.

Republican equality not only militates against the political dominance of any one man; it also entails a conception of virtue as the
sacrifice of personal interest for the sake of the common good. In
the preface to his treatise *De Re Publica*, Cicero pictures his political
career as based on this imperative:

> I could not hesitate to expose myself to the severest storms, and
> I might almost say, even to thunderbolts, for the sake of the
> safety of my fellow citizens, and to secure, at the cost of my
> own personal danger, a quiet life for all the rest.
>
> (*De Re Publica*, I.iv)[7]

As if rehearsing his coming intervention in the "monstrous reign" of
Caesar, which he sees mirrored in the storms and portents that
precede the conspirators' first meeting, Cassius flaunts similar gestures
of symbolic self-sacrifice:

> For my part, I have walk'd about the streets,
> Submitting me unto the perilous night,
> And, thus unbraced, Casca, as you see,
> Have bar'd my bosom to the thunder-stone;
> And when the cross blue lightning seem'd to open
> The breast of heaven, I did present myself
> Even in the aim and very flash of it.
>
> (2.3.46–52)

In his earlier conversation with Cassius, Brutus voices a similar
commitment to altruistic action in the public interest:

> If it be aught toward the general good,
> Set honour in one eye, and death i' th'other,
> And I will look on both indifferently.
>
> (1.2.84–6)

True Romans see themselves as the disinterested defenders of the *res
publica*, "the public thing," who hold the good of the state higher,
even, than life itself.

Finally, beginning with Aristotle and continuing – with a difference
– in Machiavelli, the republic is a distinctively masculine sphere
in which debate and action, the exercise of reason and freedom,
make men truly virile. Aristotle, working from gender oppositions
deeply rooted in Greek thought and social practice, tends to assume
rather than explain why politics is the proper action of men but not
women. He opens the *Politics* by asserting that the *polis* begins in the

reproductive union of male, characterized as "the ruling and master element" paired with "a ruled element" – the female (Aristotle 1946: 3). But in fact he spends few words on the relation of husband to wife, and never addresses directly the question of whether a woman can be a citizen. He implies that, like slaves, mechanics, and children, women are "necessary" to the state but not fit to be citizens of it, because "The citizen in the strict and unqualified sense" is "a man who shares in the administration of justice and the holding of office" (93). As Wendy Brown explains, "Women and slaves stood for the function and identity of the body, and were nothing other than their bodies." The *oikos* may be a necessary part of the *polis*, but the *polis* is constructed as a realm of men "estranged from their physiological and mortal existence . . . which must be literally separated and insu-lated from the realm of necessity" that is relegated to the *oikos* (Brown 1988: 40, 37, 43).

A similar discursive linkage between men and politics, constructed through a different kind of opposition between masculine and feminine, passes from classical thought to the Renaissance through Boethius's *De Consolatione Philosophiae* (*c.* AD 524), widely read throughout the Middle Ages and the Renaissance, translated by Chaucer and by Queen Elizabeth. In J. G. A. Pocock's reading of Boethius, Virtue and Fortune are "regularly paired as opposites and expressed in the image of a sexual relationship: a masculine active intelligence was seeking to dominate a feminine passive unpredict-ability which would submissively reward him for his strength or vindictively betray him for his weakness. *Virtus* could therefore carry many of the connotations of virility" (Pocock 1975: 37).

Like Aristotle, Machiavelli linked civic activism to "manly" heroism and military glory, but instead of sealing off that realm from a femi-nized domain, he brought *virtù* into constant, strenuous engagement with Fortuna. When republican theory and practice arose in the Florentine city-states of the Italian Renaissance, as Pocock argues, "The operations of fortune were no longer external to one's virtue but intrinsically part of it" (Pocock 1975: 76), in the form of the secular, particularized give and take of civic life no longer practiced *sub specie aeternitatis*. Thus Fortune, the traditionally feminized realm of mutability and insecurity, entered into the masculine domain of citizenship, where men actively governed themselves instead of submitting to a higher authority, and reckoned with the unpredictable contingencies of politics. Once this feminine element had entered that domain, man's exercise of virtue became "that by which form was

84

imposed on the matter [or *mater*] of *fortuna*," "that by which fortune was controlled" (Pocock 1975: 161, 162).

As Machiavelli famously remarks, "Fortune is a woman" (1965: 1:92). In Hannah Pitkin's view, the opposition between *virtù* and Fortuna central to his thought bespeaks "a vision of embattled men struggling to preserve themselves, their masculinity, and the achievements of civilization, against . . . a generalized feminine power" (Pitkin 1984: 169).[8] The nature of that power, and the resistance men can marshal against it, are inscribed with subtle ambiguity throughout his writings. Directly pertinent to republican theory in *Julius Caesar*, however, is his conception, in the *Discorsi*, of a collective, fraternal virtue that contrasts with the individual *virtù* so compellingly represented in *The Prince*. In the *Discorsi*, a freewheeling commentary on the first ten books of Livy's history of Rome, Machiavelli celebrates the manly independence of the early republic and laments its erosion with the rise of imperial power. According to Pitkin, the citizen of Machiavelli's republic develops *virtù* through a vigorous civic life (*vivere civile*) comprised of "Mutuality, reciprocity, dialogue, the web of relations that constitute a public arena and create public power . . . precisely plurality, competition, diversity . . . are the source of manly strength (Pitkin 1984: 83, 82). For Machiavelli, Pitkin says, "the Romans were literally forefathers . . . an uncorrupted community of real men, competent to take care of themselves without being dependent on anyone else, sharing in a fraternal, participatory civic life that made them self-governing" (49, 48).

Thus through Machiavelli as well as Aristotle a gendered discourse of the republic came to England (Raab 1964). This complex genealogy of a gendered republic exerts its pressure on *Julius Caesar*. Plutarch isn't the only source for Shakespeare's conception of *virtus* – only the most easily identifiable one. From the play's first scene, however, it is clear that though the *idea* of the republic governs patrician mentality, in actual practice the republic has ceased to exist. The plebs have recently transferred their allegiance from Pompey to Caesar – from one strong man to the next – and the tribunes opposing Caesar do so only in the name of his counterpart and rival, rebuking the mechanics for "ingratitude" rather than for desecrating the republic (1.1.37–55).[9] Further allusions to Pompey ironize the conspirators' belief that Caesar represents the first, unique threat to republican liberty: Cassius first meets with the conspirators on "Pompey's porch" (1.3.126), and speaks of another encounter at "Pompey's theatre" (1.3.153), one of many munificent gifts that endeared him to the populace. Plutarch, with even sharper irony than Shakespeare, sets the assassination of Caesar in this theatre. Through these allusions to Caesar's predecessor, as through Casca's account of the crown being offered to Caesar (1.2.217–72), Shakespeare dramatizes the disjunction between the conspirators' conviction that Caesar alone threatens the republic and the more longstanding, complex realignments that have already transformed it into something else. A single charismatic leader can now gain power over – and from – the people, bypassing Rome's "noble bloods." Thus Cassius's appeal to the republic and Brutus's commitment to the general good can be read as ideological in Althusser's sense: in their vision of the republic, these patricians represent to themselves an imaginary conception of their real relation to the Roman state (Althusser 1971: 164–5). In his treatise on friendship, *De Beneficiis*, Seneca remarks that Brutus

> imagined that such a citie as this might repossesse her ancient honour, and former lustre, when vertue and the primary Lawes were either abolished, or wholly extinguished . . . oh, how great oblivion possessed this man!
>
> (Seneca, transl. Lodge 1614: 30–1)

Brutus and his fellows imagine themselves as the ethical and political core of the republic, but in reality, they are being squeezed out by the constituency they despise: the people.[10]

Instead of holding monarchy, aristocracy, and democracy in balance, the republic has fostered the division of the aristocracy into factions and the rise of military superheroes. The republic, in fact, has generated what it was designed to oppose: the concentration of power in one man's hands. In assuming that they can simply repeat the original Brutus' *coup d'état* by toppling Caesar, these two Romans have elided history. Blinded by their class identity as patricians, they see themselves as a "breed of noble bloods" upholding a sacred precedent, and as pitted against "one man" who was once their peer. In this scene, while Brutus and Cassius ponder their status as Caesar's "underlings," they hear the masses roaring for him – but fail to notice that those masses have become his power base. Though in person Caesar may fall short of the mystique he generates, he knows how to inspire public adulation – but for Brutus and Cassius, the people hardly exist, and Casca's account of how Caesar refused the crown drips with aristocratic disdain for "the tag-rag people."

Shakespeare represents the people, however, not as the touchstone against which the conspirators' ideological blindness may be measured but rather as a body that clings to republican tenets as fiercely as do its social superiors. For why, according to Casca, did the people cheer for Caesar when he refused the crown?

> still as he refus'd it, the rabblement hooted, and clapp'd their chopt hands, and threw up their sweaty nightcaps, and uttered such a deal of stinking breath because Caesar refus'd the crown . . .

(1.2.250–3)

The people adore Caesar most when he *refuses* the crown. Seemingly, they too are captured by the republican ideal (even though incapable of seeing how their adoration for Caesar undermines it). Then Brutus's fear that "the people / Choose Caesar for their King" must be mistaken. Or is it? For when Caesar "perceiv'd the common herd was glad he refus'd the crown, he pluck'd . . . ope his doublet, and offer'd them his throat to cut" (1.2.270–2). He is obviously playing to the gallery in what amounts to a parody of serving "the general good" (his gesture echoes the breast-baring of Cicero, and of Cassius) in order to milk the crowd's approval and then, perhaps, get himself crowned.[11]

It doesn't lie within the people's power alone to confer the crown, however, for it is Antony who offers it, and in the next scene Casca says "the senators to-morrow / Mean to establish Caesar as a king" (1.3.88–9). Other patricians ignore the republican mandate against monarchy; though the conspirators view themselves as representing "Rome," they are but a single faction. However, because Brutus embodies and articulates for them a republican ideal in which they as a class aren't a faction but a united whole who in effect stand for the state, they rally round him. As Antony's funeral oration demonstrates, though, the man who can convince the masses that Caesar – in high republican fashion – was devoted to *them* can rule Rome. As Sigurd Burckhardt argues, Brutus and the conspirators aren't guilty of treachery, nor is their conception of the republic "right" or "wrong": it is simply an anachronism (1968: 9).

In this play, republican ideology can be adopted or coopted by any ambitious man so as to violate its basic tenets – without him or his enemies even realizing it. The play dramatizes its plasticity in a supremely ironic, ambiguous episode that directly enables the assassination. Metellus Cimber's servile "couchings," part of the ruse the conspirators devise so they can gather around Caesar to stab him, elicit from Caesar the same kinds of metaphors for the same kinds of republican ideals that Brutus and Cassius employ. His blood, he says, won't be thawed or melted by emotional appeals such as Metellus Cimber's, for he is, just as Brutus enjoined the conspirators to be,

> constant as the northern star,
> Of whose true-fix'd and resting quality
> There is no fellow in the firmament . . .
> I do know but one
> That unassailable holds on his rank,
> Unshak'd of motion; and that I am he,
> Let me a little show it . . .
>
> (3.1.60–2, 68–71)

When Caesar sounds most republican, though, he also sounds most egotistical and arrogant, claiming superiority over any "fellow in the firmament" because he is immune to personal appeals. It is tempting to read these moments as confirmation of the conspirators' fears that Caesar would be king. Such a reading would securely oppose monarchy to republican equality, and egotistic power-mongering to altruistic power-sharing. But in my view, his insistence on his own superiority to any fellow Roman is only seemingly unrepublican. Rather, Caesar's obsession with coming out on top is part and parcel of the agonistic ethos that has overtaken "the general good" as keystone of the republic. At the same time, it is what makes Romans specifically masculine.

THE TEETH OF EMULATION

The republic as an ideology is intricately bound up with the basically agonistic, highly competitive nature of the Roman ruling elite. Cassius's vignette of his swimming match with Caesar (Shakespeare's invention, an addition to his Plutarchan source materials) captures the routine intensity of competition central to the definition of Romans as men:

> For once, upon a raw and gusty day,
> The troubled Tiber chafing with her shores,
> Caesar said to me, "Dar'st thou, Cassius, now
> Leap in with me into this angry flood,
> And swim to yonder point?" Upon the word,
> Accoutred as I was, I plunged in
> And bade him follow; so indeed he did.

The torrent roar'd, and we did buffet it
With lusty sinews, throwing it aside
And stemming it with hearts of controversy.
(1.2.107–16)

Buffeting the torrent, stretching their lusty sinews on a raw and gusty day, the two Romans are displaying their mettle – their masculine toughness and stamina. Puns on this sort of mettle and "metal" as in iron or steel run through the play, contrasting with references to "the melting spirits of women."[12] As the story continues, Caesar doesn't simply lose the race. Rather, he starts to sink, calls to Cassius for help, and Cassius "as Aeneas . . . Did from the flames of Troy upon his shoulder / The old Anchises bear" (1.2.111–14) carries him to safety. Wayne Rebhorn notes the ironic contrast between Aeneas as the supreme emblem of *pietas* and Cassius's use of the emblem to suggest "the triumph of one man over another" (1990: 83). In the anecdote Cassius tacks on to this one, he goes even farther to denigrate Caesar by feminizing him, telling of a moment in the Spanish campaign when, afflicted with a fever, the pale and shaking Caesar cries out to his comrade "Give me some drink" – "like a sick girl," Cassius says (1.2.126–7).

The swimming match presented here as a spontaneous, gamesome challenge at a casual moment was institutionalized in Roman political life as the *cursus honorum*, aptly translated by Leo Braudy as "the race-track of honors" (1986: 61). Through a series of electoral contests for state office, patricians won the race for power and prestige, fell behind, or just managed to keep in the running. The play's first scene ironically recalls one of the biggest races ever, the rivalry of Caesar and Pompey: the tribunes rebuke the people for celebrating Caesar's triumph – but only because the tribunes themselves are embittered supporters of the defeated Pompey.

Caesar and Pompey were allies before they were enemies; Brutus first supported Pompey, but when Pompey fell, became Caesar's favorite; Brutus and Cassius, friends and confederates bound by shared ideas, quarrel bitterly. It is relations between men, not between men and women, that inculcate *virtus*, and male friendships are indistinguishable from politics itself, from which women are formally excluded. Like politics, they are innately rivalrous, shifting ambivalently between alliances and enmities, because the concept governing them is emulation, from the Latin *aemulari* to rival. As noted in chapter 1 (see p. 15), the *OED* defines emulation as "to copy or imitate with the object of equalling or excelling." Joel Fineman comments on the tension between those two aims: "emulation is the paradoxical labor of envy that seeks to find difference in imitation" (Fineman 1980: 151). As Rebhorn notes, emulation is "an unstable combination of identification and rivalry, love and hate" (1990: 77). And finally, the rival can be internalized, the emulative self split in two. Plutarch describes Julius Caesar as scorning his "prosperous good success . . . as if that which he had present were stale and nothing worth. This humor of his was no other but an emulation with himself as with another man" (*Life of Julius Caesar* 5: 59).[13]

But how can emulation coexist with "the general good"? The republic with its balance of powers and the *cursus honorum* of electoral office might have served to keep emulation within ideological bounds; personal ambition might have fulfilled itself in serving the general good. But historically, it didn't: Miles remarks that "As the glory and wealth that could be won in the service of a growing empire increased, so did the intensity of competition among aristocrats . . . the leading figures in this new, highly charged, heady atmosphere of political competition did not fit the more restrictive molds of Roman politics" (1989: 261). That is the precipitating cause of the conspiracy. As the play opens, Caesar "comes in triumph over Pompey's blood," a colossus dwarfing the patricians who were formerly his fellow con-testants, on his way to an actual race – the "course" forming part of the celebration of Lupercal (Liebler 1981). Republican ideology is already in crisis, for emulation has generated the biggest winner of them all, who could become king and cancel out the republic.

The conspirators' assumption that all Romans are brothers, united by their shared belief in the republic, is flatly contradicted by an equally Roman spirit of emulation. In the character-orientated criti-cism mentioned earlier, Cassius bears the burden of an idiosyncratic envy, in contrast to the supposedly altruistic Brutus. But Brutus, in fact, is not free from the drive to excel over his fellow republicans; rather, he competes in precisely republican terms which, paradoxi-cally, make civic altruism the touchstone of distinction among men.

A close look at a key moment, the soliloquy in which Brutus tries to work out a justification for murdering Caesar, will demonstrate this contradiction. Brutus begins with a conclusion: "It must be by his death" (2.1.10) and then works backward to adduce reasons. The first one is impeccable: "I know no personal cause to spurn at him, / But for the general," he declares, echoing an earlier affirmation of his willingness to risk death for "the general good." As Brutus struggles to explain how Caesar threatens "the general," he does not name his desire to be crowned. Surprisingly, this Brutus *is* willing to brook a king in Rome. Rather, it is how being crowned "might change his nature" that gives Brutus pause. In trying to move from the conditional "might" to some surer statement of the danger lurking in Caesar's ambition, Brutus draws on maxims of doubtful applicability: "It is the bright day that brings forth the adder" (14), for example. He falters when his own direct observations fail to support the conclusion he seeks: "to speak truth of Caesar, / I have not known when his affections sway'd / More than his reason" (19–21). Then he turns to "a common proof," as follows:

> lowliness is young ambition's ladder,
> Whereto the climber upward turns his face;
> But when he once attains the upmost round,
> He then unto the ladder turns his back,
> Looks in the clouds, scorning the base degrees
> By which he did ascend.
>
> (2.1.21–7)

The ambitious Caesar climbs up the ladder of advancement, which is composed of "lowliness," his inferiors, the "base degrees" of men whom he is at first willing to look in the face, but on whom he turns his back when he has gotten to the top. This ladder, its climber, and his fellows who serve him in his advance epitomize the institutionalized emulation of the Roman state. Implicitly, Brutus figures as one of those "base degrees" by which Caesar attains "the topmost round." It is this vision of being trampled on by Caesar that enables Brutus to get to the end of his soliloquy, to "fashion it thus" even though he has to admit that "the quarrel / Will bear no colour for the thing he is" (28–30: to make the leap beyond logic and proof to kill Caesar.

In the cultural milieu of Elizabethan England in 1599, Shakespeare had good reason to be interested in the emotional sway that emulation held over men. Quite simply, it was central to the ethos of England's nobility and gentry; rank conferred on them a personal sense of superiority honed by the particular method of their humanistic education. Rebhorn comments that "Rhetorical training, which served as the core of that education, was basically a training in imitative, competitive disputation and rivalrous display" (1990: 97). Exemplars played a key role in this education; like Gabriel Harvey (see chapter 1, p. 12), boys and men singled out noble Romans from history as worthy of emulation. This habit was encouraged, one might add, by Plutarch's *Parallel Lives* with its conveniently arranged pairs of worthies whose strengths and weaknesses were cross-referenced and compared. Furthermore, the economic and political upheavals of sixteenth-century England caused enormous social mobility while leaving the structure of degree itself intact, as Lawrence Stone has demonstrated – so that emulation became necessary to survival in the upper ranks as well as a marker of rank in itself.

More specifically, Eric Mallin notes,

> The proliferation of emulous factions was a crucial component of Elizabeth's method of rule. From the beginning of her reign, the queen had employed factionalism as a kind of ecosystem. To prevent challenges to the monarchy, the nobles were encouraged to conceive of one another as the sole obstacles to positions of greater and greater strength.
>
> (Mallin 1990: 146)

Up to a point, faction fueled by emulation served the queen's purposes. As Lawrence Stone explains, like other powerful monarchies emerging in the sixteenth and seventeenth centuries, the Tudors developed a bureaucracy that they made dependent on the crown for support. "By the 1580s the key to advancement lay at the Court," because the queen controlled such an array of offices, gifts, and favors that both gentry and nobles had to garner influence with her through the assiduous networking of attendance at court. The lack of a standing army, which eliminated military action as a traditional avenue to favor and power, exacerbated the importance of royal patronage to the elite, creating what Stone calls "an explosive demand for office under the Crown in the decades after 1585" that was "out of all proportion to the rewards that could reasonably be expected." He estimates the ratio of applicants to positions under Elizabeth as 2:1 for the aristocracy, 5:1 for the 500 leading country families (Stone 1967: 213–14). Nonetheless, at court emulation continued to be a typical "method of advancement" (151).

Moreover, in the 1580s and 1590s, with an increasing parsimony as her years and the cost of the war with Spain advanced, Elizabeth's scale of giving dropped to just over half what it had been earlier – and half of that went to Essex (Stone 1967: 216). At the same time, the continuing threat from Catholic Spain, as well as recurrent Irish rebellions, lent ideological urgency to the protracted rivalry between those supporting the Cecils, who as statesmen advocated peace with

Spain and Ireland, and those following the Earl of Essex, who agitated for war and sought every opportunity for military distinction.

Elizabeth, the anomalous "woman on top" in a patriarchal society, used not only political differences but also patriotic rituals to keep (male) courtiers from challenging her authority: the annual Accession Day tilts, chivalric displays of martial prowess.[14] By encouraging her courtiers to sublimate into quasi-theatrical form the emulation that her foreign policy prevented them from realizing on the battlefield, the queen "deployed chivalric conventions to maintain the order of the court." According to Richard McCoy, these tournaments were "a classic safety valve, allowing a socially sanctioned and carefully regulated release of aggressive energies," a purely symbolic means of self-aggrandizement (1989: 24). For example, Frank Whigham reads George Peele's account of the 1590 Accession Day tile as "a display of parity through emulation, reaffirming unity in submission to the queen and the consolidating class codes" (1984: 80). Through elaborate conceits of self-presentation, lavishly costumed "knights" insinuated delicate compliment to the queen as a way of angling for lucrative court posts or monopolies.

Yet by the 1590s, such rituals increasingly became vehicles for emulation rather than safety-valves. As the queen grew older, as the inevitable change of power loomed nearer, the generation then coming to age resented more and more Gloriana's power to limit its scope of action. Mallin detects in court tournaments "a deep, gender-related insincerity: dedicated masculine self-interest took precedence over obligatory chivalric service to a woman" (1990: 157). In contrast to Whigham, McCoy sees the 1590 tilt as marked by Essex's conspicuous emulation. When George Clifford, Earl of Cumberland, took his place as the new champion for the queen, Essex, by dressing in mourning for Sir Philip Sidney (who had died three years before), upstaged Clifford and "declared himself the heir to a worthier line of chivalric heroism" (1989: 82). Indeed, Essex's entire career, culminating in the rebellion of 1601, bespeaks the failure of ritual to contain rivalry. Recklessly heroic in military exploits abroad and insistent on his preeminence at court, Essex was "seen by his contemporaries as an exemplar of emulation," Rebhorn demonstrates, and should be viewed as – like Julius Caesar in Shakespeare's play – "an extreme case of *typical* aristocratic behavior" (1990: 100, 106).

In images strikingly similar to Brutus's ladder, Shakespeare also portrays emulation in two plays set in Greek society where the agonistic tradition of western culture was first established: *Timon of Athens* and *Troilus and Cressida*. In *Timon*, the Poet pictures Fortune enthroned on "a high and pleasant hill," its base "rank'd with all deserts, all kind of natures / That labour on the bosom of this sphere / To propagate their states." When Timon, "one man beck-on'd from the rest below" advances to the top where Fortune is throned, his "rivals" are "translated" to "slaves and servants," but when Fortune spurns him, he is cast ruthlessly down to be trampled on by others (1.1.65–90).[15] In *Troilus and Cressida*, the Trojan War provides a quintessentially emulous context for all relationships (Mallin 1990). Ulysses, arguing that the Greeks can't win the war because, lacking any respect for their generals, they are split into factions competing with each other, uses an image like Brutus's:

> The general's disdain'd
> By him one step below, he by the next,
> The next by him beneath: so every step,
> Exampled by the first pace that is sick
> Of his superior, grows to an envious fever
> Of pale and bloodless emulation.

(1.3.129–34)

Ulysses returns to this kind of image in his extended admonition to Achilles, when he is trying to persuade him to resume fighting and take on Hector's challenge. The route to honor, he says, is a narrow "strait,"

> Where one but goes abreast. Keep then the path;
> For emulation hath a thousand sons
> That one by one pursue. If you give way
> Or hedge aside from the direct forthright,
> Like to an entr'd tide they all rush by
> And leave you hindmost;
> Or, like a gallant horse fall'n in first rank,
> Lie there for pavement for the abject rear,
> O'er-run and trampled on. Then what they do in present
> Though less than yours in past, must o'er top yours . . .

(3.3.155–63)

Brutus's ladder of ambition, Timon's hill of Fortune, and Ulysses' narrow, crowded path are fantasies of isolated humiliation: a single man is pictured as falling behind a crowd of rivals, of whom only one can gain the summit, be the sole winner. The reader is encouraged to identify with this solitary loser, but only momentarily, because the image warns us not to fall behind, not to be trampled on, but to "stay the course" (as George Bush urged in the 1988 presidential election), chasing the chimera of being "one man" above all others.

Throughout *Julius Caesar*, Brutus is presented as the one Roman to whom the conspirators look for leadership. Cassius casts him in the ancestral role of Rome's savior; Cinna yearns, "O Cassius, if you could but win the noble Brutus to our party" (1.3.140–1); and Casca thinks Brutus's participation "will change to virtue and to worthiness" whatever appears offensive in the conspiracy (1.3.157–60). The conspirators want Brutus to *represent* the republican principles of egalitarian liberty that the daily agonistic practices of their own social and political life contradict. Brutus readily supplies that representation, suppressing emulation by binding them together as a group, rejecting individual oaths to rely on their internalized, collective commitment to the republic.

Superseding Cassius as the instigator of the conspiracy, Brutus becomes its architect. At precisely those points at which he fulfills his function as the voice of republican purism, however, he also pursues a not-so-subtle one-upmanship against Cassius.[16] In a single line, Cassius suggests that the conspirators take an oath; Brutus, in a twenty-five-line rebuttal appealing to the virile courage, faultless honesty, and Roman birthright of his fellows, deems it superficial. Cassius urges that Cicero be included in the conspiracy; Brutus vetoes it on the grounds that Cicero won't take direction. Cassius proposes killing Mark Antony as well; Brutus opposes him, in a long speech fashioning the murder as a ceremonial sacrifice and the conspirators as its priests. In each instance, as many critics have noted, Brutus makes a tactical error. This succession of blunders marks the ideological fault line of *Julius Caesar*, the point at which republican idealism and emulation meet and clash. Earlier, when Cassius gloated over his success in bending Brutus's "honorable mettle," Cassius saw persuasion as a seduction, in which he was the active partner and Brutus the feminized one who lacked the firmness to resist ("For who so firm that cannot be seduc'd?" 1.2.309). He even fantasized a counterpart competitive moment, in which he, unlike Brutus, remained firm:

> If I were Brutus now, and he were Cassius,
> He should not humour me . . .
>
> (1.2.311–12)

No longer seducible, Brutus blocks his seducer's pragmatic suggestions with a firm, masculine wall of principle. In this oblique contest
Brutus wins because he finds the most resonant and compelling
rhetoric by which to represent the conspiracy as a noble enterprise
for the general good of Rome. Republican principle has become the
stake in a contest of emulation in which Brutus competes to distinguish himself as the Roman most devoted to the republic. His character no less than that of Cassius, and that of Caesar, is conceived
and shaped in terms of the contradiction between republican virtue
and Roman emulation.[17]

Shakespeare goes out of his way to make this point in a little-
noticed brief scene devoted to Artemidorus (act 2, scene 3). After
reading aloud his statement warning Caesar of the conspiracy,
Artemidorus comments,

> My heart laments that virtue cannot live
> Out of the teeth of emulation.
>
> (2.3.11–12)

A few lines later Caesar, determined to be first in republican virtue,
brushes Artemidorus aside, saying "What touches us ourself shall be
last served" (3.1.8). The emulation that imbued him with a *virtus*
supreme among Romans is literally the death of him.

A VOLUNTARY WOUND

Brutus, of course, isn't so firm as he appears to his co-conspirators.
And it is precisely his reluctance to murder Caesar that brings out
the feminine in the play – that gives rise to the famous scene between
Brutus and Portia on the eve of the assassination. Here his image of
himself as savior of the republic is splintered by those "passions of
some difference" he reluctantly alluded to in his first encounter with
Cassius, passions now reflected in Portia's observations of his behavior
and anxieties about what it portends.

The scene depends on our prior knowledge that, as Portia suspects,
Brutus does have "some sick offence within [his] mind." We realize
that her intuitions are well founded, for in two brief soliloquies
following the long one in which Brutus justifies the murder, he admits
– but only to the audience – that his "genius" (immortal spirit) and
his "mortal instruments" (his powers as a man) are at war in contemplating "the acting of a dreadful thing" (2.1.61–9), a conspiracy
that is "monstrous" (2.1.77–85). In taking over the direction of that

conspiracy and articulating the republican principles I discussed earlier, Brutus represses these sentiments. But they return in the shape of Portia's fears and specifically, in her wound.

At first Portia urges her husband to confide in her, "within the bond of marriage," asserting "by the right and virtue" of her place as his wife that he ought to tell her what is troubling him. But then she changes tack, and more delicately presses a bolder claim:

> I grant I am a woman; but withal
> A woman well reputed, Cato's daughter.
> Think you I am no stronger than my sex,
> Being so father'd, and so husbanded?
> Tell me your counsels, I will not disclose 'em.
> I have made strong proof of my constancy,
> Giving myself a voluntary wound
> Here, in the thigh: can I bear that with patience,
> And not my husband's secrets?
>
> (2.1.294–302)

Women – untrained in reason, dwellers in the *domus* excluded from the *forum*, and susceptible in the extreme to the affections – lack access to "constancy," meaning control over the affections, adherence to rationally-grounded principles like those of the republic, firmness.[18] It is men who are firm, women who aren't. Sir Thomas Elyot states that woman's inconstancy is "a natural sickeness" (Elyot 1937: 254).

Constancy, part of the complex of Roman values that constitute *virtus* in this play, can be traced specifically to Stoic philosophy, which enjoyed a strong presence in English letters, through the prominence of Boethius's *De Consolatione Philosophiae* as mentioned earlier; the writings of Cicero, who eclectically assimilated Stoic ideas; and Seneca's *Epistles*, translated by Lodge in 1614. Both Cicero and Seneca were included in the standard grammar school curriculum (Baldwin 1944). In addition, translations of the Stoics, beginning with Tiptoft's "englishing" of Cicero's *De Amicitia* in 1481, abounded. The Stoic writers enjoyed a revival in the 1590s, just before the play was written, marked by the appearance of Sir John Stradling's *Two Bookes of Constancie*, a translation of Justus Lipsius' explication of Stoic philosophy, *De Constantia* (Kirk 1939). As John Anson notes, "for the Elizabethans, neo-Stoicism resuscitated a distinctly Roman ethos; to be a Stoic meant, in effect, to be a Roman" (Anson 1967: 13).

While neither the Stoics nor their Renaissance mediator Lipsius conceive their philosophy as gender-specific, the terms in which they pose its leading postulates are the same as those in which masculine and feminine were commonly framed (Maclean 1980). Building up parallel oppositions between Reason and Opinion, Soul and Body, Constancy and Inconstancy, Lipsius roots constancy in reason; to obey reason is to be "lord of all lusts and rebellious affections" (Lipsius 1939: 81). In certain Christian discourses, women have ready access to and attain such lordship; in the Latin heritage on which Shakespeare draws, it is rarer and comes harder. As Thomas Lodge writes in the preface of his translation of Seneca, "to subdue passion is to be truely a man" (quoted in Lipsius 1939: 29).

If ever a body of literature, comprising poetry, drama, and history in both verse and prose, inscribed the primacy of man as warrior, ruler, father, and bard, it would seem to be Latin literature. Where do women fit in this world? For the beginnings of an answer, we might turn to Plutarch's life of Julius Caesar. It opens,

> At what time Sylla was made lord of all, he would have had Caesar put away his wife Cornelia, the daughter of Cinna Dictator. But when he saw he could neither with any promise nor threat bring him to it, he took her jointure away from him. The cause of Caesar's ill will unto Sylla was by means of marriage. For Marius the elder married his father's own sister, by whom he had Marius the younger; whereby Caesar and he were cousin-germans.
>
> (*Life of Julius Caesar* 5: 1)

Similarly, in the first few pages of Plutarch's life of Brutus, we learn that Brutus's mother, Servilia, was the sister of Marcus Cato the philosopher, that same Cato who was Portia's father; Brutus too married his "cousin-german." Servilia, Brutus's mother, was thought to have had a love affair with Julius Caesar, whence arose the tradition that Brutus was Caesar's son (*Life of Marcus Brutus*, 6: 185). Women held no public offices and only in extraordinary circumstances did they even speak in public, but as objects of exchange in marriage they were crucial to the weaving of political alliances and the continuity of the dynasties which formed the basis of the Roman power elite. One feminist critic has astutely described them as having "a double status as outsider within"; excluded from public life, they were essential to its continuity as wives, mothers, and daughters (Joplin 1990: 10). In *Julius Caesar*, evidences of the exchange of women are elided (Shakespeare doesn't even mention that Cassius and Brutus are brothers-in-law); it is a man, not a woman, who mediates the originary moment of Brutus's emergence into political agency; and it is men who engage each other's passions – as friends, as rivals, as Romans on the stage of history. What is Portia's role, then, in the play's representation of Roman masculinity?

In Rome and in Shakespeare's England, whatever the actual scope of women's activities, home was held to be the woman's place: the *domus*, from which word domestic is derived, a private dwelling set in opposition to the public forum of politics. But the scene between Portia and Brutus can't be contained within a public–private opposition, in the manner of the character-orientated criticism mentioned earlier, because though Brutus, ruminating in his orchard, has already admitted his scruples about killing Caesar, he has done so in the fully politicized context of the nascent conspiracy. Rather, since Portia's suspicions echo Brutus's earlier admission that killing Caesar seems "a dreadful thing," her appearance privatizes and more importantly, feminizes his hesitation. In terms of "the general good" as Brutus's republicanism defines it, individual moral scruples must be overcome; if such scruples are associated with a woman, and voiced only in the home, all the more reason to disregard them. An opposition between private scruples and public action, however, does parallel an opposition between feminine fear and masculine constancy. It is such distinctions that underpin the construction of Brutus as a tragic hero who, though he entertains moral strictures against killing that are associated with the feminine and the private, must embrace a man's duty and repress them in the name of defending an abstract concept of the public weal. Portia and Calphurnia worry and warn husbands who actually share at least some of their fears but who, once those fears are voiced by women, gain as it were a heroic warrant to override them and act in accordance with "masculine" virtue. As Linda Charnes states, "Literature is filled with male heroes who must renounce their 'privacy' in order to achieve renown" (1993: 96).

In the orchard scene, Portia concedes her inferiority as a woman, but nonetheless seeks entitlement to the constancy of a man, first through descent from her father, known for his rigid morality and for resisting submission to Caesar by killing himself; next, through affiliation with Brutus who, Plutarch notes, "studied most to follow [Cato] of all the other Romans." Portia shows, as it were, a fine discernment in this strategy of constructing herself as a man, for as I suggested earlier, men mutually confirm their identities as Roman through bonds with each other. Brutus can trust Portia only as a man.

Plate 2 Portia Wounding Her Thigh, Elisabetta Sirani, 1664 (Stephen Warren Miles and Marilyn Rose Miles Foundation Purchase Fund, Herbert F. Johnson Museum of Art, Cornell University). While in the background woman servants engage in the traditionally feminine activity of carding yarn, by bearing her self-inflicted wound Portia emulates "masculine" virtue.

It is above all by wounding herself that she imitates a man's constancy. That wound destabilizes the gendered concept of virtue in several ways. First, that this virtue might be imitated by a woman de-naturalizes it and suggests that it isn't native to the male gender; it is learned behaviour. Portia's "voluntary wound," as Gail Paster shows, is the opposite of a quintessentially feminine "inability to stop bleeding which is one aspect of womanly incontinence" (Paster 1993: 94). Second, the site of Portia's wound, in her thigh, hints ambiguously at a genital wound – what psychoanalysis would take to be the wound of castration, signifying that she as a woman lacks the phallus, symbol of power in a patriarchal society. Seeking to articulate symbolically the dominant masculine ideal of constancy, she also evokes symbols of femininity. In the words of Madelon Sprengnether, "she reveals the underlying paradox of the play, which equates manliness with injury, so that the sign of masculinity becomes the wound" (1986: 96). Her wound anticipates the suicidal wounds of Brutus and Cassius. Like hers, they are "voluntary wounds," cultural markers of the physical courage, autonomy, constancy that count as manly virtue; but at the same time, they demonstrate the fleshly vulnerability, the capacity to be penetrated, that marks woman. In a discursive operation akin to that of the fetish, constancy is haunted by its feminine opposites, making Portia's wound ambiguously, undecideably feminine *and* masculine. Or, to put it another way, the constitution of manly virtue requires the repression of the feminine, and the repressed returns.

The encounter between Portia and her husband, cut short by the arrival of the last conspirator, ends with his promise to "construe" to her the outward signs of his self-division. Evidently, he does; Portia reappears in act 2, scene 4, distraught and anxious for news of events at the Capitol. Now struggling for the constancy to keep Brutus's dangerous secret, she has been reinscribed into the category of woman, and her distress naturalized: "I have a man's mind, but a woman's might" (2.4.8); "Ay me, how weak a thing / The heart of woman is!" (2.4.39–40), she cries. We do not see her onstage again, but she returns to trouble the text and its construction of Brutus in a famous crux. Portia's death is announced twice in act 4, scene 3: first Brutus tells Cassius about it (146–56); then when Messala also broaches it (180–94), Brutus gives no sign that he already knows she is dead.

The longstanding debate over which version is "earlier" or "later," what Shakespeare meant by the supposed revision, and whether it is a revision at all has hinged on the implications of these two moments for the characterization of Brutus – not on what they suggest about Portia (Clayton 1983). Critics who think Brutus either disingenuous or lacking in compassion not to reveal his knowledge of the death to Messala or react emotionally to it argue that the second revelation was meant to be cancelled; critics who see him as admirably self-controlled in true Stoic fashion hold out for "duplicate revelation." The judgment depends not only on how the critic interprets Brutus's character but also on how he (they are all male) values the traits he finds in it. Some want Brutus's first announcement unqualified by what they see as the calculated masking of the second; others welcome a second demonstration of Brutus's self-control. Since the second revelation doesn't necessarily conflict with the first, and since the scene can be read and acted to make sense with both, with one, or with neither, the question is undecidable and the crux functions as a litmus test of the critics and the cultural norms of heroic masculinity they endorse. In any case, in both passages Brutus is restrained, not to say impassive, while Cassius exclaims "O insupportable and touching loss!" Whether one stresses Brutus's constancy or his display of it before his two comrades, both are hallmarks of Roman masculinity.

Not only in the announcement of her death, but also in the "strange manner" of it, Shakespeare abandons his earlier ambiguity and reinscribes conventional sexual difference. Furthermore, though he followed rather closely Plutarch's account of her wound and her struggle to keep Brutus's counsel, Shakespeare edits out the suggestive particulars of her death. Plutarch says that, due to "the weake constitution of her body" she fell sick; then,

> determining to kill herself (her parents and friends carefully looking to keep her from it), [she] took hot burning coals and cast them into her mouth, and kept her mouth so close that she choked herself.
>
> (*Life of Marcus Brutus*, 6: 236)

This account allows her the sort of agency proper to Brutus and Cassius themselves as Stoics and Roman heroes who will allow no man dominion over them. It also seems to parody the constancy Portia tried to claim by her wound, and found so hard to maintain once she learned the secret of the conspiracy; here, indeed, she keeps her mouth "close," and Plutarch commends her "for courage and constant mind" because "she shewed herself as stout in defence of her country, as any of us" (*Life of Marcus Brutus*, 6: 204). Shakespeare, in contrast, has Brutus say only that "she fell distract, / And her attendants absent, swallow'd fire" (4.3.154–5), depriving her of the agency and dignity that she has in Plutarch. Her crazed, bizarre act of self-destruction reinserts her firmly into the feminine, while Brutus's suicide signifies his *virtus*.[19]

In the succeeding scene (2.2), Shakespeare reworks the themes of male heroism, female fear, wounds and constancy, now focussing on Caesar. Again a Roman wife confronts her noble husband with her fears; again *virtus* is both constituted through and subverted by the feminine. The terrible portents that frighten Calphurnia first evoke Caesar's serene and eloquent assertion of constancy in the face of "death, a necessary end" (2.2.32–7). Then he relents, agreeing to stay home, but vacillates between vaunting that he wills the change and seizing the excuse she offers him. Finally he agrees to call it *her* fear, not his, that keeps him from the Capitol. Again a woman provides the alibi for a man's fearfulness, but here the displacement doesn't serve to validate a heroic commitment to public action, as in Brutus's encounter with Portia.

Rather, Calphurnia's dream-image of Caesar's statue, twice recounted, further ambiguates the multiple, contradictory images of Caesar as both Colossus and sick girl, mighty in his triumph over Pompey, yet childless and deaf. Decius transforms the portentous imagery of bloodshed, betrayal, and hypocrisy in Caesar's account of the dream into an odd but suggestively Roman vision of a nursing mother:

> Your statue spouting blood in so many pipes,
> In which so many smiling Romans bath'd,
> Signifies that from you great Rome shall suck
> Reviving blood . . .
>
> (2.2.85–7)

In this version Caesar's blood doesn't just "run," it spouts; the vigor before attributed to the "lusty Romans" who bathed their hands in it is now imputed to Caesar, who takes Brutus's place as Rome's restorer. Decius's version recalls the legend of Romulus and Remus who, suckled by the she-wolf, were thus enabled to found the Roman state. The feast of the Lupercal, being celebrated as the play begins, was named for and associated with the she-wolf's bounty, according to Plutarch: rituals of purification and fertility evoke the wolf at several points (*The Life of Romulus*, 1: 87–8). The feast was also associated with Romulus's physical strength, which was in turn linked to the earth's fertility. Hence, as in the play, the victors in its games touch barren women to make them bear (1.2.6–8). Plutarch suggests many parallels between Romulus and Caesar: both sought to found a line of kings, slew their rivals, were reputed to be tyrants, and were stellified after death. Caesar revived veneration of Romulus, and even considered taking his name. In Decius's flattering vision, through, Caesar is the nurturing mother, not the suckling king-to-be. Swayed by this image of mammary vigor, the inconstant Caesar reverses himself once again and departs for the Senate and his death. His constancy, like his refusal of the crown, seems transparently an act, a pretense at being the firm Roman, belied by his "feminine" mutability and identification with maternal rather than masculine styles of power.

It is the assassination itself that resoundingly feminizes Caesar.[20] His punctured, bleeding body makes men cry, and Antony likens his wounds to eyes streaming with tears, or "dumb mouths" that "ope their ruby lips" to beg an orator to speak for them, because like women they cannot plead their own cause. In an extravagant image, Antony characterizes himself as that very orator, putting "a tongue / In every wound of Caesar that should move / The stones of Rome to rise and mutiny" (3.2.230–2). Antony's rhetoric, his "tongue," is indeed the phallic instrument that transforms Caesar's inert, passively bleeding body into a vehicle of political power. The physical presence of Caesar's corpse is, of course, crucial to the project Antony describes in these lines. Cleverly he first points to the holes in Caesar's mantle made by the individual conspirators, evoking from the crowd "gracious drops" of tears to match the drops of Caesar's blood. Then, when he lifts that mantle, he can use the sight of the wounds themselves to produce the first cries of revenge from the crowd.

Revenge, as Antony evokes and shapes it, has a feminine character. Its matrix is pity and tears, the release of tender and passionate feelings which are then easily transmuted into "Domestic fury and fierce civil strife" reminiscent of the Furies or the crazed female worshippers of Dionysus who, in Euripides' *Bacchae*, are capable of rending their children limb from limb. Antony predicts that

> Blood and destruction shall be so in use,
> And dreadful objects so familiar,
> That mothers shall but smile when they behold
> Their infants quartered with the hands of war,
> All pity choked with custom of fell deeds . . .
> (3.1.265–9)

In a familiar Shakespearean sequence (compare Lady Macbeth's image of dashing her baby's brains out, and Volumnia's comparison of giving suck to wounds bleeding), maternal love is the touchstone of a generalized human "pity" seen as the last, failed bulwark against unbounded violence. Unrestrained emotions deaf to the general good and inaccessible to reason overtake the Roman republic and its new leaders. Antony and Octavius ruthlessly eliminate their enemies and exploit their allies. Brutus and Cassius, who in their different ways sought to be constant to the general good, fall to petty quarreling. In answer to Brutus's criticisms, the formerly steely Cassius melo-dramatically proffers his breast for a death-blow (4.3.99–100), and apologizes for his "rash humour" by saying he got it from his mother. When Caesar, once the embodiment of *virtus* as conqueror of Europe and Asia, victor over Pompey, has been feminized and brought low, the most fearsome and destructive images of the feminine possess Rome. Again, one might say, the repressed returns.

Shakespeare's Brutus is a tragic hero, I believe, in the sense that in him the contradictions embedded in his culture are set at war. In the first place, as a Roman, paradoxically he acts both for the general good and out of emulation, in that he wants to stand above other men – in his devotion to the general good. When Portia voices her fears and scruples, she brings to light a further contradiction. His motives for the murder having already been masculinized in the context of republican ideology, his misgivings about it are feminized when Portia voices them, which allows him to deny them as "femi-nine" and thus to assert his manly virtue in acting upon his political convictions.

Mark Antony eulogizes Brutus as "the noblest Roman of them all," because "He only, in a general honest thought / And common good to all" murdered Caesar (5.5.68–72). Voicing the same cherished ideal of the republic that Brutus stated when he reasoned his way into the conspiracy, Mark Antony sees him as he saw himself, and as others saw him. Many critics have taken his words as the final word on Brutus, without seeing any irony in them. For Mark Antony is surely guided not by the general good but by vengefulness and ambition, and the triumvirate of which he is a member rules by fiat and terror – yet he too proclaims the idea of the republic as a government of and for "the common good." But perhaps it is more significant that he envisions one man only in that republic who triumphs – in virtue – over all the rest.

105

NOTES

1 This and all subsequent quotations from *Julius Caesar* are taken from the Arden 2 Shakespeare, ed. T. S. Dorsch (1988).

2 I am indebted to Wendy Brown's *Manhood and Politics: A Feminist Reading in Political Theory* (1988) for her explication of the opposition of *polis* to *oikos*, and to Jean Elshtain's *Public Man, Private Women: Women in Social and Political Thought* (1981), which elucidates the formation of the public–private opposition in relation to gender.

3 The following critics have helped me to understand the play's formation of the subject in relation to social formations; none of them, however, deals with the gendered aspects of those formations. Focussing on religious and ritualistic elements, Naomi Conn Liebler sees the conspiracy as an "attempt to change the old religious order" of Rome into a new, secular, political one (1981: 175–96). While she uncovers a rich, interesting substructure of allusions to Roman religion and its role in Roman history, I am not persuaded that the play rests on a "ritual ground" to which politics is opposed. Gayle Greene's illuminating scrutiny of rhetoric as a tool of manipulation and self-deception engages complex epistomological questions (1980: 67–93). John R. Velz learnedly explores relations between oratory and power (1982: 55–75). Ralph Berry locates the play's meaning in a Roman conception of "the self as a reflection of ancestry" imaged in statues as "a kind of externalized self" (1981: 325–36). Gail Kern Paster perceptively remarks on "the dangerous intimacy of civic life" in Rome that fosters a tension between "the collective spirit" and its product, "the heroic individual" (1985: 58–90). Sharon O'Dair (1993: 289–307) argues that "the legal status of the Republic, not the character and deeds of Caesar," is at issue, and focusses on the tension between friendship and citizenry (without, however, delineating what constitutes the republic). Jonathan Goldberg assimilates the play's Romanness, in Foucauldian fashion, to a conception of royalist ideology as always-already constituting the subject: "Public life is pervasive. There is no privacy, no retirement, no place to shift a scene or change a costume" (1989: 168). Two essays in particular influenced my thinking about the workings of ideology and class in *Julius Caesar*. Richard A. Burt shows how characters are always positioned within social discourse – which he designates too broadly, to my mind, as "Rome," without discriminating between historical periods or ideologies (1991: 109–27). Wayne A. Rebhorn's argument that emulation is the "fundamental drive" within the Roman aristocracy comes closest to mine. He searchingly analyzes the compound of identification and rivalry that leads them as a class, in his view, to destruction. I am indebted to his richly historicized presentation of emulation as the hallmark of the Elizabethan aristocracy; while I share his view of the importance of emulation in *Julius Caesar*, I see it as a cultural practice that contradicts republican ideology, rather than as a "fundamental drive" or "character type" (1990: 78).

4 Miles argues that "Shakespeare had little if any access to the original Latin terms in which his Roman subjects would actually have thought and expressed themselves," so that his Romans "reflect the values and

perspectives captured in the language of Plutarch's sixteenth-century translators" (1989: 272). In my view, Miles overestimates the historical distance between a Roman sense of character as both expressed in and defined by public action (282) and the passionate pursuit of public honors and fame that typified the ruling elite in Shakespeare's England. Furthermore, Shakespeare did read Latin, and had access to many of the same texts on which Miles, a historian of Rome, bases his understanding of the late republic as "a society in which political action provided the principal standard for judging personal character and questions of value" (272).

5 Goldberg's remarks on the staging of this scene support my reading of it as the moment in which the public domain gives birth to the subject: "These offstage events punctuate those onstage; this is the only moment in all of Shakespeare when the backstage area is conceived of as one on which the action onstage depends, one continuous with action onstage" (1983: 167). While Goldberg takes the staging as indicating "the continuity of inner life and outer life," as I do, he then shifts emphasis to the determinative force of the public: Brutus, he says, "emerges as a public figure," without subjectivity distinct from public role.

6 Laura Mulvey, drawing on Lacan's mirror phase, theorizes this process; "This mirror-moment . . . constitutes the matrix of the imaginary, of recognition/misrecognition and identification, and hence of the first articulation of the 'I' of subjectivity" (1988: 60–1).

7 Lost until 1820, this text was unknown to Shakespeare or his contemporaries; I quote it because it epitomizes Cicero's view of civic life in the republic as expressed throughout his writings.

8 For a view of Machiavellian *virtù* that differs from both Pocock's and Pitkin's, see Kahn (1986). She argues that in Machiavelli no clear-cut distinctions between Fortuna and *virtù* can be made, because *virtù* is defined only in relation to the shifting contingencies of politics, the realm of Fortuna, so that it is virtually conflated with Fortuna. Thus "To recognize which situations require which kinds of imitation finally necessitates that the prince imitate the absolute flexibility of fortune itself" (77).

9 Pompey came to prominence in the struggle between Marius and Sulla, the two rivalrous leaders who preceded him and Caesar, by 81 BC. Granted extraordinary powers by the senate, Pompey swept the Mediterranean clean of pirates and defeated the Persian king Mithridates, making himself in effect the uncrowned emperor of Rome's eastern territories and earning the soubriquet *Magnus*. Locked in rivalry with Julius Caesar, who defeated him at Pharsalus in 48 BC only four years before he himself was assassinated, Pompey held more power and authority than any one man in Rome ever had. As one of the Nine Worthies, he was a familiar figure in Elizabethan popular culture (see chapter 1, p. 13).

10 Braudy comments on the historical irony of this ideological gap: "The constant self-presentation of the Roman upper class, their preoccupation with theatre, ritual, and the re-staging of history, indicates the ease with which men on either side of a crucial political issue could believe that they alone represented the true Rome" (1986: 61).

11 As Velz points out, "an atmosphere of tableau, posture, and pageant" marks the play (1968a: 150). Caesar's gesture of "offering his death" is repeated several times, notably during the assassination, when Caesar says "*Et tu, Brute?* – Then fall Caesar!" (3.1.77). Antony alludes to this moment in his funeral oration (3.2.185–91), and Brutus declares himself willing to die for Rome in his (3.2.46–8). In my view, the repetition of this motif dramatizes the interpellation of all the major characters, no matter what their position in the conflict, in the ideology of self-sacrifice for the public good.

12 Brutus remarks that Casca was "quick mettle when he went to school" (1.2.293); in the next scene, that mettle is shaken when he experiences the storm and its prodigies, "when all the sway of earth / Shakes like a thing unfirm" (1.3.3–4), and argues with the unshaken Cassius that "It is the part of men to fear and tremble" (1.3.54) at such moments. Brutus asserts that the conspiracy has reasons strong enough "to steel with valour / The melting spirits of women (2.1.120–1), spirits he contrasts to "th'insuppressive mettle" of the conspirators (2.1.134). Caesar contrasts his unshakeable constancy to "that which melteth fools" (3.1.39–42).

13 The brief biography of Julius Caesar in Thomas Cooper's *Thesaurus Linguae Romanae et Britannicae* (1565) calls him "Firste of all the Romanes," and states, "Of this man and Pompei it was said, that they weare of so haute courages, that the one could not abyde an equall, the other a superior."

14 I am indebted to Lawrence Stone's *The Crisis of the Aristocracy 1558–1641* (1967), which discusses in detail numerous social practices of the Tudor and Stuart elite structured by emulation: see especially "Office and the Court," 183–232. Yates (1975) first called attention to the political importance of chivalry for Elizabeth; see also Strong (1977). McCoy (1989) provides astute analysis of chivalry as an attempt to solve the problems created, in large part, by emulation; Whigham (1984) charts the emulation embedded in codes of courtiership. See also Watson (1984) and Antony Esler (1966).

15 For an extended reading of this speech as a paradigm of masculinity in relation to Fortuna as its matrix, see Kahn (1987).

16 In the 1959 essay that challenged the prevailing idealization of Brutus, Gordon Ross Smith debunked his virtues as "flamboyant and specious," listing fourteen occasions on which he "demands control for its own sake" and arguing that he "could not bear the thought of anyone's being able to rule over him" (368–72). Gayle Greene provides a probing analysis of Brutus's use of rhetoric to avoid facing moral questions (1980: 78–84). Gary Miles's portrait of Brutus as naive, self-deceived, and exemplifying "the essential weakness of all humanity" (1989: 279) follows a more recent critical tendency toward total disenchantment with Brutus.

17 As readers have noticed, Brutus can be paired with both Cassius and Caesar. Moody Prior (1969) remarks that until after the assassination, Brutus gains respect at the expense of Cassius; then in the quarrel scene, Cassius is presented more sympathetically than Brutus; finally when Titinius compares Cassius's death to the setting of Rome's sun, as a noble Roman he approaches the level of Brutus. Norman Rabkin (1967) argues

persuasively that in two successive scenes, 2.1 and 2.2, Brutus and Caesar are paralleled as "flawed giants" who both put country before self, yet in doing so reveal their vanity; he thinks the parallel reinforces the revenge tragedy structure of the whole play. While I recognize the patterned differences of character between Brutus and Caesar, I think their common ideological formation as Romans and republicans works at a deeper, more determining level. Rabkin's interpretation fits my own in its stress on the impulse toward civic altruism that Brutus and Caesar share, but I see the contradictions inherent in republican ideology, rather than revenge structure, as governing dramatic action.

18 Compare the definition of *consto, constare* (to be constant) in Cooper's *Thesaurus*: glossing a phrase from Cicero, *Per se ipsum constare*, Cooper says, "To be of himselfe: without any to depende of . . . to be like himselfe: to be always one," which implies a contrast to the dependency and volatility held typical of women.

19 Boaistuau (1574) lists among the aberrant appetites of pregnant women the desire to eat "hotte burning coales" (sig. Dix^v). If we take Brutus's reference to Portia's "condition" (2.1.236) to indicate not just her female-ness but a possible pregnancy as well, then the manner of her death emphasizes her gender even more.

20 Comparing the imagery of Caesar's bleeding body to the similar descrip-tion of Lavinia in *Titus Andronicus* as "a conduit with three issuing spouts," and also to a contrasting metaphor of bloodletting as deliberate physical purgation in *Coriolanus*, Gail Kern Paster brilliantly interprets Caesar's corpse as "marked with the shameful stigmata of ambiguous gender, especially the sign of womanly blood" (1993: 94), womanly because his bleeding, like menstruation, is involuntary and uncontrollable. Paster, though, attributes to the conspirators a quasi-conscious motivation to feminize him; I see that feminization, rather, as an epiphenomenon of their enactment of republican *virtus* in assassinating him.

5

ANTONY'S WOUND

... For with a wound I must be cured.

(4.15.78)[1]

It is possible that *Antony and Cleopatra*, rather than *Coriolanus*, was Shakespeare's last Roman experiment.[2] It is surely his most daring and original – an attempt to transmute Roman matter and style into a glittering if unstable new alloy of mettle and mutability, a Rome drawn to, repelled by, and finally fused with what is Other to it. The play refuses to confine itself to one genre: famously, it is tragedy, comedy, history, and romance all at once. As a "love tragedy," it is a generic oxymoron, and probably better classified as "resolutely tragicomic ... a tragic experience embedded in a comic structure" (Adelman 1973: 52). Still, genre can't fully explain the disconcerting relation between "realistic manner" and "romantic matter" noted by Leslie Thomson: the legendary hero and heroine who are petty and grand by turns, who declaim and then squabble, whose conduct so often belies their rhetoric (1989: 77–8). Michael Neill identifies hyperbole, in Puttenham's term "the overreacher," as the play's basic rhetorical and structural principle: aiming high, it often tumbles into anticlimax, creating the "perceived gap between expectation and performance" that is the leitmotiv of so much interpretation (Neil 1994a: 68).

Yet many have also – perhaps in reaction to this stylistic and generic hybridity – read the play in terms of a mutually confirming chain of binary oppositions labeled "Rome" and "Egypt." War and love, public and private, duty and pleasure, reason and sensuality, male and female, then, form the framework within which the play means. And its meaning is that of a love story laced with cultural conflict, a Roman warrior seduced by an Egyptian queen. This schematic binarism, however, only replicates a binarism undeniably at work in the play,

110

while keeping us from gaining critical perspective on it.[3] Even when readers resist taking sides, to argue that the play's treatment of contrasting value systems is ambiguous or equivocal, the poles of ambiguity or equivocation remain those of Rome or Egypt. Furthermore, this chain of oppositions has become naturalized – taken for a perennial, inevitable structure of choice. In that structure, Antony's Romanness is implicitly unified and coherent, Cleopatra's Egyptianness an external threat to it. Finally, to pose the question of the play as a choice between Rome and Egypt is to posit the terms of that choice as equal and independent, as though "Egypt" like "Rome" possessed its own autonomous cultural authorization.

Such a stance ignores the historical specificity of the narrative Shakespeare dramatizes, and the political circumstances determining the creation of that narrative. Furthermore, it fails to take full account of Antony's ambivalence and the more radical instabilities of his subjectivity. Shakespeare's "Herculean" hero both overflows the measure of *virtus* and fails to meet it (Waith 1962; Adelman 1973: 132–9). Never merely the "firm Roman" of the model constantly before him, he is yet drawn toward Rome by his investment in the race for power as much as he is pulled away from it by Cleopatra. Ernest Schanzer compares him to "a chronic deserter, forever changing sides in the struggle"; unlike most other critics, Schanzer doesn't take the love story as the play's only point of orientation (1963: 145). A concurrent story of homosocial relations – the rivalry, enmity, identification, and love that combine to inscribe Antony within *virtus* – is interwoven with the love story, but has found relatively little critical attention. Acted out in the troubled partnership of Antony and Caesar, another crucial difference besides those of male and female, Egyptian and Rome, drives the play's action – a difference within *virtus* and within Rome.

Classicists have long recognized that in the struggle for domination between Antony and Caesar, preeminent Augustan writers such as Virgil, Ovid, and Horace served the ideological purposes of Caesar's party. By fusing the xenophobia that fostered Roman national identity with patriarchal gender ideology, they demonized Cleopatra as Rome's most dangerous enemy, a foreigner and woman ruler whose power was fatally inflected by her sexuality. As Lucy Hughes-Hallett says, "Cleopatra was Rome's enemy, and we in the West are Rome's heirs. The notion of Cleopatra that we have inherited identifies her as being the adversary, the Other . . . an Oriental, and a woman" (1990: 4).[4] Though Plutarch qualified this opposition

111

to some extent, his life of Antony, on which Shakespeare based his play, still encodes it. To view that play, then, as organized by the contrast of independently constituted cultural value systems is to ignore the profound bias at work in the construction of that opposition *per se*.

Even more importantly for my purposes, the intended result of Octavius Caesar's campaign against Antony wasn't simply to vilify the foreign queen as Rome's arch-enemy, but to eliminate Antony as a credible rival. Actually, Cleopatra was only the means to that end. By magnifying her supposedly monstrous appetites for both power and sexual pleasure, Caesar and the writers enjoying his patronage were able to diminish Antony as a traitor to Rome "fatally debilitated" by love for her, "to subsume him and render him invisible" – and thus to present Caesar as the only true Roman fit to rule (Hughes-Hallett 1990: 39).

Shakespeare's play then, isn't only *about* a struggle between two superheroes for sole dominance over the Roman Empire; in a historical sense, the Augustan materials on which it draws actually *constitute* part of that struggle. The play is thus doubly determined by homosocial rivalry. In dramatizing the story of Antony and Cleopatra, Shakespeare fell heir to a legacy of representation on which the Latin curriculum and the *studia humanitatis* of the Renaissance were founded, a legacy organized by and centering on the mythic construction of Octavius Caesar as the destined victor in a prolonged power struggle who instituted the *pax romana* that ushered in the Christian era. Virgil sees Octavius's victory as decreed by the gods; we can see it as exemplifying a pattern of agonistic rivalry already familiar in both Roman history and Shakespeare's Roman works. Their contest for mastery is at least as important in Shakespeare's play as the love story. In Caesar and Antony Shakespeare dramatizes the homosocial bonding that is Rome's hallmark. On an ideological level, this rivalry not only guides the sword that, however awkwardly, gives Antony the "bungled" wound that sends him to a hero's death; it also guides his life.

A PAIR OF CHAPS

As in *Julius Caesar* and *Coriolanus*, in this play Shakespeare replicates the dyadic structure of male relationships in Plutarch: "the significant pair-bonding is always male . . . and perpetually competitive, because one will always gain one's identity only by destroying a double or parodic mirror image" (Kinney 1990: 181). Antony and Caesar don't

112

mirror each other as do Brutus and Cassius, fellow republicans, or Coriolanus and Aufidius, equally matched martial giants. Rather, their bonding is a specific instance of what Eve Kosofsky Sedgwick calls homosocial desire, "the affective or social force, the glue, even when its manifestation is hostility or hatred or something less emotively charged, that shapes an important relationship" (1985: 2). Despite the obvious contrasts of character that distinguish Antony and Caesar, they mirror each other in a blinding desire for *imperium*. That is "the affective or social force, the glue" that binds them. Emulation binds them precisely because they are rivals for power, as Caesar's eulogy to Antony suggests:

> O Antony,
> I have followed thee to this; but we do lance
> Diseases in our bodies. I must perforce
> Have shown to thee such a declining day,
> Or look on thine: we could not stall together
> In the whole world.
>
> (5.1.35–40)

This "disease" is a cultural one, an agonistic style of interpellating men as rivals in an all-or-nothing contest.

Early in the play, his conversation with the soothsayer dramatizes this choice, revealing the hold that the homosocial bond of emulation has on him:

Antony: Say to me, whose fortunes shall rise higher, Caesar's or mine?
Soothsayer: Caesar's.
Therefore, O Antony, stay not by his side.
Thy daemon – that's thy spirit which keeps thee – is
Noble, courageous, high, unmatchable,
Where Caesar's is not. But near him thy angel
Becomes afeared, as being o'erpowered; therefore
Make space enough between you.

(2.3.15–23

That this advice is uttered by a soothsayer makes Antony's rivalry with Caesar seem fated, rather than socially inscribed, and mystifies it. The Soothsayer is Egyptian; that Egypt was widely held to be the seat of ancient, occult wisdom intensifies that mystification. Notice, though, the terms in which Antony confirms the Soothsayer's prediction that he is "sure to lose" (2.3.25–6) against Caesar in any game:

"The very dice obey him. . . . / If we draw lots, he speeds; / His cocks do win the battle still of mine . . . and his quails ever beat mine" (2.3.33–8). The speech hints at the casual dailiness of such competitions; recall the impromptu swimming contest between Cassius and Julius Caesar. Precisely because they are ordinary pastimes, though, they define a pervasive cultural pattern of homosociality: men playing with, and against, each other. Suetonius relates a parallel moment in his life of Augustus: when Agrippa and Augustus together consult an astrologer about their future career, the astrologer prophesies great good fortune for Agrippa, then flings himself at Augustus's feet in token of the preeminent future awaiting the emperor – on that will totally eclipse Agrippa's (Suetonius 1979: 107).

"If thou dost play with him at any game," says the Soothsayer, "thou art sure to lose" (2.3.23–4). This defiance of the law of odds can be seen as a kind of cultural critique phrased as prophecy. If Antony were able to avoid "playing" with Caesar, his own "unmatchable" genius would shine. But Antony can't avoid it because his very identity is always already constructed in terms of that game. Significantly, the Soothsayer doesn't advise Antony to abandon Cleopatra. Rather, he wants the hero to preserve his "lustre" – his charisma, fame, authority – by keeping his distance from Caesar. At first that is exactly the course Antony takes, toward Egypt, where not only his pleasure but also his advantage, in distance from Caesar, lies. His genuine fascination with Cleopatra notwithstanding, she also serves as an alibi for gaining the distance from Caesar that he seeks in order to excel him.

The play's rivalrous dyads constantly re-form into trios, then revert to dyads, for third parties give the fractious "brothers" cause to part as much as they also make peace between them. The play opens with Cleopatra's mocking picture of Antony subordinated both to Caesar and the "shrill-tongued Fulvia" (1.1.28–34), and pulled back and forth between them. Fulvia's wars against Caesar help stir up his quarrel with Antony. Then, with Fulvia dead, the threat of Pompey's crescent power draws them together again. But Pompey counts on the alliance fraying once again: "'Twere pregnant they should square within themselves" (2.1.46), and ultimately, he is right. The Soothsayer scene provides the salient example of this pattern of failed mediations between rivals. Antony has just patched up his quarrel with Caesar and bound himself anew to him as "brother" by marrying Octavia. Precisely at this moment, he feels the itch of emulation again, the urge to match himself against Caesar: "Whose fortunes shall rise higher . . . ?". Enobarbus predicts that Antony and Caesar won't stay together, for "that which is the strength of their amity [Octavia] shall prove the immediate author of their variance" (2.6.124–6) – and he too is right. The unhappy Octavia stands between them, "Praying for both parts" and lamenting, "Husband win, win brother, / Prays and destroys the prayer; no midway / 'Twixt these extremes at all" (3.4.15–20). Like the Sabine women rushing between their husbands and their fathers, like Volumnia pleading with her son not to destroy Rome, Octavia counts on the bonds of marriage and on her kinship with men to supersede their rivalry with each other. Striving against the dominant institution of politics in Shakespeare's Rome, she is bound to fail. As Claire Kinney remarks, "The mediating female is gradually obliterated; Rome's central relationship is between male rivals," the female term being suppressed while the male one is doubled (1990: 180).

Emulation configures all relations between men in Rome. In the aftermath of the successful campaign against Parthia that he waged on Antony's behalf, Ventidius rejects the suggestion that he pursue the enemy further to gain recognition and reward, on the grounds that "Who does i'th'wars more than his captain can / Becomes his captain's captain," his rival rather than his follower, and risks loss of favor (3.1.21–2). Paradoxically, Ventidius "could do more to do Antonius good, / But 'twould offend him," so he refrains (3.1.25–6). But in a further paradox, he aborts the campaign to *pursue* his ambition by not offending Antony; he "rather makes choice of loss / Than gain which darkens him" (3.1.24–5). In contrast, Enobarbus seems to stand aloof from emulation like a Horatio or a Banquo, outspoken, cynical, lacking ambitions of his own.[5] It isn't rivalry that impels him to consider abandoning his leader, but disappointment in Antony's lack of judgment and loss of honor. When he considers the merits of staying, however, he too thinks in terms of agonistic rivalry:

> he that can endure
> To follow with allegiance a fall'n lord
> Does conquer him that did his master conquer
> And earns a place i'th'story.
>
> (3.13.43–6)

When Enobarbus calls Caesar and Antony "a pair of chaps" that "grind the one the other," he catches a paradoxical complementarity in their rivalry; two parts of a single ideological mechanism, they produce each other as heroes. Like a pair of animals snarling over a

115

piece of meat ("throw between them all the food thou hast," 3.5.12), they are leveled, put on the same quasi-instinctual plane, however different their personal styles, by their interpellation into a dominant social mode.

Yet however "Roman" Antony is as Caesar's rival, in another sense he fails to fit the mold. The embracing irony of the play is that Antony never returns to the heroic Roman image of fixed and stable identity from which – according to the testimony of nearly every character in the play – he has only temporarily departed. Janet Adelman remarks, "Antony himself is the primary object of desire for all the major characters" (1992: 177), Roman and Egyptian both: they all yearn for him to "be Antony." Cynthia Marshall concurs: "Antony is always someone else's version of Antony, never himself" (1993: 387). In his passion for Cleopatra, he "o'erflows the measure," escapes the mold, and crosses the boundary between Roman and Other. By thus violating the cultural codes in which masculinity is written, he risks the loss of his very identity.[6]

As in *Coriolanus*, "a deep sense of the fragility of masculine identity in face of the female Other" threatens a Roman hero. Cleopatra, doubly Other in terms of gender and culture, shakes the very foundations of *virtus* in Antony. However, "the heroic ideal, with its profoundly agonistic ethos [provides] the classic expression of . . . differentiation" from the female Other (Neill 1994a: 110). In the form of rivalry with Caesar, this agonistic heroism enables Antony to shore up his Roman virtue. Repeatedly, Cleopatra draws Antony to her and divides him from Caesar and all that is Roman; repeatedly, he spins back into Caesar's orbit, to the familiar, if fatal, games of emulation. Antony's attraction to Cleopatra, rather than simply feminizing him in the service of her lust (as the Romans believe), in fact enters into the dynamics of rivalry. His surrenders to her wily charms, combined with her perceived betrayals, impel him to reassert his masculinity and his Roman identity precisely through his emulous bond with Caesar.

Once Antony is again established in the East with Cleopatra, he seems bent on provoking Caesar to reengage in hostilities with him. He spurns Octavia, and sets up a new dynasty and a counter-empire with its own Egyptian religion. For his part, Caesar eliminates Lepidus on his own and keeps the spoils for himself, angering Antony, then dares him to fight at sea. It is as though Antony, and Caesar as well, have sought this moment of direct confrontation since Antony, following the Soothsayer's advice to avoid defeat at Caesar's hands, left Rome. While that passive avoidance preserves his alliance with Caesar, it also keeps their rivalry from being acted out, even in quail fights or games at dice. When the fleets and armies gather at Actium, the pent-up competitive urge that makes Antony the man he is finds expression in his determination – in defiance of all military advice – to take Caesar's dare, and fight at sea.

As Linda Fitz demonstrates, Shakespeare's departures from Plutarch's account "mitigate Cleopatra's culpability" for Antony's defeat (1977: 310). More than that, his play dramatizes the Roman construction of her agency *as such* – as an ideological reading of events that differs from what can be known about them but effectively *becomes* what is known about them.[7] The queen phrases her intention of being present at the battle in precise, limited terms: because Egypt bears a "charge" – assumes expenses and contributes forces – in the war, and because insofar as she is Egypt's "president," she is politically speaking a man, entitled to move in a man's sphere (3.7.15–17).

Concerning the single most important military decision of the battle, whether to fight by sea or by land, while Plutarch says that Antony, "subject to a woman's will . . . for Cleopatra's sake . . . would needs have this battle tried by sea" (64), Shakespeare clearly puts that decision in Antony's hands, and makes his rivalry with Caesar Antony's determining motivation:

Antony: Canidius, we will fight
        With him by sea.
Cleopatra: By sea, what else?
Canidius: Why will
        My lord do so?
Antony: For that he dares us to't.
Enobarbus: So hath my lord dared him to single fight.
                                    (3.7.27–30)

As Fitz notes, Plutarch doesn't mention Caesar's dare (1977: 311). The intrusion of a nameless soldier at the end of the war council, simply to argue – without opposition from Antony – against the decision to fight by sea, emphasizes the hero's reckless determination to fight his rival (3.7.60–6). This episode seems deliberately shaped to make two related comments on Antony's reasons for the decision. First, that he isn't influenced by Cleopatra at all, but rather, impelled on his own to pursue the rivalry with Caesar. Second, that no matter what Antony actually says or does, he and his fellow Romans are disposed to construe her presence as influence, and her influence as,

117

simply, emasculating domination. "So our leader's led, / And we are women's men," exclaims Canidius (3.7.60–6). Here Shakespeare departs from Plutarch to distinguish clearly between Roman perceptions of Cleopatra's influence over Antony as feminizing him, and Antony's decision, wholly his own, to take Caesar's dare.

Once the decision to fight Caesar by sea is made and acted on, the issue then becomes why Cleopatra flees the scene. The only clue we are given is her plea,

> O my lord, my lord,
> Forgive my fearful sails! I little thought
> You would have followed.
>
> (3.11.53–5)

which suggests that, like Rosalind's swoon at the sight of a napkin soaked in Orlando's blood, the queen has involuntarily testified to her essential feminity, demonstrating her unfitness for battle rather than the insidious intention to lead men into it with which Canidius, Scarus, Enobarbus and Antony credit her. But when Antony insists "thou knew'st too well . . . thou knew'st . . . You did know" (3.11.55, 58, 64), she doesn't deny it but merely pleads "Pardon, pardon" (3.11.66) which still leaves the question of what she intended up in the air. Later Enobarbus declares that "Antony only," impelled by "the itch of his affection" (3.13.3–12), is to blame for following her – which settles the question of her lover's responsibility for his shameful flight, without at all exculpating his still inscrutable beloved for allegedly provoking him to it. Thus the idea that the woman who holds or tries to hold political power will end by robbing the male of both political and sexual power, however it is qualified or complicated, persists. Whatever Cleopatra intended, if she hadn't been present in battle, Antony wouldn't have "violate[d]" his "Experience, manhood, honour" (3.10.22–3).

But the Soothsayer, of course, speaks truth; if Antony plays with Caesar at any game, he is sure to lose. And when he does, he and all his followers blame the loss on Cleopatra, whose sudden, unexplained flight from battle lends itself perfectly to that recourse. In the dizzying succession of defeats and victories, quarrels and reconciliations that follow upon Actium and culminate in Antony's death, he undergoes an experience of self-loss or self-violation that is triggered not so much by defeat at Caesar's hands as by betrayal at Cleopatra's: not defeat *per se*, but what is perceived as domination by a woman, is what unmans Antony (Sprengnether 1989; Wheeler 1980). The figures of speech that construct his shame and dishonor recuperate its putative cause: Cleopatra's flight. Antony cries, "I have fled myself," "I followed that I blush to look upon," "Let that be left / Which leaves itself" (3.11.7, 12, 19–20). To follow Cleopatra, to do what she did, is almost to *become* Cleopatra: "unqualitied," no longer either Roman or a man.[8] Countering the undertow of this feminization is the bond of rivalry with Caesar; even though it brings defeat, it does not produce the loss of gender identity, amounting to a sense of extinction, that her betrayal causes. Through that bond; Antony struggles to reconstitute his *virtus*: his status and his manhood as a Roman.

All the strategies he uses are combined in the scene of Thidias's humiliation (3.13): Antony seeks single combat with Caesar, displaces his own loss of manhood onto the hapless Thidias, and denigrates Cleopatra as wanton and faithless. At this point, Caesar has refused Antony's challenge to single combat by offering "courtesy" to Cleopatra if she hands Antony over to him (13–16), making her the wedge, as it were, by which he might pry the lovers apart and eliminate Antony. The hero's only chance of survival, let alone victory, rests on her loyalty. As in the battle, he is again dependent on, vulnerable to, a woman. By reiterating his challenge to Caesar, Antony seeks to return the struggle to a man's world, to the one-on-one structure of single combat that doesn't involve Cleopatra. The terms of his challenge stress his age and his opponent's "rose of youth," denigrating him as "the boy Caesar" (17–28), whose lack of maturity Antony equates with cowardice, even with childishness (Snyder 1980: 205–6). Differences in age here signify positions in a male status hierarchy in which "boys" serve "men". This test of personal mettle, "sword against sword, / Ourselves alone" will prove that only the more mature, "grizzled" Antony belongs at the top of that hierarchy (25–8).

The arrival of Thidias with his smooth-tongued flatteries re-triangulates the struggle, again making the queen the crucial middle term between the two men, and shifts it into a sexual register. When Thidias kisses Cleopatra's hand, he acts as his master's proxy; his gesture signifies that Caesar has the power to take Antony's woman from him. Essentially, she is the spoils of battle, and belongs to the victor. By having Thidias whipped till he whines "like a boy" (101–3), Antony would again strike at Caesar's claim of superiority, impugning the victory of a mere boy and reinstating himself, symbolically, as possessor of the spoils. As Thidias is dragged off to be stripped of manhood, Antony turns to Cleopatra to demote her from queen to whore. Not only has she given herself to those he considers his equals, Pompey and Caesar, she has abused him by showing favor to a mere hired servant, "a fellow that will take rewards" (126). The standard by which he judges her measures, again, status among men rather than female virtue; what matters most isn't that she has been, he considers, unfaithful to him, but that she has leveled him with Caesar's servant. While Antony condemns Cleopatra for her supposed desertion, he is conspicuously magnanimous toward the deserter Enobarbus. The hero blames himself for his comrade's defection, but projects onto a woman the ignominy of a defeat that he himself brought on. He may have lost authority, but she is merely "a fragment of Cnaius Pompey's" (120–1) – a mindless object of male appetite, already scorned when he first raised her to favor.

Though Caesar isn't present at this scene, he is its intended audience. Addressing the bleeding, abject Thidias, Antony makes him the message as well as the messenger:

> If that thy father live, let him repent
> Thou wast not made his daughter . . .
> Henceforth
> The white hand of a lady fever thee;
> Shake thou to look on't. Get thee back to
> Caesar,
> Tell him thy entertainment . . .
>
> (138–44)

Hindered from proving his own manhood to Caesar in single combat, Antony virtually emasculates another man – a helpless underling – to assert his claim on Cleopatra over Caesar's. Caesar may be the intended audience; Cleopatra is the actual one. In this theatre of cruelty Thidias stands in for her. Watching him cringe, she becomes witness of her own subordination, queen though she may be, in this Roman world of ruthless domination. The tongue-lashing Antony gives her finds its counterpart in the stripes Thidias gets, and hints at her fate should she actually betray her lover: she will be humiliated and despised as a whore. Though both the rhetoric and the spectacle of Thidias's whipping are mere show – symbolic surrogates for the sexual and political leverage Antony has lost – the scene serves to demystify Antony's "loss of self," the melting of his charisma, through dramatizing the gendered physical modes by which a Roman hero actively carves out his place in the hierarchy of power and status. As

120

Jonathan Dollimore argues, "power is a function not of the 'person' . . . but of place . . . relative to one's placing in the power structure" (1984: 209). Antony without his power isn't Antony, and his power is always already configured in relation to Caesar.

EROS AND THE SWORD

Even – or especially – when Antony finally loses to Caesar, his struggle to hold his place in that emulous pairing doesn't end. In fact, it continues by means of the sword, not raised against Caesar in single combat, but turned against himself. Almost invariably, critics call Antony's attempt to kill himself "bungled" or "botched," and most of them consider it a theatrical and moral disaster. Some thirty years ago, Derek Traversi declared, "Even in his suicide Antony is revealed as a botcher" (1963: 177).[9] Critical consensus hasn't changed: two recent editors of the play share this estimate. In his introduction to the Cambridge edition, Michael Neill calls Antony's suicide "shocking bathos . . . which deliberately courts embarrassed laughter" (1994b: 76), and John Wilders, editor of the Arden 3 *Antony and Cleopatra*, terms it an "ineffectual attempt . . . both painful and ridiculous" (1955: 30). Cynthia Marshall thinks it "radically disrupt[s]" Antony's access to heroism and makes him look "foolish onstage" (1993: 402).

These judgements testify not necessarily to Shakespeare's artistic failure, but rather to the culturally problematic nature of suicide in the Renaissance as well as now.[10] While often paying lip service to Stoic rationales for suicide, critics tend to forget that suicide has a history. As historians Michael MacDonald and Terence Murphy comment in their study of suicide in early modern England, "There has been in every era a hermeneutics of suicide, a set of institutions, proceedings, and beliefs that identified suicidal deaths and assigned them meanings" (1990: 221). Even a definition of the term is contingent on cultural categories of honorable and dishonorable death: at different moments in European history, religious martyrs and recklessly daring soldiers have been stigmatized as suicides or celebrated as heroes. The word itself doesn't appear in ancient Latin, but is, rather, an English derivative from Latin compounds meaning "self killing" (Grisé 1982: 23; Griffin 1986: 69). In contrast, the Roman lexicon of suicide emphasized rationality and free will. In the phrase *mortem sibi consciscere*, used with regard to public acts, the verb *consciscere* meant to approve of, determine, resolve upon. *Voluntaria mors* or voluntary death carried no connotation of violence or perversity and

121

again, associated the act with freedom of the will and rationality. When referring to the execution of suicide, the Romans spoke of *sua manu*, the hand signifying freely willed action (Grisé 1982: 24–7; Griffin 1986: 69).

Though such associations were, as I shall argue, strongly present for many early modern readers and theatre-goers, they had to compete with a well-engrained Christian prohibition. In *The City of God* Augustine construes suicide as a sin on two grounds. First, he classes suicide with murder as a violation of the first commandment. Second, he argues that, like Judas who "despaired of God's mercy and in a fit of self-destructive remorse left himself no chance of a saving repentance," the suicide commits the sin of turning away from grace (1972: 27, I.16). Throughout the Renaissance, iconographic tradition linked the rope and the knife to despair as a terrible sin (Wymer 1986: 22–6).

On the other hand, precisely the secular ideals of honor that Augustine deplored were revived and revalidated by humanistic study of Roman history and literature (Wymer 1986: 1–3, 11–18), so that another discourse of exemplary – and specifically Roman – suicides emerged. "What educated Elizabethan could have been ignorant of the deaths of Lucretia, Cato, or Brutus? Their encomiums could be read by every schoolboy with little Latin and less Greek," McDonald and Murphy comment (1990: 87). More than rationales derived from Stoicism, these familiar exemplars imbued suicide with the dignity and honour of the Roman past. For example, Filippo Strozzi, the Florentine republican implicated in the assassination of Alessandro de'Medici, left a suicide note asking that "he might at least be permitted to have his place with Cato of Utica and the other great suicides of history" (Wymer 1986: 16). Finally, when Shakespeare wrote *Antony and Cleopatra*, "suicide had become one of the ways of defining Roman mores and Roman character in the theater" (Wymer 1986: 134; Charney 1961: 209). It figures prominently in a number of Roman plays, among them *Appius and Virginia* by Webster and (?) Heywood (1559–67), Chapman's *Caesar and Pompey* (1605–13), Jonson's *Sejanus* (1605), and Fletcher's *Valentinian* (1610–14). One need not have been educated to be familiar with suicide as a marker of specifically Roman honour.

Either discourse, Christian or secular, was troubled by the other. Because the defense of one's honor and the preservation of a good name into posterity were as central to the ethos of the ruling elite in Renaissance England as in Rome, such secular rationales for suicide commanded respect, despite anxious concerns about sin and salvation. Lodowick Bryskett approvingly cites "the aunceient Romanes, who held it the part of a stout heart, for a man to kill himself rather than to suffer shame or servitude," mentioning Cato, Cassius, and Brutus (1972: 182–3). Despite this degree of respect for Roman exemplars, however, "no actual suicide was praised as an honorable death before 1650" (MacDonald and Murphy 1990: 92–3). We can hear some of this tension – or confusion – between humanistic and Christian conceptions in Sir Walter Raleigh's suicide note to his wife, written in 1603 during his imprisonment in the Tower on a charge of treason:

> That I can live to thinke howe you are both lefte a spoile to my enimies, and that my name shal be a dishonor to my child I cannot; I cannot indure the memorie thereof. . . . I knowe it is forbidden to destroye our selfes but I trust it is forbidden in this sorte, that we destroye not ourselves dispairinge of gods mercie.
>
> (Latham 1939: 40)

Raleigh struggles to reconcile what religion has taught him with his gentleman's sense that death is preferable to dishonor (MacDonald and Murphy 1990: 96–7).[11]

Montaigne's essay on suicide is also a sensitive register of this cultural ambivalence. Near the beginning, he declares (using the Latin term for suicide), "The most voluntary death is the fairest." He then reverses himself to invoke the familiar Christian metaphors (adapted from Plato's *Phaedo*) of the world as God's garrison and the suicide as a deserter from his appointed post. Finally, he bypasses any absolute religious prohibition against suicide to explore, through myriad classical instances (and one from the Old Testament), "occasions sufficient to justify a man's decision to kill himself." His cautious conclusion, "Unendurable pain and fear of a worse death seem to me the most excusable motives for suicide," tempers respect for the rationality and dedication to honour that shaped Roman constructions of suicide with a certain awareness that from a Christian point of view, there can be no excuse (1975: 251–62).[12]

Rather than dismissing Antony's death as a theatrical fiasco, then, we would do better to identify the codes that gave meaning to Roman suicides, in order to determine how, filtered through Renaissance perspectives, they might also configure Antony's. As MacDonald and Murphy remind us, there is a historically specific hermeneutics of suicide.[13] At first glance, the exemplary suicides so often cited in Renaissance texts – Lucretia, Brutus, Cato – seem to illuminate Antony's only by contrast, for they died as martyrs to their political principles, for the sake of "freedom" against "tyranny." No such claim can be made for Antony. And no Roman hero could be more different from Antony than the flinty, pious, republican Cato. Yet a comparison of Antony's with Cato's "voluntary death" as related in Plutarch's *The Life of Cato Utican* reveals a significant element in common that suggests Antony's death is better than a bungle. Granted, Shakespeare is staging a suicide in the theatre, whereas Plutarch is narrating one in a biography. But in fact, by Plutarch's time suicide had actually become "a fashionable cult" with its own conventions of performance, in which Cato's death served as a much-imitated model. Persius (d. AD 62) states that every schoolboy had to recite the speech of the dying Cato, and when, surrounded by friends, Seneca the Younger took his life, he summoned his secretaries so he could dictate his will and his philosophical reflections for the imagined audience of posterity as well (Griffin 1986: 198, 66–7).

A leader of the resistance to Julius Caesar's growing power, Cato found himself at his enemy's mercy when Caesar, having defeated Pompey at the battle of Pharsalia (48 BC), marched on Utica. In his account of Cato's last evening, Plutarch stresses the patriot's calm rationality and the firmness of his resolution to die "rather than be bound to a tyrant for injustice" (1895a: 174). The evening begins like any other: Cato takes the customary bath and dines with his male friends, his sons, and some guests from the city. They constitute, in effect, his audience. His well-known intentions require no announcement, but are tacitly suggested when he engages in a philosophical debate on the proposition "that only the good man is free" (1895a: 175): only through death can he maintain republican virtue, and he freely chooses death. He then reads Plato's *Phaedo* twice. In a sense, *Phaedo* is his script, for it is clear that he views the death of Socrates, an act profoundly consistent with his philosophy, as a model for his own.

As night comes on, Cato asks for his sword; when it is not brought, he repeats the request, which again is not fulfilled. At last, he angrily strikes the servant who fails to bring it, crying out "that his son and his servants would deliver him naked into the hands of his enemie," and demanding,

Why dost thou not bind thy father (my sonne) his hands behind him, that when Caesar commeth, he may find me in case not

124

to defend my selfe? I do not desire my sworde to hurte my selfe, for if I had any such minde, I need but holde my breath a little, or give but a knocke of my head against the wall onely, and dispatch my self quickely.

(1895a: 176)

Cato understands his sword not as an instrument of self-murder but as a military weapon to be used against his enemy Caesar rather than against himself. With his sword, he can cheat that enemy of the triumph he seeks: to subject Cato to the utter humiliation of defeat. Without that sword, Cato sees himself as defenseless in a kind of single combat with Caesar for the prize of honor.

Yet when, after the long night of reading and philosophical conversation, Cato finally grasps that sword, because his hand is swollen from the blow he gave his servant, he fails to kill himself instantly. In fact, his "bungle" is much worse than Antony's: he is found "all of a gore bloud, and the most part of his bowles coming out of his bodye, him selfe being yet alive, and seeing them." To defeat Caesar, he is forced to "tare his bowels with his own hands" (1895a: 178). Yet, what might seem to be a fiasco like that attributed to Antony is hailed by the Romans as the act of "a free man [with] an invincible mind" (1895a: 178); moreover, for the Renaissance Cato is a favorite, frequently cited exemplar of integrity and courage. Caesar's reaction to Cato's suicide bears out Cato's understanding of that act:

O Cato, I envy thy death, sithe thou hast envied mine honor to save thy life. For in deede, had Cato been contented Caesar should have saved his life, he had not so much impared his owne honor, as he had augmented Caesar's glory.

(1895a: 178)

In other words, Caesar requites Cato's "envy" of the glory Caesar might have won (by defeating Cato but sparing his life) with his own "envy" of the honor his rival wins through suicide – which is nothing diminished by his failure to kill himself with a single blow and the horrific mutilation that results.[14]

It is this strain of emulation in Cato's suicide that Montaigne rehearses in his essay "Of Cato the Younger," in which he laments what he sees as a contemporary tendency to debunk the actions of virtuous men instead of emulating them in the positive sense – fashioning oneself according to their examples. Calling Cato "truly a model chosen by nature to show how far human virtue and

125

Plate 3 Julius Caesar on a Triumphal Chariot, 1599. Woodblock on paper by Andrea Andreani after Mantegna. The last in a series of nine depicting Caesar's triumph. Caesar, crowned with laurels by an angel, is preceded by a medallion quoting him: "Veni, vidi, vici" (I came, I saw, I conquered), and by a placard praising him as "divine, most lenient, first, best, greatest." Andreas Andreani. Italian. active 1540/46-1623. *Julius Caesar on a Triumbhal Chariot Drawn by Two Horses* from *The Triumbh of Caesar*.

constancy could go," Montaigne concludes by quoting five Latin poets in praise of Cato and arranging them in ascending order of poetic achievement, as though holding his own competition for laurels. Significantly, all except the last praise Cato by alluding in some way to emulation in the sense of trying to outstrip a rival, and two specifically represent Caesar and Cato as rivals for virtue. Martial seems to echo Caesar's reaction to Cato's suicide, "Let Cato outdo even Caesar, while he lives," and so does Horace: "This earth of ours he subjugated whole, / Excepting Cato's unrelenting soul" (1975: 171–2). Though Montaigne is interested in models of virtue for the sake of virtue *per se*, he conceives this modeling in terms of an emulous pair – and he views Cato's suicide, however imperfectly executed, as a model of virtue. While Antony isn't a philosopher-patriot like Cato, still, Montaigne's view of Cato suggests that smoothness of execution was not – for the Romans or for the Renaissance – a criterion of suicide's dignity or moral value. It also encourages us to shift our focus to the way suicide might articulate the problematic structures of masculinity; especially, those of emulation.

What propels *Antony and Cleopatra* to its double catastrophe of suicides is deeply implicated in such structures: Caesar's triumph. Though not enacted onstage, through compelling reiterations it comes to have the imaginative force of an event materially realized and witnessed. These massive public spectacles were awarded by the Roman senate to those who had led major military campaigns resulting in significant conquests. By the triumph of Paulus Aemilius in 168 BC, they had become tantamount to apotheosis of the *triumphator*, conferring an almost magical authority and glamor upon him. Captive rulers were a stock feature of the triumph, demonstrating not only Rome's domination over a foreign state but also the personal victory of a Roman leader over a foreign prince (Warren 1970: 65; Payne 1962: 85–7, 106–9).[15]

In *Antony and Cleopatra*, Caesar's triumph seems to happen over and over, twice anticipated by both hero and heroine in four vivid descriptions of some length, and often referred to by others. Recounted from the perspective of the captive forced to be an object of the common gaze in that spectacle, all the scenes stress the loss of physical autonomy and the shame of not being able to control who looks at one's body. Antony imagines that Caesar will "hoist . . . up" Cleopatra "to the shouting plebeians." She too sees herself being "hoist[ed] up . . . to the shouting varletry" and along with her women, "uplift[ed] . . . to the view" of all. But Antony's vision differs significantly from

Cleopatra's in stressing his loss of status to Caesar specifically rather than his debasement by contact with commoners: he pictures himself

> with pleached arms, bending down
> His corrigible neck, his face subdued
> To penetrative shame, whilst the wheeled seat
> Of fortunate Caesar, drawn before him, branded
> His baseness that ensued?
>
> (4.14.73–7)

For Antony, this shame would be like sexual penetration for a boy or a woman, entering into his body and proclaiming his submission – in this case, to one formerly his equal, his rival, his "great competitor." Caesar drawn in his chariot doesn't merely precede Antony as victor; he writes "baseness" onto his very body, as with a brand.

In Plutarch's *Life of Paulus Aemilius*, the defeated king Perseus is similarly feminized. He entreats the Roman not to be led in triumph, and Aemilius, "mocking (as he deserved) his cowardly faint heart," implies that the king can commit suicide instead. Plutarch comments: "Howbeit his heart would not serve him, he was so cowardly, and made so effeminate . . . that he was contented to make one among his own spoiles" (1895f: 237).[16] In his comparison of the lives of Antony and Demetrius, Plutarch makes a similar judgement. He considers Demetrius's death to be "the more reproachefull. For he suffered him selfe to be taken prisoner . . . to serve his mouthe and bellie, as brute beastes doe," while Antony, even though his death was cowardly and miserable, "yet was it before his bodie came into his enemies hands" (1895d: 93). Due, in part, to the moral suasion embodied in Roman exemplars, this motivation could still be held laudable in the Renaissance. In *The Anatomy of Melancholy*, for example, Burton commends "Publius Crassus, Censorius, and Plancus, those heroical Romans, to make away themselves, than to fall into their enemies' hands" (Burton 1927: 371). Sir Walter Raleigh was said to have justified his suicide attempt in 1603 similarly, claiming that he stabbed himself "in order that his fate might not serve as a triumph to his enemies" (quoted in Greenblatt 1973: 116).

Antony's determination to die in order to defeat Caesar of his triumph, then, would have found a certain sympathy in a Renaissance audience, no matter how that death was accomplished. In the episodes that lead up to and surround his death – the ruse of Cleopatra's own demise, the unexpected suicide of Eros, Dercetus's theft of the bloody sword – Antony's commitment to his rivalry with Caesar never wavers, while his love for Cleopatra follows the rise and fall of his military fortunes. When he is victorious, he basks in her admiration; when defeated, he spurns her as the "triple-turned whore" that no Roman can trust, and seeks to reinstate himself as Caesar's rival.

Cleopatra lies to Antony because she desperately wants to regain his love. Reasonably enough, she thinks she has lost it when he rages at her, envisioning her humiliation in Caesar's triumph as his own revenge on her for presumably betraying him (4.12.32–40). She flees without a word to take refuge in her monument from his fury as much as from Caesar. His next speech identifies the sequence of events that follows from this moment as a pair of conflicting, ideologically scripted scenarios that intertwine to configure his suicide. He compares himself to Hercules in his death-throes, furious, writhing, caught in the fire of a woman's treachery:

> The shirt of Nessus is upon me. Teach me,
> Alcides, thou mine ancestor, thy rage.
> Let me lodge Lichas on the horns o'th'moon,
> And with those hands that grasped the heaviest club
> Subdue my worthiest self. The witch shall die.
> To the young Roman boy she hath sold me, and I fall
> Under this plot. She dies for't. Eros, ho!
>
> (4.12.43–9)

Hercules' wife Deianira, mistakenly thinking that the shirt Nessus gave her had been dipped in a love potion, sends it to Hercules to regain his love. Nessus, however, has actually poisoned the shirt, which sets the hero on fire. In rage and torment, Hercules blames the wrong person and punishes Lichas, the messenger, who brings the shirt, by hurling him over the sea; like his supposed ancestor, Antony too blames the wrong person. As Hercules destroyed Lichas, so he would wreak his vengeance on the queen; both the god and the hero act on the mistaken belief that a woman has entrapped them.

Like Deianira's gift of the shirt, Cleopatra's lie about her death is intended to restore the Herculean hero's love for her, specifically by dispelling his impression that "she has packed cards with Caesar." When Mardian brings the message that with Antony's name on her lips, she has killed herself, he says, "My mistress loved thee, and her fortunes mingled / With thine entirely" (4.14.24–5). He speaks explicitly to Antony's belief that she loved herself or Caesar more than Antony, and implicitly to the accusation that she betrayed him to his rival.

Despite the implication that she died for love of him, however,

Antony construes her suicide as a death not for love but for honor. He rewrites the female scenario of duplicity in service of love that is encoded in the Lichas image into a male scenario of honor reclaimed through death. Having arrived at "the very heart of loss" – defeat by Caesar, accomplished (he thinks) by Cleopatra's betrayal – Antony feels emasculated in a sense that is as much political as sexual. "O, thy vile lady!," he cries to the eunuch at first, "She has robbed me of my sword" (4.14.22–3). Without his sword, he is neither male nor Roman; his deepest need, then, is to reclaim his Roman (masculine) identity. The only means of reclaiming it is suicide because, as Cato's example suggests, suicide itself is the ultimate expression of homosocial rivalry. Through suicide, Antony will regain his sword. Or, more precisely and ironically, the false report of her suicide sent by the supposedly emasculating Cleopatra shows him the way to regain it.

This restoration is accomplished, though, only through intricate explorations of the positive and the negative poles of bonds between men that have little to do with Antony's love for her, and much to do with the values that configure Roman manhood. For Eros, the servant on whom he relies to help him die, Antony's suicide entails a conflict between a loyalty justified by Antony's *virtus* and a loyalty inspired by love. The prolonged, ambivalent course of Enobarbus's detachment from Antony prefigures this conflict. At first, repelled by his master's defeat and dishonor, he leaves Antony; then he dies – evidently from shame at his own failure to return that master's love. A similar tension between conflicting imperatives recurs in Antony's relations with Eros, whose name ivites an allegorical reading. Twice Eros appears in close association with Anthony's armour. First he helps Anthony to put it on (4.4) and then, answering the command, "unarm Eros" (4.14.35), to take it off for the last time – figuring the uneasy coexistence of lover and soldier within Anthony. However, a close look at the scene (4.14) in which Eros agrees to kill Antony but then turns the knife against himself suggests a different meaning for that name, as a signifier of love specifically between men.

As the scene begins, Antony laments to Eros his loss of "visible shape": his inability to maintain the public identity and self-image of a world conqueror, humiliated as he is by defeat in battle and by what he perceives as Cleopatra's betrayal of him. The prospect of suicide consoles him: "there is left us / Ourselves to end ourselves" (4.14.21–2). That will restore his shape. After Antony takes in Cleopatra's message, at first he seems to be shifting his allegiance from "Rome" to Cleopatra. He takes off his arms, symbolically ending

130

"The long day's task" of his vocation as warrior. Possessed by love and racked by grief, he dismisses Eros, and in a short soliloquy, elaborates a vision of death as a lover's reunion in Elysium with Cleopatra in which, "like Dido and her Aeneas," they will "make the ghosts gaze" (4.14.51–4). In thus rewriting Virgil's Aeneas in his own image – not as the empire-builder who abandoned Dido, but as a lover faithful to her after death – Antony reminds us of his departure from that Virgilian model of *virtus*, and seems to be modelling his death on Cleopatra's, as a final, uncontestable affirmation of love.

But no sooner does he send Eros away than he begins to call him back. Antony's soliloquy is prefaced and concluded by urgent summonings: "Eros! – I come, my queen. – Eros! – Stay for me," and "Come, Eros, Eros!" (4.14.50, 54). Here Eros's name might well seem an allusion to Antony's passion for Cleopatra, making the character a displaced allegorical representation of the eros that, fused with honor, would symbolically reconcile "Egypt" and "Rome." Read as *double entendre*, the panting cadences would then suggest that Antony envisions suicide as the very consummation of his passion for Cleopatra. But read literally as commands to the servant whom he will ask to assist him in dying, the phrases construct his suicide as "Roman" in a different sense than that of rivalry with Caesar.

Like Brutus and Cassius in the earlier Roman play, Antony doesn't contemplate committing suicide by his own hand; rather, he relies on a comrade (in this instance, a servant) to accomplish his death, thus making suicide, which etymologically speaking means the killing of oneself, a misnomer. It is, rather, an affair between men. Eros's return in answer to his master's summons initiates a reinscription of Antony's death, as escape from a feminizing shame and restoration of the honor that is a crucial component of his manhood, rather than as a *Liebestod* affirming his allegiance to Cleopatra and all she represents. Reminding Eros of the oath he swore to kill Antony on his command, the hero condemns himself "to lack the courage of a woman" if he doesn't seek his own death, and reminds Eros, "Thou strik'st not me, 'tis Caesar thou defeat'st" (4.14.68).

Suicide then assumes its place as Antony's last gesture in the contest that has defined him, the only means left to him of besting his rival. But Eros resists his master's command to draw his sword and strike. Torn between respect for the code that preserves honor by self-murder, on one hand, and simple affection on the other, the servant recoils from the task. Antony then describes the "penetrative shame" he expects to suffer in Caesar's triumph. Only through death at the hands of Eros, by means of a sword representing what is martial, manly, and Roman, can Antony triumph over Caesar. Eros, faced with the choice of following either the letter of his oath, to kill his master whenever honor should require it, or its spirit, love for Antony that supersedes that code of honor, fulfills the implication of his name and kills himself for love, saying "Thus do I escape the sorrow / Of Antony's death" (4.14.94–5). This poignant gesture complicates our sense of homosocial relations in the play's world, counterbalancing the agonistic masculinity acted out by the aristocratic characters, and reinforcing class difference in the altruistic devotion of servant to master.

Shakespeare dramatizes a similar conflict in *Julius Caesar*, when Cassius's follower Pindarus keeps the oath he took when Cassius saved his life and kills his master, but then is ashamed of his action (5.3.36–50). This suicide is counterbalanced by that of Titinius, who kills himself after Cassius's death, purely out of love for him (5.3.80–90). In a similar balance of personal love against adherence to a code of honor, Brutus rejoices, when no fewer than three of his comrades refuse his request to be killed, "that yet in all my life / I found no man but he was true to me" (5.5.34–5), then finds equal satisfaction in the honor he wins when Strato agrees to help him die. Just as he read in Mardian's account of Cleopatra's supposed suicide not a testament of love but an exemplar of honor, Antony ignores the implication of his follower's dying words, and finds in Eros's action only what is "brave" and "valiant," "A nobleness in record."

Left to his own devices, Antony then performs his notoriously "bungled" suicide, and achieves not death but a wound: the wound Cleopatra has tricked him into, the wound that makes him merely a dead weight. Inert and bleeding, his body is awkwardly hauled up to the queen's monument, in an odd reversal of gender roles, by Cleopatra and her women. What are we to make of Antony's failure to realize fully the cultural entitlement Roman suicide promises him? It is undeniable that, as Cynthia Marshall has recently argued, "Wounded, bleeding, and lacking agency, Antony takes on a typically feminine position [and] . . . troubles an audience's notions of what it means to be a (masculine) hero" (1993: 403).

But that is precisely the point. That Antony fails to perform his suicide effectively exposes it *as* a performance like Cato's, intended to effect an ideological transformation whereby he can regain the Roman virtue he lost in being defeated by Caesar. His suicide caps a sequence of moments in which, through some specific breach of or conformity

132

with heroic decorum, Antony loses, gains, and again loses that virtue. When he followed Cleopatra's ships at Actium, he "violated[d] . . . manhood" (3.10.22–30, admitting "I have fled myself" (3.11.7), then in the Thidias scene reasserted it by reducing Caesar's messenger to womanish humiliation. Furthermore, if Cleopatra, invoking and following precisely the same "high Roman fashion" of self-murder, can make herself as "marble-constant" as a man, doesn't that demonstrate that this performance supposedly reserved for men can be appropriated by women who have the courage and the flair to execute its rituals properly? Similarly, Lucrece seizes for herself the honor of manly death through self-murder, as Portia seeks to prove her constancy through a "voluntary wound." That Cleopatra calls it a "fashion" – something actively shaped by human intervention – reminds us of its complex historicity. That suicide could be understood to wipe out shame, restore manhood, vindicate honor would not have seemed farfetched, despite Christian teaching, to early modern audiences, but it would also have marked Rome's historical difference from themselves. Already a social performance in Cato's time, it became a textual and dramatic performance in Shakespeare's; a marker of Romanness, but one that also registered the discomfort and misgivings inspired by Christian prohibition.

The awkwardness of staging Antony's dying moments has bothered many critics, actors and directors. It even bothered Plutarch, who says, "It was a hard thing for these women to do, to lift him up" (1895d: 80). The stage historian Richard Hosley argues that a winch, pulley, and harness would have been used to lift Antony fourteen feet above the level of the main stage to the gallery (Hosley 1964), and performance critic William Worthern worries about "a high monument aloft, a missed handhold, a flimsy railing," that might threaten " a slapstick catastrophe, as Antony plummets to the stage [floor]" (Worthen 1986: 295).[17] These anxieties about the deployment of Antony's body in stage performance, I suggest, do more than emphasize Antony's "bungle." If suicide plays out homosocial rivalry to its limits, transforming defeat at a rival's hands into victory, and inscribes collaboration in suicide as autonomy, by rendering Antony physically powerless this scene also exposes the contingencies that attend these cultural fictions. Antony's physical presence has previously been configured according to a canon of the warrior body. This body is either armored (we watch Cleopatra and Eros put Antony's armor on before his penultimate battle, 4.4) or firmed by ascetic regimens (recall Antony's diet of horse urine, berries, bark, and "strange flesh" on the retreat from Modena (1.4.57–72). The wounds it suffers are voluntary and thus confirm the warrior's courage and will – all the more so if they are grievous or mortal.[18] Once Antony's sword thrust fails to kill him instantly and merely renders him helpless, he can no longer be imagined in terms of the warrior body. However, as the soldiers bearing Antony arrive at Cleopatra's monument, the lovers greet each other in a perfectly poised duet representing him as a victorious warrior:

Antony: Not Caesar's valour hath o'erthrown Antony,
            But Antony's hath triumphed on itself.
Cleopatra: So it should be, that none but Antony
            Should conquer Antony; but woe 'tis so.

                                                  (4.15.14–18)

Compare the stage direction, which reads "They [the Roman soldiers bearing him to Cleopatra's monument] heave Antony aloft to Cleopatra" (4.15.38). The disparity between stage action and rhetoric exposes these ringing assertions of triumph over Caesar as purely ideological constructions built up of words disjunct from the wounded body they reconfigure.

This exposure continues when, after his death, Antony's sword refuses to stay in place as the signifier of his Roman manhood. A minor character named Dercetus grabs it, saying "This sword but shown to Caesar with this tidings / Shall enter me with him" (4.14.116–17). The weapon then enters a context of ambition and misrepresentation that subverts the altruistic service of Eros and Antony's idealized emulation.[19] For Dercetus bears it off to Caesar, disingenously presenting himself as Antony's loyal servant who risks death in approaching his master's enemy. He tries to curry favor with that enemy by proffering Antony's sword as a precious relic marking the death of a Roman martyr:

> that self hand,
> Which writ his honour in the acts it did,
> Hath, with the courage which the heart did lend it,
> Splitted the heart. This is his sword;
> I robbed his wound of it. Behold it stained
> With his most noble blood.
>
>   (5.1.21–6)

Hand, honour, heart; sword, wound, blood: the key words of Dercetus's bogus tribute starkly epitomize the components of *virtus* –

and at the same time, render them ironic as signs and images to be manipulated in the striving for advancement that organizes the Roman subject, whether common soldier or world conqueror. Dercetus's plan doesn't bring him the notice he hopes for, however. Instead, his speech and his war trophy precipitate Caesar's tearful eulogy to Antony as his rival, which reprises the essence of emulation: its paradox and its ambivalence. Maecenas anticipates the paradox by remarking, "When such a spacious mirror's set before him, / He needs must see himself" (5.1.34–5). As when Cassius offered to serve as Brutus's "glass," revealing his "hidden worthiness" (1.2.54–7, 67–9), one man confirms himself in masculine virtue through a specular relationship to another man.

Antony reflects Caesar in the immediate sense that their rivalry can only end in the death and defeat of one or the other; it is literally a classic zero-sum game. So the image of Antony's sword stained with his blood calls to Caesar's mind the fate he might well have met, making Antony the image of himself in defeat. The mirror also suggests the "equalness" to which Caesar refers in his last line: whatever their temperamental differences, they possessed a similar quotient of the qualities that make up a hero, and each was worthy to compete with the other. Most profoundly, though, they are rendered mirror images of each other by their common fashioning in the ideology of *virtus*. They are, as it were, devoted to each other by the rivalry they share. Their "equalness" spawns a relentless striving for its opposite, the ultimate difference of total victory and total defeat: that is the paradox at the heart of emulation. What Caesar calls "our stars" we can see as the shaping power of an ideology materialized and acted out in the Roman political system and the expanding empire it generates. His reference to their rivalry as fated recalls Antony's conversation with the Soothsayer in the early moments of the play, which mystified emulation in a similar way. The wheel has come full circle.

This sense of their implacable rivalry, though, is counterbalanced by this ruefully passionate tribute:

> But yet let me lament,
> With tears as sovereign as the blood of hearts,
> That thou, my brother, my competitor
> In top of all design, my mate in empire,
> Friend and companion in the front of war,
> The arm of mine own body, and the heart

Plate 4 Frederick Chatterton's opulent production of *Antony and Cleopatra*, Drury Lane Theatre, 1873 (*The Illustrated London News*). Antony's wound is transformed into Cleopatra's lament. Reproduced with permission of the Huntington Library, San Marino, California.

Where mine his thoughts did kindle – that our stars,
Unreconciliable, should divide
Our equalness to this. . . .

(5.1.40–8)

Caesar suspends syntactical completion of the sentence with five lines
of epithets expressing the quality of his love for Antony. Caesar calls
him brother, competitor (a term which includes the senses of "rival"
and of "partner" both), mate, friend, companion, the arm of his body,
even his very heart – Shakespeare heaps up the synonyms – in short,
the person above all others to whom Caesar considers himself bound
by intimate, affectionate ties. This sequence climaxes in "the heart /
Where mine his thoughts did kindle" (45–6), a phrase in which the
two men become inextricable from each other, fused in heart and
mind. Whether he "really" means this (in view of the harsh criticism
he has leveled at Antony throughout the play) is beside the point:
what he means by it is that his enmity coexisted with this intense
identification – perhaps even enabled it. That is the ambivalence of
emulation.

AGAIN FOR CYDNUS

By spending his last moments with Cleopatra, Antony, it cannot be
denied, attests to his love for her – a love that sets him decisively
apart from his Roman comrades. That love makes him a split subject
who strives to embrace, as Carol Thomas Neely asserts, "Cleopatra's
sexuality, duplicity, and difference from him and find them compatible with his manhood" (1985: 150). But even in her arms, with death
upon him, he portrays himself as "a Roman by a Roman / Valiantly
vanquished" (4.15.59–60), countering the undertow of her attraction
for him by evoking a reciprocity with Caesar that, even though fatal,
insures Romanness.

Roman suicide cannot possibly offer a woman – let alone a woman
like Cleopatra – the kind of cultural entitlement it promises a man.
Cleopatra's commitment to the Roman ethos falls within a different
problematic, and means differently from Antony's even though both
face the same pair of alternatives: life as Caesar's captive, or suicide.
On the one hand, Cleopatra's presence in Caesar's triumph would
make her doubly abject: defeated not only in her own name, but in
the name of Antony, and thus merely the signifier of one man's final
victory over the other. As in the scene of Thidias's whipping, she would

be the spoils that proclaim Caesar the victor. On the other hand, suicide does defeat Caesar of the additional victory he yearns for: her presence at his triumph. Further, it seems to grant her a truer autonomy than any she enjoyed as queen; like Juliet, she seizes on her "power to die," and exploits it to the fullest. Finally, as a spectacle executed with her elegant theatricality (no bungler she) and rich with imagistic suggestions of feminine fecundity and sensuality, her death seems to constitute a strong counterstatement to *virtus*.[20] Conceived and enacted by her as a way of imposing her fiction on Caesar's history, every detail is contrived to bespeak her queenliness, through the many allusions to her robe and crown culminating in Iras's eulogy, "It is well done, and fitting for a princess / Descended of so many royal kings" (5.2.320–1). Moreover, as Lorraine Helms points out, the queen's death is staged "without father, master, husband, hero, shareholder, or journeyman" (1992: 560); it is exclusively a female enterprise.

Another cluster of haunting images, however, is finely orchestrated to affirm not her majesty and autonomy, but rather her power to incite male desire – tantamount, from the Roman perspective, to feminizing the men who are drawn to her. Shakespeare alludes to his richest evocation of this power, Enobarbus's description of her first meeting with Antony, when she says "I am again for Cydnus / To meet Mark Antony" (5.2.227–8). The figs and the asps elegantly evoke the plenitude of pleasure, the fecundity that she and her maids exult in. Comparing death to "a lover's pinch, / Which hurts, and is desired" (5.2.289–90), she recalls the dynamic of making hungry where most she satisfies that is expressed in the spectacle on the river.

If, however, as Carol Neely says, "Death renders female sexuality benign" – if it is only at the moment of death that the desire Cleopatra provokes loses its power to feminize the male subject – then surely Shakespeare hasn't escaped the constraints of the Augustan tradition on which he draws (1985: 161). Furthermore, it isn't death *per se* that renders her infamous sexuality benign, but rather, death conceived as marital consummation through reunion with Antony as her husband; conceived, even, as wifely duty to a dead husband. Through such terms, Shakespeare reconstructs his heroine as a Roman wife allowed just enough autonomy to choose death as testament of her love for her husband. By fusing her identity as queen with a new identity as wife, suicide decontaminates her infamous sexuality. Helms rightly terms it "an achieved rite of passage through eroticism into marriage" (1992: 559). When Antony dies "a Roman, by a Roman / Valiantly vanquished," he affirms the continuity of his identity. But Cleopatra dies not only to defeat Caesar but also to claim the new title of wife precisely *by* joining Antony in death, a feminine rationale for death that has the kinds of classical precedents cited by Montaigne in his essay "Three Good Women." There he praises, for instance, the woman who had herself tightly bound to her fatally ill husband's waist, so that as they leapt to their deaths from a window, he would die in her arms, and Arria, who stabs herself and then removes the dagger to tell her husband (who faces certain political assassination) that it didn't hurt, giving him courage to do the same (1975: 563–9).

Nicole Loraux's remarks on the deaths of women in Greek tragedy suggest a continuity in Greco-Roman patriarchal inscriptions of the wifely death, and a context for Cleopatra's. Invariably, says Loraux, the heroines of Greek tragedy withdraw to the marriage chamber, "the narrow space that tragedy grants to women for the exercise of their freedom ... the space where they belong ... Even when a woman kills herself like a man, she nevertheless dies in her bed, like a woman." Thus female characters confirm tradition, but "at the very moment that they are innovating," for "Wives in death win a renown that goes far beyond the praise traditionally granted to their sex" (1987: 23, 24, 29). In Greek tragedy, wives die offstage and unseen – whereas Cleopatra's death is a *coup de théâtre* of great power. But part of that very power, I suggest, derives from the honorific identity of wife that this mode of death grants her. Only when she is divested of royal power save for its trappings, only when her erotic potency is symbolically circumscribed by marriage, does the *jouissance* always associated with her and her realm lose its emasculating threat. Only then the endless cycle of satisfaction and arousal ends, in the identification of the marble constancy of death with marital consummation: "Husband, I come!" (5.2.281).

NOTES

1 All quotations from *Antony and Cleopatra* are taken from *The New Cambridge Shakespeare*, ed. David Bevington (Cambridge: Cambridge University Press, 1990).

2 Bevington (1992: A1–A21) gives 1608 as the latest possible date for the writing of *Antony and Cleopatra*, and on the basis of style and allusions, dates the writing of *Coriolanus* around 1608 as well. There is no clear evidence of the order of their composition.

3 Recently this binarism has been seriously challenged by critics arguing that "love" and "war," Egypt and Rome, aren't opposites but rather,

mutually constituted and compromised. Jonathan Dollimore holds that in *Antony and Cleopatra*, "sexual desire is not that which transcends politics and power, but the vehicle of politics and power" (1990: 486), while for Linda Charnes, it is "an act of misrecognition" to see the lovers as actually achieving the transcendence of politics that they claim (1992: 7).

4 Hughes-Hallett, who is neither a literary scholar nor a historian and who does not write exclusively for an academic audience, draws on both classical scholarship and feminist theory in her study of the cultural history of Cleopatra's representations. In classical scholarship, both literary and historical, the role of the Octavian party in shaping the conception of Antony and Cleopatra that prevails in Augustan writers and their successors is well documented. See, for example, Tarn and Charlesworth (1965) and Grant (1972).

5 See Neely's discussion of Enobarbus as a divided figure with "mixed roots in comedy and tragedy," whose ambivalence she reads as subtly mirroring Antony's and resolved only in his suicide, in which he "debas[es] himself to ennoble his flawed master" (1985: 151, 155).

6 The play dramatizes a struggle to define Antony's identity in which nearly all the characters participate, and which has long prompted contrasting interpretations of it. Discussion reached a new level of insight in the work of Richard P. Wheeler and Madelon Gohlke. Wheeler views Antony in terms of a polarity in Shakespearean heroes between fear of and longing for merger, on the one hand, and desire for autonomy that results in isolation on the other (1980). Gohlke views him in terms of the masculine fantasy that "femininity signifies weakness, while actual women are perceived . . . as enormously powerful," a perception which "institutes the structures of male dominance designed to defend against such an awareness" (1980: 180). Some critics understand him in terms of "a classical 'Roman' notion of fixed and stable identity" which is eventually exposed as "chimerical and ultimately self-destructive" (Neill 1994a: 85, see also Kinney 1990 and Singh 1989). Others view his identity as radically contingent; Jonathan Dollimore argues that Antony's *virtus*, in any case a product of power relations rather than an essential quality, is "under erasure" – rendered obsolete by the *realpolitik* of empire (1984: 204–17). Cynthia Marshall interprets Antony in terms of "an interior space between governing self-image and performance in the world . . . the space inhabited by melancholy" (1993: 388). Another group of critics finds reason to celebrate him as enlarging or innovating conventional terms of heroic masculinity. Carol Neely, while seeing gender roles in the play as "polarized . . . within a patriarchal framework," thinks Antony accepts Cleopatra's difference from him and finds it "compatible with his manhood" (1985: 150). Peter Erickson finds that Antony develops an alternative or reformed masculinity with a "liberatory, subversive quality" through an identification with maternal bounty (1985: 134). Janet Adelman takes this idea further, to read the play as "a contest between male scarcity and female bounty as the defining site of Antony's heroic masculinity" (1992: 177).

7 Ania Loomba remarks, "Shakespeare does not simply indicate a stereotype but depicts it as constructed by various male perspectives in the

140

play . . . such a construction is then challenged and dismantled" (1989: 75). In my view, it isn't dismantled, but continues to shape the characterization of Cleopatra to the end of the play.

8 The figure of the eunuch, closely associated with Cleopatra, has hinted at Antony's "unmanning" since the play's first scene. Philo derides Antony as "the bellows and the fan / To cool a gypsy's lust," and the stage direction immediately following reads, "*Flourish. Enter Antony, Cleopatra, her ladies, the train, with eunuchs fanning her.*" Subsequently, when Cleopatra seeks diversion from thoughts of the absent Antony, she calls for Mardian, and banters with him about his "unseminared . . . affections" – which quickly remind her of lovemaking with Antony (1.5.8–35). Mardian's lack calls forth Antony's fullness. This sequence is repeated in another scene, in which Mardian first "stands in" for Antony, when the queen asks him to play billiards with her; his sexual deficiency then gives rise to thoughts of Antony. But this time, her image of catching Antony like a fish suggests the familiar iconography of pleasure's baited hook and its emasculating effects; lack effaces fullness. Finally, the defeated Antony, already contemplating suicide, greets Mardian (now acting as the queen's messenger) with "O, thy vile lady, / She has robbed me of my sword!" (4.15.23–4). As in the entrance of the eunuchs in the first scene, Antony's turn from Roman war to Egyptian passion is associated with a loss of virility. An unpublished paper by John Whitney (1993) first suggested a connection between Antony and Mardian to me.

9 Among the very few who don't share this consensus, McAlindon suggests simply that the suicide follows decorum, and compares it to the depiction in Garnier's play and the Countess of Pembroke's translation of Garnier, in which "there is not the slightest suggestion . . . that the suicide was deficient in Roman nobility because it was not immediately effective" (1973: 200). See also Brower (1971: 317–53).

10 The following discussion of suicide is much indebted to the many-faceted historical analysis of MacDonald and Murphy (1990) and the well-informed literary interpretation of Wymer (1986). See also Sprott (1961) and Noon (1978).

11 When he was imprisoned in the Tower again in 1618, his keeper Sir Thomas Wilson reported, "He took occation to comend the magnanimity of the Roamyns who wold rather taek ter deaths by ther own hands then endure any that were base and reprochfull" (Latham 1939: 54).

12 Compare Robert Burton's remarks on suicide in *The Anatomy of Melancholy*. Posing the question of whether it is lawful to commit suicide, Burton first cites schools of ancient philosophy, which all give assent to suicide as a form of liberty; then exemplars – Cato, Dido, Lucretia, Cleopatra, and Brutus, who "voluntarily died to avoid a greater mischief, to free themselves from misery, to save their honour, or vindicate their good name." He then pivots to declare, "But these are false and Pagan positions, profane Stoical Paradoxes, wicked examples . . . impious, abominable, and upon a wrong ground," citing Church Fathers in support of this condemnation. But he concludes the whole discussion by wondering, "Who knows how he may be tempted? . . . We ought not to be so rash and rigorous in our censures as some are; charity will judge and hope

the best; God be merciful to us all!" (1927: 370–4). Compare also John Donne's treatise on suicide, *Biathanatos*, written in 1608 (when *Antony and Cleopatra* may also have been written). He declares that the grounds for judging the morality of suicide are "obscure and steepy and slippery and narrow, and every error deadly" (quoted in Rudick and Battin 1982: lxxxiii).

13 Margaret Higonnet sees a radical shift in attitudes toward suicide at the end of the eighteenth century, "from a moralistic but potentially heroic vision of suicide to a more scientific yet demeaning acceptance of the act as illness . . . interpreted as a set of increasingly feminine symptoms" (1986: 69–70). Perhaps such a shift could help account for the dismissive judgements on Antony's suicide that prevail today.

14 The emulation between Cato and Caesar was played out after Cato's death when Cicero wrote a laudation of him, which provoked Caesar's *Anticato* (neither has survived); poems praising Cato by Martial and Horace followed, and Lucan makes him a hero of him in his *Pharsalia*, while Virgil includes him on Aeneas's shield as a significant figure in Roman history but as a lawgiver, removed from rivalry and war (*Aeneid* 8.670). See Taylor (1949: 170–1).

15 After Pompey's conquest of Pontus and vast eastern territories in 66 BC, he is said to have led nearly 300 captives in triumph (Payne 1962: 106). However, when Julius Caesar celebrated his triumph after defeating Pompey in 48 BC, according to Plutarch, "he did offend the Romans . . . bicause he had not overcome Captaines that were strangers, nor barbarian kings, but . . . the sonnes of the noblest man in Rome" (1895b: 5, 57). Shakespeare may be conflating this distinction between Roman and foreigner by projecting the shame of a foreign captive onto a Roman defeated by a Roman.

16 Surrey's sonnet on Sardanapalus, "Thassyryans king in peas with fowle desyre," pursues a similar association between suicide and masculinity but in a contrasting narrative. The king, "who scarce the name of manhode dyd retayne / Drenched in slouthe and womanishe delight," having "lost his honor and hys right," finally "murdred hym self to shew some manfull dede" (Surrey 1964: 29).

17 See Thomson (1989) for a thorough consideration of the staging questions and a highly interesting interpretation of their relationship to the play's structure and meaning; see also Neill's succinct analysis (1994a: 363–7).

18 Gail Kern Paster elucidates this distinction between gendered bodily canons of bleeding. On one hand, in the "naturally grotesque" woman bleeding is construed as "open, permeable, effluent, leaky;" on the other, as in Coriolanus's battle wounds, bleeding is "rather physical than dangerous" (1.5.17–19), because "Such blood is voluntary in two senses: it is shed as a result of action freely undertaken, and it is shed virtually at will" (1993: 92, 96–7).

19 Neill comments that Dercetus's theft reveals "the ultimate hollowness of those properties in which Roman masculinity is publicly invested" (1994a: 120). Without making such a judgment, I want to trace the discursive construction of those properties.

20 Anne Barton argues that Cleopatra's suicide "redeems the bungled and
    clumsy nature of Antony's death," in part by scripting Octavius into a
    part in her tragedy, instead of playing the role of captive in his triumph
    (1973: 19).

6

MOTHER OF BATTLES
Volumnia and her son in *Coriolanus*

From my mother's sleep I fell into the state . . .
(Jarrell 1969: 144)

War is a man's work . . . The male . . . wants to think that he's fighting for that woman somewhere behind, not up there in the same foxhole with him. It tramples the male ego. When you get right down to it, you have to protect the manhood of war.
(Gen. Robert H. Barrow, commander of the US Marines,
quoted in Hartsock 1989: 134)

During the fall and winter of 1990–91, all over the world people watched a familiar scene on television: members of the US armed forces engaged in the business of war, this time in the Persian Gulf. Clad in bulky, camouflage-printed fatigues, they all looked like soldiers. Of course, some of them were women. Though women's branches of the Navy and Army had participated in World War II, the Korean War, and the war in Vietnam, this time it was different. No longer mainly secretaries and nurses, though technically they still did not fight in direct combat, women in large numbers took on the same jobs essential to combat – and the same risks – as their male comrades. But an even more radical break with hallowed tradition appeared along the economic fault-lines revealed by the Gulf War when we learned that *mothers* numbered among those troops: mothers of infants, mothers of several children, divorced mothers, and single mothers. Because they needed the money, they had joined the reserves or the regular forces, little thinking they would be called up and shipped halfway across the globe from their children.

War is a "gendering activity" more stringent than most, in which "the discourse of militarism, with its stress on 'masculine' qualities, permeates the whole fabric of society, touching both men and women"

(Higonnet *et al.* 1987: 4). In the paradigmatic war narratives of western culture, women stay at home and men make war to protect them; women are figured as being "naturally" dependent on men, who should be "naturally" warlike and brave (Cooper *et al.* 1989: xiii). Classic discourses of war in Homeric epic or modern journalism oppose masculinity to femininity, battlefront to homefront, public to private, while also framing them as complementary. The disruption and violence of war thus evoke – and insist on – a profoundly conservative gender binarism that in peacetime can be taken for granted. In "militarist and misogynist rhetoric," Joan W. Scott comments, "gender relations are seen as timeless and unchanging, outside social and political systems," and deployed to insure social stability. The private/public binarism reinforces that of gender, both being critical to the formulation of the "nationalist or patriotic ideologies" underpinning war (Scott 1987: 27–8).

These constraints have been eased only for women who avoid motherhood. Virgin warriors such as Camilla in the *Aeneid* and Joan of Arc, instruments of a higher power, are singled out as divine exceptions; Amazons are exceptions of another sort in rejecting and violating masculinist constructions of womanhood. Virgins and Amazons are alike in eschewing motherhood either actually or symbolically (a popular Greek etymology derives the word from "without breast," referring to amputations allowing them to draw the bow rather than nurse the baby). When Queen Elizabeth I spoke to her troops at Tilbury and offered to take up arms herself, she spoke as an exception – a virgin queen. Citing the conundrum "How long will women make war? As long as women have children," Nancy Huston states, "It is the act of giving birth itself which is considered to be profoundly incompatible with the art of dealing death." Rather than fixing childbearing and warmaking in static opposition and thus recuperating conventional gender binarism, however, she argues, "neither phenomenon can be said to have symbolic precedence, and therefore only the *interaction* between the two can be the object of analysis" (Huston 1986: 119, 131).

The interaction between mothering and warmaking has a social and literary history that begins in ancient Greece: typically, it is oppositional, hierarchical, and complementary. The same epic tradition that opposes women to war also represent mothers as arming their sons. In the *Iliad*, Thetis helps arm Archilles, as Venus arms Aeneas in the *Aeneid*; both mothers symbolically authorize their sons' masculine vocations as warmakers, but do not bear arms themselves, remaining on the feminine side of the gender divide (Cooper *et al.* 1989: 13). In Athens, a gendered ideology counterposed *oikos*, the immanent, need-related realm of women, children, and slaves to *polis*, the realm of male citizens "that exists for the perfection of man's political nature" (Brown 1988: 36, 39–40). Only when a woman bore a child to her husband did she enter irreversibly into the *oikos* to which they both belonged; but the rule that "only those who were able to defend the city in wars could be citizens (*politai*)" totally excluded women from *polis* (Cantarella 1987: 31). This hierarchical yet complementary pattern also prevailed in Sparta, where according to Plutarch, "it was forbidden to inscribe the names of the dead upon their tombstones, except for men who had fallen in war and women who had died in childbirth" (Loraux 1981: 37; Huston 1986: 131): both had presumably fulfilled the highest civic duty proper to their genders.

One version of the Spartan complementarity between motherhood and the martial ethos appears in a text available to Shakespeare, Plutarch's *The Sayings of Spartan Women*. The great majority of speakers in these vignettes are mothers, who either excoriate their sons for not meeting the highest standards of courage on the battlefield, or, rejoicing that their sons have died bravely, conspicuously eschew grieving for them. Two examples typify the style and point of the sayings:

> One woman sent forth her sons, five in number, to war, and standing in the outskirts of the city, she awaited anxiously the outcome of the battle. And when someone . . . reported that all her sons had met death, she said, 'I did not inquire about that, you vile varlet, but how fares our country?' And when he declared that it was victorious, 'Then,' she said, I accept gladly also the death of my sons.'
>
> Another, hearing that her son had been slain fighting bravely in the line of battle, said, 'Yes, he was mine.' But learning in regard to her other son that he had played the coward and saved his life, she said, 'No, he was not mine.'
>
> (1931: 461–3, 465–7)

While the mothers show not the slightest sign of conflict between affection and patriotism, the implied reader is expected to shudder at but nonetheless admire such maternal sacrifice. The vignettes depend on a tension between two constructions of the maternal: that a mother should prize her sons above all else, and that a mother produces sons for the state, to which she owes them.

146

In Roman culture, "women enjoyed enormous power as mothers" (DuBois 1985: 203), but unlike Greek women who served the state only in bearing sons, in rearing them Roman women were considered "a fundamental instrument of the transmission of a culture" (Cantarella 1987: 134). Writing in the late first century AD, Tacitus approvingly recalls the time when "every citizen's son, the child of a chaste mother," was raised by her and not a hired nurse. He praises "the mothers of the Gracchi, of Caesar, of Augustus [who] directed their children's education and reared the greatest of sons" (quoted in Lefkowitz and Fant 1982: 141–2). Cornelia, mother of the Gracchi, figures prominently in Plutarch's biography of her sons, Tiberius and Caius. He emphasizes her part in making them "more civill, and better conditioned, than any other Romans in their time" so that "education prevailed more in them, than nature." In the biography's conclusion, as Cornelia recounts her sons' deaths "without shedding teare," declaring "that they had such graves, as they had deserved," she echoes Plutarch's Spartan women (Plutarch 1985h: 236, 275).[1]

In the relationship between its hero and his mother, Shakespeare's *Coriolanus* offers a troubling, richly problematic treatment of the cultural nexus between bearing children and bearing arms. In this play, probably written between 1605 and 1610, Shakespeare moves the feminine from the margins where he placed it in *Julius Caesar* to the center, making Volumnia a major character. He follows Plutarch in leaving the father's place vacant, but enlarges the mother's role considerably to make her pertinent at every moment to the tragic action. Volumnia's considerable authority derives equally from her social identity as a mother and from her identification with the masculinist, militarist ideology of Rome. She embodies in an exaggerated, intensified form a construction of motherhood not only normative in Roman culture but still influential today in wartime.

Insofar as Volumnia acts within the established feminine parameters by bearing and rearing a son, the play conforms to conventional gender binarism. Her complicity with Roman militarism is no less conventional. But it is precisely because Volumnia holds such power over her son as a mother that her advocacy of the dominant martial ideology gives her a crucial political leverage. As a mother, she is of course subjected by the dominant ideology – but she is also instrumental to it, and thus central to the play's critique of *virtus*. Thus the play dislodges "mother" as a representational category from its oppositional place in the masculinist discourses of war and of *virtus*, making it a contestable term that cannot be placed securely on

147

either side of a male/female, public/private, warmaking/mothering binarism (Bower 1991: 33).[2]

With the birth of her "man-child," Volumnia seized such access to the political sphere as Rome offered her, through the "natural," physical offices of bearing and rearing him. In this play, the principal characters' bodies are a material representation of ideology; in mother and son Rome inscribes itself, and they embody its cultural text. "There's no man in the world / More bound to's mother," Volumnia claims (5.3.158–9).[3] In this suggestive metaphor, Shakespeare echoes Plutarch but shifts his meaning significantly. Plutarch's Volumnia says, "No man living is more bounde to shewe himself thankefull in all partes and respects," referring specifically to the child's duty to be grateful to the parent for his nurture and education (Plutarch 2: 147). In the play, "bound" implies not just a specific moral obligation, but a connection equally physical and emotional that bespeaks the totalizing indebtedness of son to mother.

Both son and mother share a sense of physical connection. At the climactic moment of her arrival in Antium to beg him not to destroy Rome, Coriolanus calls her "the honour'd mould / Wherein this trunk was fram'd" (5.3.22–3); earlier he used the same word for his own body, "This mould of Martius" (3.2.103). She exults, "Thou art my warrior; / I holp to frame thee" (5.2.62–3). The words "mould" and "frame" both suggest that the womb has power to shape the fetus, as distinct from the father's more exiguous contribution to its beginnings. "Mould" means not only friable earth or topsoil, but also "earth regarded as the material of the human body" and "dust to which the human body returns after death" (*OED*); it evokes the mythic connection between women, earth, and death. Because mould also means "a pattern by which something is shaped," as does "frame," it suggests that Volumnia has played not only the maternal but also the paternal role in childbearing as established in the prevailing Aristotelian medical model: she has supplied both matter and form. In accord with this model, paternity is conventionally proven by the child's resemblance to its father, as when Volumnia refers to her grandson as her son's "epitome . . . / Which by th'interpretation of full time / May show all like yourself" (5.3.68–70). But Coriolanus is, rather, the epitome of his mother; his father is only alluded to (perhaps) once, when Volumnia admits, in a moment of relative modesty, that she only helped to "frame" her son.

Her role as genetrix, however, serves as metaphor for her more powerful part in "framing" her son's temperament and value system.

148

That too is imaged in the physicality of her motherhood: "Thy valiantness was mine; thou suck'st it from me," she declares at another pivotal moment (3.2.129). Cicero, referring to Cornelia as an exemplary mother, says "her sons were brought up not so much at their mother's breast as by her speech" (Lefkowitz and Fant 1982: 206). While Cicero distinguishes the ideological indoctrination performed by the mother from the physical nurture she provides, Shakespeare conflates them, evoking through the physical bond of nursing the emotional undertow of Volumnia's dominating authority over – or of – her son.

When Cominius nominates Coriolanus for consul, he declares, "Valor is the chiefest virtue" (2.2.84). Here Shakespeare makes a play on words, identifying valor as the virtue, or essence, of *virtus*, manliness (Rackin 1983: 69). In thinking of the "valiantness" with which she suckled her sons as hers, Volumnia claims to possess the phallus, the prime signifier of masculinity in Rome, but identifies it with a signifier of femininity: mother's milk. Masculinity belongs first to the mother; only she can pass it on to a son. This construction contrasts with one common to many cultures, and certainly prevalent in early modern England: that the male child must be separated from the maternal environment at a certain age, and definitively located in a men's world in order to realize his masculinity.[4]

Volumnia's account of her son's coming of age continues the interpellation seen in the image of nursing him, evoking the same relational complex of mother and son, masculine and feminine, mothering and warmaking:

When he was yet but tender-bodied, and the only son of my womb; when youth with comeliness plucked all gaze his way; when for a day of kings' entreaties, a mother should not sell him an hour from her beholding; I, considering how honour would become such a person – that it was no better than picture-like to hang by th'wall, if renown made it not stir – was pleased to let him seek danger where he was like to find fame. To a cruel war I sent him, from whence he returned, his brows bound with oak. I tell thee, daughter, I sprang not more in joy at first hearing he was a man-child, than now in first seeing he had proved himself a man.

(1.3.5–18)

The speech emphasizes her investment of maternal affection in him as the passive object of her gaze, and her achievement in transcending that affection to invest, as it were, in government bonds – in the honor he wins in "a cruel war." Infused with the milk of her "valiant-ness," he leaves her womb to prove himself a man, but she hastens and controls that martial rite of passage. His brows may be "bound with oak," but he is still "bound to his mother." The distinction and separation of male from female that is normal to male rites of passage, and normally then succeeded by passage through a male status hier-archy, is here confounded and conflated. Though Volumnia raises her son in the name of the father, in doing so she exercises a uniquely maternal power that eludes patriarchal controls over women.

This cultural short-circuit can be understood in terms of Kristeva's analysis of the "mother-woman's" place as

> rather a strange 'fold' (*pli*) which turns nature into culture, and the 'speaking subject' into biology . . . this heterogeneity, which cannot be subsumed by the signifier, literally explodes with preg-nancy – the dividing line between nature and culture – and with the arrival of the child – which . . . gives her a chance, albeit not a certainty, of access to the other, the ethical. These peculiarities of the maternal body make a woman a creature of folds . . .
>
> (1986: 115)

The word *volumen*, from which Volumnia's name may be derived, means that which is rolled, a coil, whirl, wreath, fold, eddy, or a roll of writing – a book or volume or part of one (Lewis 1890). The name can be associated with the complex interior circular spaces of the female reproductive organs as well as with the religious and legal textual inscriptions that delineate the social formation. In Shakespeare's play, Volumnia and *virtus*, womb and state, mother and son form a metaphorical and dramatic coil or fold which can be unrolled only for the purpose of analysis.

This coil is no less ideological. In a bizarre image to which several feminist critics have devoted great attention (Adelman 1980, 1992; DuBois 1985; Sprengnether 1986), Volumnia offers a striking para-digm for the social and psychological structures that bind her perfor-mance as a mother to his performance as Rome's champion fighter:

> The breast of Hecuba
> When she did suckle Hector, look'd not lovelier
> Than Hector's forehead when it spit forth blood
> At Grecian sword contemning.
>
> (1.3.40–3)

In the parallel and opposition of nursing mother and bleeding son, several implications emerge. First, the gaze segments the persons that are its objects: it is her breasts, not Hecuba, and his forehead, not Hector, that we see. The flowing breast as metonymy for the woman rather straightforwardly defines her *raison d'être*: to suckle future warriors. The forehead, a rather curious metonymy for the warrior, more subtly defines his, as Gail Kern Paster notes: "The seat of reason itself will bleed voluntarily from contempt rather than involuntarily from an enemy's external blow" (1989: 287–8). As much as flowing breast and spitting forehead serve to distinguish male from female, and involuntary maternal nurture from the warrior's fully willed bleeding, the passage also implies a causal connection, a teleology. What the mother infuses into the baby he then releases as a warrior; she nurses him so that he may later turn dependency into aggression in a socially adaptive way (Adelman 1992: 132). She nurses him in contempt, as it were, of erotic options; she uses her body not to make love, but to help make war. But the instrument of aggression is, interestingly, not a sword but a wound, a wound that behaves like a sword, spitting forth blood against the sword-wielding enemy. The image denies Hector's vulnerability, for the wound, instead of impairing his ability to fight, constitutes his weapon (Adelman 1992: 132).

This odd, arresting image linking maternal breast to masculine wound and sword resonates through the ensuing seven scenes dramatizing the Roman army's successful siege against the city of Corioles and victory over the Volsces. Though she is, of course, absent from these scenes, the Roman mother's emotional and political presence is evoked every time her son appears, "bleeding, assaulted by the enemy" (1.4.61), "as he were flay'd" (1.6.23). "mantled," "smear'd," or "mask'd" in blood (1.6.29, 69, 1.8.10). Indeed, in image and action Coriolanus embodies the implications of Hector's sword-like wound. Coriolanus reads his bleeding to signify not his vulnerability but rather his success as a fighter ("'tis not my blood / Wherein thou see'st me masked," he vaunts, 1.8.9–10). Not only does he speak of his sword conventionally as the soldier's typical equipment ("We with smoking swords," "he shall feel mine edge," 1.4.11, 29); he is even identified with – or *as* – a sword, in Lartius's commendation: "Oh, noble fellow! / Who sensibly outdares his senseless sword, And when it bows, stand'st up" (1.4.52–4). Swords may bend; Coriolanus, despite his many wounds, remains erect and keeps his cutting edge. This image of the warrior as his weapon is dramatized when Coriolanus appeals for volunteers to carry out an assault against the Volscians'

151

prime warrior and his troops; the stage direction reads, "*They all shout and wave their swords.*" The hero then cries, "O me alone! Make you a sword of me!" and "*They all take him up in their arms, and cast up their caps*" (1.6.75–6).[5] In this enacted interpellation of the hero as his country's sword, Coriolanus realizes the implications of Hector's spitting wound as an image of *virtus*: he is the quintessential Roman subject, the national ego-ideal that common soldiers are supposed to imitate but can never equal. As such he is both singular and isolated because he embodies an abstraction, but also fused with the masses subjected by means of that ideal – an ambiguity perfectly mirrored in the interplay between him and the mass at this moment. First he calls for the superior soldier, or "many so minded," to follow him as their leader, the exemplar of *virtus*; then, when they lift him up, he calls upon them to supply the shaping power that makes him Rome's sword, the weapon of its national will.

When Coriolanus is forced to move from field to forum, however, the play begins to reveal the self-cancelling nature of a masculinity that is maternally authorized. Volumnia now becomes a dramatic presence onstage and an agent in the deepening political crisis of which her son's political candidacy is part. The electoral ritual (3.1) requires two things of Coriolanus: that he use words to dissemble what he feels, and that he show his wounds to the people. Both words and wounds are linked problematically to gender difference. Curiously, though he seeks wounds with unparalleled zeal, he cannot bear to have them spoken of, not only before the people but among the patricians as well. It is this reluctance, fused with his contempt for the plebs, that ultimately (assisted by the tribunes' scheming) ruins his candidacy and leads to his banishment. In battle he could avoid confronting language as a symbolic order, a system of sounds that are signs; he could speak with his body, in a pre-linguistic code of representation that the play often alludes to. Significantly, we first see Coriolanus's martial body language through his mother's words: "Methinks I hear hither your husband's drum; / See him pluck Aufidius down by th'hair ... / Methinks I see him stamp thus" (1.3.29-30, 32). Many references to Coriolanus's "grim looks" and the "thunder-like percussion" of his voice similarly represent him through his hyperbolically warlike physical traits. Acting out rather than articulating the martial identity his mother transmits to him, in battle he stays closer to the infantile scene of its transmission.[6]

The words from which Coriolanus most wants to flee are words of praise inspired by his wounds, many and highly visible. Yet even when he rejects the praises wounds elicit, he does so in a way that recalls them: "I have some wounds upon me, and they smart / To hear themselves remembered" (1.9.28–9); "I had rather have my wounds to heal again / Than hear say how I got them" (2.2.69–70). The wound is a sensitive register of the contradictions arising from Volumnia's maternal appropriation of the Roman code of masculinity. As Mary Douglas comments regarding the human body as an image of society, "Interests in apertures depend on the preoccupation with social exists and entrances, escape routes and invasions. If there is no concern to preserve social boundaries. I would not expect to find concern with bodily boundaries" (Douglas 1970: 82). Wounds were the apertures that marked Coriolanus's precocious entry into manhood as a young boy; in the electoral ceremony, which constitutes a second rite of passage, wounds are meant to validate his membership in the governing elite of Rome.

But given Volumnia's position as the arbiter of *virtus* for her son, his wounds function like a fetish: he must mention them, but only to prevent mention of them.[7] Even as they evoke the female aperture, they deny it, for only sword-wielding men are enabled to seek wounds, whereas women are born with them. Wounds signify martial prowess rather than a "feminine" physical frailty. The warrior who survives his wounds asserts the impregnability of the male body, whereas in terms of the Roman code of femininity, the woman's "wound" implies pregnability – her capacity to bear sons. "Every gash was an enemy's grave" (2.1.155), says Menenius of the hero's hacked body, but the hero survives, and keeps on fighting. Coriolanus needs his wounds, needs them desperately, for two contradictory reasons: to please his mother and to assert his manliness. It is as proof of his manliness that they please her, but in pleasing her, they also bind him the more closely to her – and to the state that determines their meaning. In a scene that almost caricatures her investment in his injuries while locating it in the Roman political processes, she tabulates them and gloats over them:

Volumnia: Oh, he is wounded; I thank the gods for't ... I'th'shoulder and i'th'left arm: there will be large cicatrices to show the people when he shall stand for his place. He received in the repulse of Tarquin seven hurts i'th'body.

Menenius: One i'th'neck, and two i'th'thigh – there's nine that I know.

Volumnia: He had, before this last expedition, twenty-five wounds upon him.

Menenius: Now it's twenty-seven . . .

                                           (2.1.120, 146–54)

Because Volumnia is inescapably identified with the wound as a patrician signifier of manliness, any social recognition of Coriolanus as man, warrior, or civic leader also reinscribes him as her nursling.

When he stands for the consulship, Coriolanus is forced not just to hear words but to speak them, to use language in a way that exaggerates or carries to the extreme its symbolic properties; honoring custom but violating his nature, he must employ verbal formulas of humility in speaking to the people and, for the first time in his life, mask the contempt he ordinarily heaps on them. When Volumnia intervenes directly in the political process for the first time, to persuade her son to regain the consulship, the political stability of Rome lies in her hands. In one sense, the scene recapitulates the original scenario of Volumnia's power as Roman mother: because she first made him a man, now she only can sway him and enable his passage from warrior to civic leader. But the scene's dominant metaphor, theatricality, also deconstructs that scenario. In humbly begging the people's pardon, Coriolanus, like an actor, is to play a part:

Coriolanus: Would you have me
              False to my nature? Rather say I play
              The man I am.

Volumnia: O sir, sir, sir.
              I would have had you put your power well on
              Before you had worn it out.

Coriolanus: Let go.

Volumnia: You might have been enough the man you are,
              With striving less to be so . . .

                                         (3.2.14–20)

In suggesting that his masculinity might be only a costume he wears (like Macbeth's "borrow'd robes"), artificial rather than natural, Coriolanus flirts with a truth that would disrupt the binary oppositions on which Rome is based.[8] His mother dismisses that suggestion, but only succeeds in subverting the idea of masculinity further: enough, less, more – how does a man know when the measure of his gender is exactly right? As she proceeds to coach him in this new role of artful, accommodating politician, she stresses the deferential gestures he must make: doffing his hat, kneeling, bowing his head in humility (3.2.73–80). This body language is precisely the opposite of the intimidating, aggressive displays she previously identified with and reveled in; its contrivance is all the more evident. However differently they are played, both soldier and consul are cultural scripts for maleness. Though Volumnia has not written them, she associates her role as mother in "making" her son with coaching him in those roles, and thus exerts a powerful pull on him: "as thou hast said / My praises made thee first a soldier, so, / To have my praise for this, perform a part / Thou hast not done before" (3.2.107–10). However, in calling what he regards as his very self – being a soldier – a part he plays, her speech also de-essentializes maleness.

At first her strategy seems to work: Coriolanus agrees. Even as he is agreeing, though, he portrays the new role in terms of transformation to the feminine, and recoils from it. He equates it with "some harlot's spirit" and envisions the feminization of his voice – that "thunder-like percussion" or "battery" that is the hallmark of his warrior identity – as the price of seeking the people's voices (3.2.112–21). Panicked at recapitulating the "double bind" of a masculine role that puts him once again in his mother's debt, he has recourse to the familiar male/female binarism that identifies the feminine with acting and duplicity, and the male with natural, essential truth. But such "truth" is already undone by the theatrical metaphor – if both the warrior's ferocity and the politician's "insinuating nods" are the man's part, and he learns them both from a woman who thereby serves as his cultural father.

By the end of the tragedy, when Rome celebrates Volumnia as its savior, "the mother has replaced the son as cynosure" (Paster 1985: 89). Using psychoanalytic paradigms, several critics have focussed on Volumnia's role in her son's intra-psychic contradictions, without exploring the social construction of that role (Adelman 1992; Wheeler 1980; DuBois 1985; Sprengnether 1986). By looking briefly at Volumnia's supreme moment in the play (5.3), I want to examine that construction: her placement as mother in Roman patriarchy. I will be concerned with the occluded symbolic as distinct from the overt social configurations of gender.

In the Rome of this play, not only does the hero lack a father – none of the father surrogates wields much authority or wields it effectively. This vacuum of patriarchal power is accentuated when both the general Cominius and the politican Menenius fail in successive missions to Coriolanus; the women then move in, and succeed.

155

Volumnia, Virgilia, and Valeria as mother, wife, and sister (of Publicola, exemplary statesman and soldier) are linked alliteratively and identified in terms of their kinship to men so as to suggest as a group the place of women in Rome. Virgilia's name connects her subordinate role as wife to the *pietas* or filial piety central to Rome's national epic. Valeria, the sister, who in Plutarch instigates the women's visit to Antium, has little to say in Shakespeare. But when Coriolanus addresses her as "The moon of Rome, chaste as the icicle / That's curdied by the frost from purest snow / And hangs on Dian's temple" (5.3.65–7), Shakespeare points to what is symbolically at stake for Rome in this final crisis. Chastity, the female counterpart of *virtus*, is what makes women socially valuable in Roman patriarchy, as I have argued with regard to *Lucrece* (Kahn 1976: 61). If women can be encouraged to resemble Diana in lacking any desires of their own for men, their wombs can the more effectively be controlled by men in ways that serve the state. "Dian's temple" recalls the national cult of Vesta, in which virgins guarded the sacred fire representing the continuity of Rome. It hints at the symbolic confinement of women's sexuality – their desires and their wombs – within the ideology of chastity, which is in turn connected to the social practices of kinship and marriage (Kahn 1976: 50).

Plutarch's Valeria suggests a more revealing cultural paradigm for women's role in the Roman state, however, when she urges its women to follow "the daughters of the Sabynes . . . in former age, when they procured lovinge peace, in stead of hatefull warre, betweene their fathers and their husbands" (1895b: 182). Livy's account of the peace-making role of the raped Sabine women stands behind Valeria's words in Plutarch and also shapes the climactic scene in *Coriolanus*: Volumnia's plea to her son, before the gates of Rome, to spare the city.

Livy explains that the Romans seized the Sabine women because, lacking the right of intermarriage with the surrounding peoples, they lacked the means of continuing their newly founded state (1967: I.ix–xii). Without access to marriageable women, Rome faced extinction. So Romulus lured his neighbors to the city with a harvest festival the name of which hints at Rome's need and its leader's purpose: the Consualia, named from *condere*, to store up. When the Sabines arrived, the Romans seized their virgins, and the others fled in panic. Thus Romulus stored up his human harvest of children, assuring the Sabine women that they would "become co-partners in all the possessions of the Romans, in their citizenship and, dearest privilege of all to the human race, in their children" (1967: I.ix.15). In time the Sabines

156

returned to attack Rome and take back their woman. Then the raped and Romanized women rushed wildly between the two armies,

> beseeching their fathers on this side, on that their husbands, that fathers-in-law and sons-in-law should not stain themselves with impious bloodshed, nor pollute with parricide the suppliants' children, grandsons to one party and sons to the other.
>
> (1967: I.xiii.2–3).

Like the Sabines, the women in *Coriolanus* are kin to both warring sides, and intercede by appealing to bonds of marriage and procreation. When Volumnia tells her son that in marching on Rome he will "tread . . . on thy mother's womb" she echoes the Sabine women who appealed to their fathers on one side, their newly acquired husbands on the other, not to stain themselves with the impious bloodshed of kinsfolk. By alluding to her womb as the source of her son's being, she makes his connection to her seem originary, total, and unquestionable, as she has before. But by identifying her womb with Rome, she also evokes the peculiar value of women to Rome as the fertile resource without which the state cannot reproduce itself, cannot continue.[9] Her appeal is not merely sentimental; rather, it is pertinent to the situation at hand, for Coriolanus plans not just to make war on Rome, but to enter its walls and destroy its women and children.

Resisting his mother's two long speeches of entreaty, Coriolanus yields only when she and the others "shame him with [their] knees" (5.3.169). With the exception of mothers, within the patrician class women commonly kneel to men, as their wives, daughters, sisters; only mothers as progenitors share in the authority and honor accorded to fathers. But because of the way she framed him to *virtus*, Coriolanus owes more than his physical existence to his mother. In kneeling to her son she reverses the usual gesture of indebtedness only to evoke more pointedly the unusual totality of his debt to her so that he will capitulate to her. But that debt is unusual only in the sense that the mother's contribution to the making of a son is normally occluded by the authority accorded to the father. In this play, the father is absent and the mother's contribution is exposed and exaggerated, not to reveal her power *per se* but rather her complicity with the father's power. In Kristeva's terms, the mother's power is folded within the father's.

Coriolanus ends ironically, with Volumnia hailed as "the life of Rome" while her son, unknown to the Romans, is hacked to death by the Volsces. In every sense, she prevails: over his desires for revenge,

POSTSCRIPT
Cymbeline: paying tribute to Rome

> The testimonies . . . lie bleeding in me.
> *Cymberline* 3.4.22–3

Cymbeline takes us back to the misty beginnings of Britain's ties with Rome, to the era following Julius Caesar's occupation of the island when the fledgling nation was still a Roman tributary. Though long grouped with the romances, this play is as much Roman as romance, its identifiably historical elements fused with the romance conventions characteristic of Shakespeare's last plays. Robert Miola puts it decisively under a Roman rubric by tracing its many echoes of theme and incident in Shakespeare's other Roman works, its allusions to Latin texts and its concern with *pietas*.[1] For my purposes, it belongs with the Roman works because like them it grapples with *virtus* as a vexted configuration of warriors, wounds, and women.

What sets it off from the other Roman works is a specific concern with British national identity. Like Romanness, however, that national identity is gendered masculine (Mikalachki 1995). As in the English history plays, in *Cymbeline* "belief in the fierce independence of England . . . [is] the sign of masculine virtue" (Adelman 1992: 206). In Roman Britain, *virtus* is necessarily a hybrid, an uneasy marriage of native stock with scion, and in the vicissitudes of Posthumus we can trace its tensions. Orphan son of a noble Briton warrior, he is banished to Rome, there loses his faith in the native British virtue that Imogen embodies, returns to fight against Britain but finally confirms his British identity by valiantly defending his country against Rome. Imogen sets the action going by marrying Posthumus in defiance of her father. The question posed in that action – "Who shall possess Imogen? To whom does she belong?" (Schwartz 1970: 224) – joins the problem of *virtus* with that of chastity, for Imogen's chastity isn't merely her own: it is a national treasure. She is princess

160

of Britain and heir to its throne (Thompson 1991: 77). Furthermore, her name, taken from Innogen, wife of Brute, the legendary founder of Britain, implies that she too will mother a new race. The motif of thesaurization that figured the feminine in *Lucrece* and *Titus* is equally important here. In Imogen Shakespeare combines the situation of Lucrece, whose chastity is the property of her husband, and that of Lavinia, whose chastity belongs to her father.

In *Cymbeline*, independence from Rome is always already compromised by a kind of co-dependence on Rome for the validation of manly virtue. Britons might fight Romans because they too adhere to the Roman *ethos* of manhood won through emulation. Cymbeline's final gesture has understandably puzzled many readers: the Britons having won their independence by conspicuous bravery, in the last twenty-five lines of the play he seems to sell them out.

> Although the victor, we submit to Caesar,
> And to the Roman empire; promising
> To pay our wonted tribute . . .
>
> (5.5.461–3)

"Although the victor," Cymbeline is driven to acknowledge Rome's preeminence, to maintain that cultural tie through a nominally hierarchical relationship that recapitulates Rome's dominance when it no longer actually obtains. Meredith Skura suggests, "Cymbeline must finally pay 'tribute' to the Rome that generated him and his ideals" (1980: 213). Perhaps we can also read his gesture metadramatically: in this play Shakespeare pays tribute to Rome as a cultural model for Britain and specifically, as source and inspiration for his own Roman works – acknowledging his own form of emulation.[2]

In defying the Roman ambassador, Cymbeline postulates a native civility pre-dating contact with Rome by recalling the first British king, Mulmutius, as the nation's lawgiver (3.1.55–63). But in fact this is the only such moment in the play. Rather, it is the oft-mentioned invasion of Britain by Julius Caesar that marks the emergence of the island into history from a barbaric past.[3] It also provides the touchstone of *virtus* for the play's older generation. In a phrase that expresses both identification and rivalry, Posthumus's father Leonatus "did *join* his honour / *Against* the Romans with Cassibelan" (1.1.29–30, my emphasis). Similarly Cymbeline, who was "knighted" by Augustus Caesar, says "of him I gather'd honour, / Which he to seek of me again, perforce, / Behoves me keep at utterance," i.e., defend (3.1.72–4), implying that honor is created reciprocally in exchanges

161

of valor between Romans and Britons. Belarius says his "body's mark'd / With Roman swords," which made him "once / First, with best of note" (3.3.56–8).[4] Cymbeline's three children all have Latin names and so does Posthumus. In the recent past, then, Britain's ruling elite validated itself by fighting against Rome, and its defeat mattered less than the honor it won against such a preeminent adversary.

But now Britain turns to the other side of emulation, asserting its parity with Rome. "Britain's a world by itself," says Cloten in response to Caius's opening reference to Caesar's conquest (3.1.2–4), and his mother follows with her own rereading of Caesar's "kind of conquest," picturing him as "twice beaten" by the "natural bravery" of Britain's seas and coast that kept him from landing. But her vivid rendering of sands that "suck up" Caesar's boats and seas that crack them is itself unavoidably indebted to Caesar's account of his invasions of Britain in *De Bellum Gallicum*, a staple of the grammar school curriculum (3.1.15–34) that was also included in Holinshed. The Queen emphasizes "The natural bravery of [the] isle . . . ribb'd and pal'd in / With rocks unscaleable and roaring waters" (3.1.19–21), to which Caesar's history offers ample testimony. Posthumus, in contrast, dwells on the Britons' capacity to learn and practice Roman military discipline:

> Our countrymen
> Are men more order'd than when Julius Caesar
> Smil'd at their lack of skill, but found their courage
> Worthy his frowning at. Their discipline,
> (Now wing-led with their courages) will make known
> To their approvers they are people such
> That mend upon the world.
>
> (2.4.20–6)

Actually, Caesar recounts several occasions on which small bands of native fighters ambush the invaders, who were weighed down by their armor and unfamiliar with British terrain (1917: iv. 26–7, 32; v.15–17). The two somewhat disparate versions of British martial strength ultimately complement each other, though, to assert that the Britons draw on native advantages while learning from the Roman model. The important point for my argument is that even when Britons assert their strength with some justice, they unavoidably call on Roman sources.[5] Rome persists as the emulous reference point for configuring Britain and its men, impelling Britons to surpass Rome

162

in order to found themselves as Britons. In *Cymbeline*, as Jodi Mikalachki argues, "British national identity is formed from the inter-action of the Roman invaders with the native land" (1995: 317).

This interaction reaches its climax in the encounter at "the narrow lane" (5.2–3) between a band of four Britons – "an old man, and two boys," plus Posthumus disguised as a peasant – and the Roman army. In a spectacular display of bravery that is first enacted, then recounted in some detail by Posthumus, against all odds these few turn the tide of battle. The Britons face imminent defeat: Cymbeline has been captured and his army is in flight. Posthumus's narrative stresses repeatedly the peculiar terrain of this fight and the initial cowardice of the Britons: the struggle takes place in "a strait lane . . . Close by the battle, ditch'd, and wall'd with turf," that is "damm'd / With dead men, hurt behind" (5.3.3–51). This narrow passage suggests two different but significantly related symbolic spaces. First, it recalls the sites of emulation projected so vividly in *Julius Caesar* ("young ambi-tion's ladder," 2.1.21–2), *Troilus and Cressida* (the steps marking "the envious fever / Of pale and bloodless emulation," 1.3.133–4) and *Timon of Athens* ("Fortune's high and pleasant hill," 1.1.65). I suggested in chapter 4 that in these tight spaces jammed with men, each one struggling to get ahead of the others and come out on top, Shakespeare expresses the intense anxiety of institutionalized competition in the Roman ethos.[6] The imagery of the Britons "hurt behind" evokes a primitive dread of bodily exposure associated with the shame of fail-ure that looms as the alternative to achieving manly virtue. Those who are valiant will face the enemy and "Stand," the repeated rallying cry of Belarius (5.3.25, 28, 31).

In *Cymbeline* isn't just one man but rather an age-graded spectrum of representative males – an old man, two boys, and Posthumus in the prime of life – who vanquish the Romans. They comprise a kind of all-male martial family, an extension of the pastoral family of Belarius and his two kidnapped sons, which is echoed in the dream vision of the Leonati (in which the mother's role is firmly subdued to the father's, sons and father forming a martial triad), and finally realized in the reunion of Cymbeline with his sons after his queen's death. Janet Adelman argues that this parthenogenetic filial unit constitutes the play's central fantasy of "pure male family from which women can be wholly excluded" which provides "a secure basis for masculine identity" (1992: 199). Certainly this heroic stand enables Posthumus to prove and claim his worth as a son of the Leonati, emulating his father and the brothers who "Died with their swords in hand" (1.1.36), and makes him a fit husband for Imogen instead of the "nothing" he was previously held to be.

At the same time, I suggest, it restates the ambivalence inherent in Britain's emulation of Rome, insofar as it closely parallels not only Holinshed's description of Haie and his sons fighting off the Danes, but also Livy's famous account of Horatius at the bridge.[7] Along with other hardy defenders of the early Roman republic such as Mutius Scaevola and Verginius, Horatius was an oft-cited exemplar of *virtus* who saved Rome from invasion by the Tarquins, preventing them from reestablishing kingship after their expulsion by Brutus. Horatius took his stand at a narrow bridge of piles across the Tiber that allowed access to the city; as the Tarquins' forces approached it, the Romans fled. Horatius, though, stood at the head of the bridge, challenging the enemy to fight him alone, and inciting his countrymen to destroy the bridge behind him. Then, having successfully held off the invaders and "given proof of valour," he leapt into the Tiber and swam to the Roman side (1967: II.x). That the play's climactic moment marking the achievement of British independence and authentic manly virtue is indebted both to native and to Roman models of valor seems to reiterate the ambivalence in Britain's emulation of Rome.

The "narrow lane" can also be read in another way, as sexual terrain, for the political plot of Britain's relations with Rome is at every point in close alignment with the love story of Posthumus and Imogen. As Linda Woodbridge argues, the lane suggests the highly defended site of Imogen's chastity, the narrow entrance to her womb (1991: 334–5). The Roman invasion of Britain at this distinctive site parallels Iachimo's invasion of her bedchamber and Cloten's parallel "siege" for her hand; thus "Imogen's perils are Britain's" (Woodbridge 1991: 335).[8] When Imogen awakes from a death-like sleep to find her bedfellow a beheaded corpse which she mistakes for her problematical bridegroom, Shakespeare confounds the sexual with the political register in a bizarre parody of the consummation that might assure Britain's future. In a manner strongly reminiscent of Lavinia's rape in *Titus*, Cloten contrives his intended revenge against Imogen as a mockery of her marriage to Posthumus. Killing Posthumus first, he would then "ravish her" dressed in her husband's clothes, "He on the ground" (3.5.141–9); Bassianus similarly served "as pillow" for Lavinia's ravishers.

Though Cloten's plan falls through, he still ends up a substitute bridegroom dressed in Posthumus's clothes and – until she works her way past his "brawns" – sexually appealing to the princess. However,

Plate 5 *Publius Horatius*, by Hendrick Goltzius, Holland, 1558–1617. From *Roman Heroes* (1586), a series of eight engravings depicting exemplars of virtus inspired by Livy's history of the early republic, and dedicated to Rudolf II, emperor of the Holy Roman Empire. The hero lifts his sword heavenward, dedicating his right hand to the defense of Rome. Reproduced with permission of Los Angeles County Museum of Art, gift of Mary Staesburg Ruiz.

165

the "lawful pleasure" from which she "oft restrained" her husband is still prevented. Indeed, these nuptials are both truncated and travestied. And Cloten, from the beginning both surrogate and scapegoat for Posthumus (Siemon 1976: 60; Adelman 1992: 215–16), is now more unsuitable than ever, a mere "trunk . . . Without his top" (4.2.353–4) while Posthumus's "root" must yet be delved (1.1.27). Neither is fit to "be jointed to the old stock" of Britain's family tree, that "stately cedar" identified with Cymbeline (5.4.142, 140). In this sequence of outrageous dramatized puns, Shakespeare reverts to something like the hybrid mode of *Titus*, the mixture of comic, grotesque, and tragic that characterized his engagement with Rome more than a decade earlier. After the dire, tragic Romes of the intervening three dramas, again he plays with Rome or rather with Roman Britain, a hybrid dramatized in a likewise hybrid form, tragicomedy.

Once Posthumus comes to believe Imogen unchaste, in the striking image that serves as the epigram for this chapter, he suffers a wound. He writes to his servant, "Thy mistress, Pisanio, hath played the strumpet in my bed: the testimonies whereof lie bleeding in me" (3.4.21–3). The sexual pun on "testimonies" noted by Janet Adelman (1992: 213) revealingly transforms the "wound" usually suffered by the woman in defloration or violation to a wound she inflicts, through her supposed infidelity, on the man's tenderest parts. These outward parts are a metaphor for the inner wound that "[lies] bleeding in" Posthumus, the "testimonies" that enter into his consciousness to shame his manhood and sully his honor. His famous soliloquy on "the woman's part" (2.4.153–86) also internalizes this injury, identifying as woman's all "motion / That tends to vice in man": he gets it from her, but it comes to reside in him. The argument of this speech is that not only the cuckolded male but all men are congenitally infected with the feminine, since there is "no way for women to be, but women / Must be half-workers" (2.4.153–4).[9]

Posthumus's response to this wound is unsurprisingly conventional: like Titus or Antony, like Claudio, Othello, or Leontes, he seeks revenge – a wound for a wound. The "bloody cloth" is meant to prove that revenge has been accomplished, and thus to restore *virtus* (5.1.1–2). Instead, this bogus proof produces in Posthumus intense guilt at supposedly murdering his wife for "wrying but a little." In a long soliloquy meditating on her "little fault" and his greater one, Posthumus finally seizes on a chance to win valor from wounds in battle as the alternative to the crippling remorse he is suffering:

'tis enough
That, Britain, I have kill'd thy mistress: peace,
I'll give no wound to thee: therefore, good heavens,
Hear patiently my purpose. I'll disrobe me
Of these Italian weeds, and suit myself
As does a Briton peasant: so I'll fight
Against the part I came with: so I'll die
For thee, O Imogen, even for whom my life
Is, every breath, a death: and thus, unknown,
Pitied, nor hated, to the face of peril
Myself I'll dedicate. Let me make men know
More valour in me than my habits show.
Gods, put the strength o' the' Leonati in me!
(5.2.19–31)

In the first three lines, Posthumus compares killing Imogen to wounding Britain as a Roman turncoat; then he turns away from both acts of betrayal to embrace a plan that combines two complementary aims. First, he resolves to die a humble, anonymous penitential death fighting for Britain in disguise, paying his life in restitution for hers. Here he would play "the woman's part" in a different sense than before; his stance resembles Imogen's as Fidele, whose name and disguise as a humble page represent the self-effacing devotion she assumes after her husband tries to kill her. But having insisted that he will remain "unknown" in his valor (27), he reverses himself; he declares that he will "make men know / More valour *in me* than my habits show" (30, my emphasis), and prays "Gods, put the strength o' th' Leonati *in me*" (line 31, my emphasis). The repeated phrases hark back to the "bleeding testimonies in me" that drove his attempt to murder his wife. In effect, the repetition suggests that he will court the wounds of battle as a way to heal the wounds of supposed sexual dishonor. Either way, masculinity is imaged in wounds, as it has been throughout the Roman works, and those wounds are both feminine and masculine, the one kind suggesting the other. That the battle takes place in a sexualized "narrow lane" further suggests the implied substitution of one kind of wound for another, and one kind of "part" for another as well. In place of "the woman's part" that bleeds within him, he will play the part – in costume as a British peasant – of Britain's manly defender. And the martial wounds he risks will reattach him to his paternal heritage: "the strength o' th' Leonati," a combination of Roman *virtus* and native British courage (Skura 1980).

167

Posthumus's valor in the narrow lane establishes him, finally, as a fit bridegroom for Imogen and future ruler of Britain. The most "Roman" episode in the play, it also reestablishes Britain's independence from Rome (until at the last moment Cymbeline restores the tribute). What stands in glaring contrast to this literally classical proof of *virtus* is Posthumus's astonishing forgiveness of Imogen without proof of her innocence; when he decides to give his life in battle for her sake, he still believes she slept with Iachimo (5.1.1–13). Of course, as readers have pointed out, this capacity to accept a woman's sexuality as an ordinary human "fault" is hedged about by the fact of Imogen's perfect innocence, starkly opposed to the Queen's utter badness, a primitive splitting by which the play defends against a full integration of the feminine into masculine consciousness. His forgiveness of Imogen is also contained by the way in which her initial spunkiness dwindles into submission. As Ann Thompson says, she "must die as an heiress in order to be re-born as a wife" (1991: 84). Furthermore, the dream vision of the Leonati and the descent of Jupiter constitute powerful reminders that a strong principle of paternal control subtends the play's action.

But Posthumus's forgiveness of Imogen is nonetheless a striking departure not only from the intransigence of Claudio, Leontes, and Othello, but from the Roman pattern of placing women in a separate domain while pairing heroes most importantly with their emulous male rivals rather than with women. Though Posthumus at first stigmatizes his wife and her seeming fault as "the woman's part," in his fifth-act soliloquy he internalizes that part and cleanses it of sexual contamination. Surely the play works as hard to enable Posthumus to accept "the woman's part" as to foster manly virtue in him. Insofar as *Cymbeline* is romance as much as Roman, we shouldn't wonder at this: forgiveness runs strong in Shakespeare's romances. And though I am ending this study of *virtus* in the Roman works with a postscript to *Cymbeline*, I don't mean to imply that in it Shakespeare arrives at some final resolution of the dilemma that has engaged him for about twenty years, since he wrote *Lucrece* in the early nineties. In a broad sense, that dilemma informs many if not all of Shakespeare's plays and poems, as a host of (mainly feminist) critics have been showing us (also for about twenty years). In the Roman works, the wound that signifies *virtus* remains an open wound in the sense of a persistent but unsuccessful attempt to fix, stabilize, delimit masculinity as a self-consistent autonomy free from the stigma of the feminine. Other contemporary versions of *romanitas* take it more or less at face value, as simply "a set of virtues . . . soldierly, severe, self-controlled, self-disciplined" (Hunter (1977: 94). Shakespeare makes it, rather, a question of sexual difference – an open question, still.

NOTES

1   Miola sees the play as "Shakespeare's valediction to Rome" in the sense that it amalgamates elements of the Roman ethos but revises them in accordance with a morally superior complex of British values: "Roman pride is balanced by humility, Roman courage by the qualities of mercy and forgiveness, Roman constancy by a capacity for flexibility, growth, and change" (1983: 207). G. W. Knight urged that *Cymbeline* "be regarded mainly as an historical play" (1947: 129) because its concern with "Britain's islanded integrity" allies it to the English history plays, and J. P. Brockbank called it "a historical romance" on the grounds that Holinshed's account of the descent and early life of Brute resembles the story of the lost princes in Wales (1958: 43–4). As noted in chapter 1, the legend that Brute, son of Aeneas, founded Britain persistently configured Britain as Rome's heir, legitimately claiming title to Roman culture and political predominance.

2   In a world-historical sense, one might say, *Cymbeline* can also be read in terms of *translatio imperii*, the *topos* of the westward progress of empire from Troy to Rome to Britain. Frances Yates explores both Elizabethan and Jacobean appropriations of Augustan Rome as prototype of a Protestant empire that would reform the Church. She shows how Cymbeline's reign, contemporary like Augustus's with the birth of Christ, "drew together British imperial and Roman imperial sacred legend in some new fusion of Britain and Rome" (1975: 43). Patricia Parker traces resonant echoes of the *Aeneid* in *Cymbeline* that evoke *translatio imperii*, "the ideology of historical transumption in which Britain, and its king, would be the fulfillment and surpassing of Rome" (1989: 206).

3   The invasion is alluded to in the first scene, with reference to Posthumus's father and brothers (discussed below), then recalled by Posthumus (2.4.20–3) and Lucius (3.1.2–10). It provides the context for the dispute over tribute between Cymbeline, the Queen, Cloten and Lucius in 3.1; crops up again in Belarius's reference to his martial past (3.3.55–60), also discussed below; and is memorialized in the Leonati of the dream-vision, who speak of "dying in our country's cause" (5.4.71–4).

4   Mikalachki, who interprets *Cymbeline* as a richly revealing document in the creation of early modern British nationalism, calls this image "a literalization of the Roman writing of ancient British history" and remarks "Without fighting the Romans, the princes will have no such marks to read by the winter fire when they are old" (1995: 315).

5   See Nearing (1949) on the complex historiography of Caesar's invasion of Britain. Roman writers such as Lucan, Tacitus, and Dio Cassius disparaged the venture and its leader, while Orosius, on whom Bede and then Geoffrey of Monmouth depended, used *The Gallic Wars* as a source but emphasized Caesar's losses in Britain. Geoffrey probably didn't know *The*

Gallic Wars; in any case, he gives a quite different account of the Roman invasion than Caesar's. The Britons defeat Caesar on his first landing, and he returns a second time to take revenge. Again he is routed, by an army three times larger than his, Roman soldiers drowning by the thousands in the Thames. In order to explain how the Romans managed to subject the Britons, then, Geoffrey invented Androgeus, a perfidious Kentish prince, whose intervention brings about the tribute (Nearing 1949).

6   Another kind of emulation, familiar from *Lucrece*, is that of the wager plot, which begins as a contest among men "for the distinction of possessing not simply the fairest but the most "virtuous, wise, chaste, constant, qualified and [least] attemptable" woman (1.5.61–2).

7   Both Nosworthy, editor of the Arden 2 *Cymbeline*, and Bullough, editor of the standard collection of Shakespeare's sources, consider Holinshed's account, which comes from volume 2 of his *Historie of Scotland*, the sole source of the narrow-lane episode. No one, so far as I know, has noticed the close parallel in Livy's Horatius.

8   Woodbridge convincingly argues that "Elizabethan England had a sense of herself as an island, perpetually threatened with invasion," that by the time of the Armada crystallized into "a siege mentality" of "The Land as Woman, society as a body threatened at its orifices" (1991: 337, 340, 341).

9   Janet Adelman reads this speech compellingly as "a fantasy in which maternal sexuality *per se* is always infidelity, always a displacement of the father and a corresponding contamination of the son ... as though Imogen's sexuality evoked the woman's part in Posthumus, making him acknowledge himself (for the first time) as born of woman" (1992: 212–13). Without denying the cogency of this reading, I am pursuing connections between the wound images that reside in their fetishistic capacity to express the "feminine" components of manly virtue.

BIBLIOGRAPHY

PRIMARY WORKS

Aristotle (1946) *Politics*, E. Barker (ed.). Oxford: Clarendon.

Ascham, R. (1570, rpt 1967) The *Scholemaster*, L.V. Ryan (ed.). Ithaca, N.Y.: Cornell University.

Augustine, St (1972) *The City of God*, D. Knowles (ed.). Harmondsworth, Middlesex, England: Pelican Classics.

Bernard, R. (transl.) (1598) *Terence in English*, Cambridge.

Boaistuau, P. (1574) *Theatrum Mundi*, J. Alday (transl.). London.

Bryskett, L. (1972) *Literary Works of Lodowick Bryskett*, J.H.P. Pafford (ed.). Farnsborough: Gregg.

Burton, R. (1927) *Anatomy of Melancholy*, Floyd Dell and Paul Jordan-Smith (eds). New York: Tudor Publishing.

Caesar, J. (1917) *The Gallic War*, H. J. Edwards (transl.). London: Heinemann.

Camden, W. (1610) *Britain, or a Chorographical Description of England, Scotland, and Ireland . . . Translated into English by Philemon Holland*, London.

Chapman, G. (1631) *Caesar and Pompey: A Roman Tragedy, declaring their Warres*, London: Thomas Harper.

Cicero, M.T. (1971) *Brutus*, G.L. Hendrickson (transl. and ed.). Cambridge, MA: Harvard University Press.

—— (1928) *De Re Publica*, C.W. Keyes (transl.). Loeb Classical Library. London: William Heinemann.

—— (1951) *De Natura Deorum, Academica*, H. Rackham (transl.). Loeb Classical Library. Cambridge MA: Harvard University Press.

Cooper, T. (1969) *Thesaurus Linguae Romanae et Britannicae*. Menston, England: Scolar.

Digges, L. (1640, rpt. 1932), in Ingleby *et al.*, vol. 1.

Donne, J. (1982) *Biathanatos*, M. Rudick and M. P. Battin (eds and intro.). New York: Garland.

Elyot, T. (1937) *The Governour*. London: J. M. Dent.

Fulbecke, W. (1601) *An Historical Collection of the Continuall Factions, Tumults, and Massacres of the Romans and Italians . . .* London: William Ponsonby.

Grafton, R. (1569) *A Chronicle At Large and Meere History of the Affayres of England and Kinges of the same, deduced from the creation of the worlde, unto the first habitation of the Islande . . .* London.

Heywood, T. (1608) *The Rape of Lucrece. A True Roman Tragedy*. London: printed for I.B.

Johnson, S. (1968) "Preface to Shakespeare," *The Yale Edition of the Works of Samuel Johnson*, A. Sherbo (ed.). New Haven and London: Yale University Press, vol. 7.

Jonson, B. (1965) *Sejanus*, J. Barish (ed. and intro.). New Haven: Yale University Press.

Lipsius, J. (1939) *Two Bookes of Constancie, Englished by Sir John Stradling*, R. Kirk (ed. and intro.). New Brunswick, NJ: Rutgers University Press.

Livy (1967) *Ab Urbe Condita* vol. 1, B. O. Foster (transl.), Cambridge MA: Harvard University Press, 14 vols.

Lodge, T. (1609, rpt. 1969) *The Wounds of Civil War*, J.W. Houppert (ed. and intro.), Lincoln, NE: University of Nebraska Press.

Machiavelli, N. (1965) *Chief Works, and Others*, A. Gilbert (transl.), Durham, NC: Duke University Press, 3 vols.

Montaigne, M. (1975) *Essays*, D. M. Frame (transl.), Stanford: Stanford University Press.

Ovid (1961) *Metamorphoses*, R. Humphries (transl.). Bloomington: Indiana University Press.

—— (1989) *Fasti*, J. G. Frazer (transl.), 2nd edn. Cambridge, MA: Harvard University Press.

Plutarch (1895a) *The Life of Cato Utican*, in *Lives of the Noble Greeks and Romans, Englished by Sir Thomas North*, G. Wyndham (intro.). London: David Nutt, vol. 5, 109–79.

—— (1895b) *The Life of Caius Marcius Coriolanus, Lives*, vol. 2, 143–90.

—— (1895c) *The Life of Julius Caesar, Lives*, vol. 5, 1–71.

—— (1895d) *The Life of Antonius, Lives*, vol. 6, 1–93.

—— (1895e) *The Life of Marcus Brutus, Lives*, vol. 6, 182–240.

—— (1895f) *The Life of Paulus Aemilius, Lives*, vol. 2, 196–242.

—— (1895g) *The Life of Romulus, Lives*, vol. 1, 68–112.

—— (1895h) *The Life of Tiberius and Gaius Gracchus, Lives*, vol. 5, 235–75.

—— (1931) *The Sayings of Spartan Women, Moralia*, vol. 3, F. B. Cole (transl. and ed.). London: Heinemann, 455–69, 14 vols.

Seneca, L. A. (1614) *De Beneficiis, Moral Essays*, T. Lodge (transl.). London.

Shakespeare, W. (1992) *The Complete Works of William Shakespeare*, D. Bevington (ed.). Cambridge: Cambridge University Press.

—— (1990) *Antony and Cleopatra*, D. Bevington (ed. and intro.). Cambridge: Cambridge University Press.

—— (1994) *The Tragedy of Antony and Cleopatra*, M. Neill (ed. and intro.). Oxford: Oxford University Press.

—— (1995) *Antony and Cleopatra*, J. Wilders (ed. and intro.). Arden 3. London: Routledge.

—— (1976) *Coriolanus*, P. Brockbank (ed. and intro.). London: Methuen.

—— (1955, rpt. 1966) *Cymbeline*, J. M. Nosworthy (ed. and intro.). London: Methuen.

—— (1988) *Julius Caesar*, T. S. Dorsch (ed. and intro.). London and New York: Routledge.

—— (1981) *King Richard III*, Anthony Hammond (ed.). London: Methuen.

—— (1969a) *Lucrece, The Poems* F. T. Prince (ed. and intro.). Arden Shakespeare Paperbacks. London: Methuen.

BIBLIOGRAPHY

—— (1971) *The Merry Wives of Windsor*, H. J. Oliver (ed. and intro.). London: Methuen.

—— (1969b) *Timon of Athens*, H. J. Oliver (ed. and intro.). London: Methuen.

—— (1968) *Titus Andronicus*, J. C. Maxwell (ed. and intro.). London: Methuen.

—— (1995) *Titus Andronicus*, Jonathan Bate (ed. and intro.). London: Routledge.

—— (1982) *Troilus and Cressida*, K. Palmer (ed. and intro.). London and New York: Methuen.

Seutonius (1979) *The Twelve Caesars*, R. Graves (transl.). Penguin Classics. Harmondsworth: Penguin.

Surrey, H. H. (Earl of) (1964) *Poems*, E. Jones (ed.). Oxford: Clarendon Press.

Udall, N. (1533) *Floures for Latyn Spekynge, Selected and Gathered out of Terence*. London.

Virgil. (1971) *The Aeneid of Virgil: A Verse Translation*, A. Mandelbaum (transl.). Berkeley: University of California Press.

SECONDARY WORKS

Adelman, J. (1973) *The Common Liar: An Essay on Antony and Cleopatra*. New Haven: Yale University Press.

—— (1980) "'Anger is my meat': Feeding and Dependency in *Coriolanus*," in Schwartz and Kahn (eds), 129–49. Reprinted in Adelman (1992).

—— (1992) *Suffocating Mothers: Fantasies of Maternal Origin in Shakespeare's Plays, Hamlet to The Tempest*. London and New York: Routledge.

Althusser, L. (1971) "Ideology and Ideological State Apparatuses," in *Lenin and Philosophy and Other Essays*. New York: Monthly Review Press, 127–86.

Anson, J. S. (1967) "*Julius Caesar*: The Politics of the Hardened Heart," *Shakespearean Studies* 2: 11–33.

Apter, E. and Pietz, W. (1993) *Fetishism as Cultural Discourse*. Ithaca: Cornell University Press.

Arthur, M. B. (1981) "The Divided World of *Iliad* VI," in H. P. Foley (ed.). *Reflections of Women in Antiquity*, New York, London, and Paris: Gordon and Breach.

Babcock, B. (ed.) (1978) *The Reversible World: Symbolic Inversion in Art and Society*, Ithaca: Cornell University Press.

Baldwin, T. W. (1944) *William Shakespere's Small Latine and Lesse Greeke*, Urbana: University of Illionois Press, 2 vols.

Barish, J. A. (1965) *Sejanus* (ed. and intro.). New Haven: Yale University Press.

Barkan, L. (1986) *The Gods Made Flesh: Metamorphosis and the Pursuit of Paganism*, New Haven: Yale University Press.

Barroll, J. L. (1958) "Shakespeare and Roman History," *Modern Language Review* 53: 327–43.

Barton, A. (1973) "'Nature's piece 'gainst fancy': The Divided Catastrophe in *Antony and Cleopatra*," inaugural lecture, Bedford College, London, 1973.

Bashar, N. (1983) "Rape in England between 1550 and 1700," in London Feminist History Group, *The Sexual Dynamics of History: Men's Power, Women's Resistance*. London: Pluto, 28–42.

173

Bate, J. (1995) "Introduction," in Bate, J. (ed. and intro.). Shakespeare, W., *Titus Andronicus*. London: Routledge.

Bayet, J. (1971) "Le Suicide mutuel dans la mentalité des Romains," in *Croyances et rites dans la Rome antique*, Paris: Payot, 130–76.

Belsey, C. (1985) *The Subject of Tragedy: Identity and Difference in Renaissance Drama*, London and New York: Routledge.

Berkin, C.R. and Lovett, C.M. (eds) (1980) *Women, War, and Revolution*, New York: Holmes.

Bernheimer, C. (1993) "Freudianism and Decadence: Salome's Severed Heads," in Apter and Pietz (eds), 62–83.

Berry, P. (1992) *Shakespeare Survey* "Women, Language, and History in *The Rape of Lucrece*," 44: 33–40.

Berry, R. (1981) "*Julius Caesar*: A Roman Tragedy," *Dalhousie Review* 61, 2 (summer): 325–36.

Blits, J. S. (1981) "Manliness and Friendship in Shakespeare's *Julius Caesar*," *Interpretation* 9, 2–3 (September): 155–67.

Boose, L. E. (1989) "The Father's House and the Daughter in It," in Boose and Flowers (eds), 17–24.

—— and Flowers, B. S. (eds) (1989) *Daughters and Fathers*. Baltimore: John Hopkins University Press.

Bower, L.C. (1991) "'Mother' in Law: Conceptions of Mother and the Maternal in Feminism and Feminist Legal Theory," *differences: A Journal of Feminist Cultural Studies* 3,1: 20–38.

Bowers, A. R. (1981) "Iconography and Rhetoric in *Lucrece*," *Shakespearean Studies* 14: 1–21.

Braudy, L. (1986) *The Frenzy of Renown: Fame and its History*. New York: Oxford University Press.

Brockbank, J. P. (1958) "History and Histrionics in *Cymbeline*," *Shakespeare Survey* 11: 42–9.

Bromley, L.G. (1983) "Lucrece's Re-Creation," *Shakespeare Quarterly* 34, 2 (summer): 200–11.

Brower, R. (1971) *Hero and Saint: Shakespeare and the Graeco-Roman Heroic Tradition*. New York: Oxford University Press.

Brown, W. (1988) *Manhood and Politics: A Feminist Reading in Political Theroy*. Totowa, NJ: Rowman.

Brucher, R. T. (1979) "Tragedy, Laugh On: Comic Violence in *Titus Andronicus*," *Renaissance Drama* 10: 71–91.

Bullough, G. (1957–1966) *Narrative and Dramatic Sources of Shakespeare* (ed. and intro.) London: Routledge and Kegan Paul, New York: Columbia University. 7 vols.

Burckhardt, S. (1968) *Shakespearean Meanings*. Princeton: Princeton University Press.

Burt, R. A. (1991) "'A dangerous Rome': Shakespeare's *Julius Caesar* and the Discursive Determination of Cultural Politics," in *Contending Kingdoms: Historical, Psychological, and Feminist Approaches to the Literature of 16th Century England and France*, Detroit: Wayne State University Press 109–27.

Butler, J. (1990) *Gender Trouble: Feminism and the Subversion of Identity*. London: Routledge.

Calderwood, J. (1971) *Shakespearean Metadrama*. Minneapolis: Minnesota University Press.

Cantarella, E. (1987) *Pandora's Daughters: The Role and Status of Women in Greek and Roman Antiquity*, M. B. Fant (transl.). Baltimore: Johns Hopkins University Press.

Cantor, P. A. (1976) *Shakespeare's Rome: Republic and Empire*. Ithaca: Cornell University Press.

Charnes, L. (1989) "'So Unsecret to Ourselves': Notorious Identity and the Material Subject in Shakespeare's *Troilus and Cressida,*" *Shakespeare Quarterly* 40, 4 (winter): 413–40.

—— (1992) "What's Love Got to Do With it? Reading the Liberal Humanist Romance in Shakespeare's *Antony and Cleopatra,*" *Textual Practice* 6,1 (spring): 1–16

—— (1993) *Notorious Identity: Materializing the Subject in Shakespeare*. Cambridge, MA: Harvard University Press.

Charney, M. (1961) *Shakespeare's Roman Plays: The Function of Imagery in the Drama*. Cambridge, MA: Harvard University Press.

Clayton, T. (1983) "'Should Brutus Never Taste of Portia's Death But Once?' Text and Performance in *Julius Caesar,*" *Studies in English Literature 1500–1900* 23,2 (spring): 237–55.

Cooper, H. M., Munich, A. A., and Squier, S. M. (1989) *Arms and the Woman: War, Gender, and Literary Representation*. Chapel Hill: University of North Carolina Press.

Danson, L. (1974) *Tragic Alphabet: Shakespeare's Drama of Language*. New Haven: Yale University Press.

Davidson, C., Gianakaris, C., and Stroupe, J. H. (eds) (1986) *Drama and the Renaissance: Comparative and Critical Essays*. New York: AMS.

de Beauvoir, S. (1953, rpt. 1989) *The Second Sex*, H. M. Parshley (transl.). New York: Vintage.

Dean, L. (1968) "Introduction," in *Twentieth-Century Interpretations of Julius Caesar*. Englewood Cliffs, NJ: Prentice-Hall.

Dessen, A. (1989) *Shakespeare in Performance: Titus Andronicus*. Manchester: Manchester University Press.

Dollimore, J. (1984) "*Antony and Cleopatra* (ca. 1607); *Virtus* under Erasure," in *Radical Tragedy: Religion, Ideology and Power in the Drama of Shakespeare and his Contemporaries*. Chicago: University of Chicago Press: 204–17.

—— (1990) "Shakespeare, Cultural Materialism, Feminism and Marxist Humanism," *New Literary History: A Journal of Theory and Interpretation* 21,3 (spring); 471–93.

—— and Sinfield, A. (eds and intro.) (1985) *Political Shakespeare: Essays in Cultural Materialism*. Ithaca: Cornell University Press.

Dorsch, T. S. (1988b) "Introduction," in Dorsch, T. S. (ed. and intro.), Shakespeare, W., *Julius Caesar*. London: Routledge

Douglas, M. (1970) *Natural Symbols: Explorations in Cosmology*. New York: Pantheon.

DuBois, P. (1985) "A Disturbance of Syntax at the Gates of Rome," *Stanford Literature Review* 2: 185–208.

—— (1988) *Sowing the Body: Psychoanalysis and Ancient Representations of Women*. Chicago: University of Chicago Press.

Dubrow, H. (1987) *Captive Victors: Shakespeare's Narrative Poems and Sonnets.* Ithaca and London: Cornell University Press.

Edwards, E. (1868) *The Life of Sir Walter Raleigh.* London: Macmillan, 2 vols.

Elshtain, J. B. (1981) *Public Man, Private Woman: Women in Social and Political Thought.* Princeton: Princeton University Press.

—— (1987) *Women and War.* New York: Basic.

Erickson, P. (1985) *Patriarchal Structures in Shakespeare's Drama.* Berkeley and Los Angeles: University of California Press.

—— and Kahn (eds) (1985) *Shakespeare's 'Rough Magic'.* Newark: University of Delaware Press.

Esler, A. (1966) *The Aspiring Mind of the Elizabethan Younger Generation.* Durham, NC: Duke University Press.

Fawcett, M.L. (1983) "Arms/Words/Tears: Language and the Body in *Titus Andronicus,*" *English Literary History* 50: 261–77.

Felman, S. (1981) "Re-reading Feminity," *Yale French Studies* 62: 19–44.

Ferguson, M. W., Quilligan, M. and Vickers, N. J. (1986a) "Introduction," in Ferguson *et al.* (1986b), xv–xxxvi.

—— (1986b) *Rewriting the Renaissance: the Discourses of Sexual Difference in Early Modern Europe.* Chicago: University of Chicago Press.

Fineman, J. (1980) "Infanticide and Cuckoldry: Shakespeare's Doubles," in Schwartz and Kahn (eds)., 70–109.

—— (1987) "Shakespeare's Will: The Temporality of Rape," *Representations* 20 (fall): 25–76.

Fink, Z.S. (1962) *The Classical Republicans: An Essay in the Recovery of a Pattern of Thought in Seventeenth-Century England.* Evanston, IL: Northwestern University, 2nd edn.

Fitz, L. T. (1977) "Egyptian Queens and Male Reviewers," *Shakespeare Quarterly* 28,3 (summer): 297–316.

Freud, S. (1925, rpt. 1961) "Some Psychical Consequences of the Anatomical Distinction Between the Sexes," *Standard Edition of the Complete Works of Sigmund Freud,* James Strachey (transl. and ed.). London: Hogarth Press vol. 19, 248–58.

—— (1927, rpt. 1961) "Fetishism," *Standard Edition,* vol. 21, 152–7.

Froula, Christine (1986) "The Daughter's Silence: Sexual Violence and Literary History," *SIGNS* 11,4 (summer): 621–44.

Garber, M. (1990) "Fetish Envy," *October* 54 (fall): 45–56.

Gohlke, M. (1980) "'I wooed thee with my sword': Shakespeare's Tragic Paradigms," in Schwartz and Kahn (eds), 170–87.

Goldberg, J. (1983, rpt. 1989) *James I and the Politics of Literature: Jonson, Shakespeare, Donne and their Contemporaries.* Baltimore: Johns Hopkins University Press.

—— (1985) "Shakespearean Inscriptions: The Voicing of Power," in Parker and Hartman (eds), 116–37.

Goux, J.-J. (1983) "Vesta, or the Place of Being," *Representations* 1 (February): 91–107.

Grafton, A. and Jardine, L. (1986) *From Humanism to the Humanities: Education and the Liberal Arts in 15th and 16th Century Europe.* Cambridge, MA: Harvard University Press.

Grant, M. (1972) *Cleopatra.* London, Weidenfeld & Nicolson.

Green, D. E. (1989) "Interpreting 'her martyr'd signs': Gender and Tragedy in *Titus Andronicus*," *Shakespeare Quarterly* 40,3 (fall): 317–26.

Greenblatt, S. (1973) *Sir Walter Raleigh: The Renaissance Man and his Roles.* New Haven: Yale University Press.

Greene, G. (1980) "'The power of speech to stir men's blood': The Language of Tragedy in Shakespeare's *Julius Caesar*," *Renaissance Drama* 11: 67–93.

——and Kahn, C. (1985) *Making a Difference: Feminist Literary Criticism.* London: Routledge.

Greene, T. M. (1982) *The Light in Troy: Imitation and Discovery in Renaissance Poetry.* New Haven: Yale University Press.

Griffin, M. (1986) "Philosophy, Cato, and Roman Suicide," *Greece and Rome* 33: 64–77, 192–202.

Grisé, Y. (1982) *Le Suicide dans la Rome antique.* Montréal: Bellarmin.

Halpern, R. (1991) *The Poetics of Primitive Accumulation: English Renaissance Culture and the Genealogy of Capital.* Ithaca: Cornell University Press.

Hampton, T. (1990) *Writing from History: The Rhetoric of Exemplarity in Renaissance Literature.* Ithaca: Cornell University Press.

Harbage, A. (1989) *Annals of English Drama, 975–1700: an analytical record of all plays, extant or lost, chronologically arranged and indexed by authors, titles, and dramatic companies by Alfred Harbage*, revised by S. Schoenbaum, 3rd edn, revised by S. Wagonheim. London and New York: Routledge.

Hartsock, N. (1989) "Masculinity, Heroism, and the Making of War," in A. Harris and Y. King (eds) *Rocking the Ship of State: Towards a Feminist Peace Poetics.* Boulder: Westview, 133–52.

Haselkorn, A. M. and Travitsky, B. S. (eds) (1990) *The Renaissance Englishwoman in Print: Counterbalancing the Canon.* Amherst: University of Massachusetts Press.

Helms, L. (1989) "'Still Wars and Lechery': Shakespeare and the Last Trojan Woman," in Cooper, Munich, and Squier (eds) 25–42.

—— (1992) "'The High Roman Fashion': Sacrifice, Suicide, and the Shakespearean Stage," *PMLA* 107,3 (May): 554–65.

Higgins, L. A. and Silver, B. R. (eds and intro.) (1991) *Rape and Representation.* New York: Columbia University Press.

Higonnet, M. R. (1986) "Speaking Silences: Women's Suicide," in Suleiman (ed.), 68–83.

Higonnet, M. R., Jenson, J., Michel, S., and Weiss, M. C. (eds and intro.) (1987) *Behind the Lines: Gender and the Two World Wars.* New Haven: Yale University Press.

Holland, N. N., Homan, S., and Paris, B. J. (eds) (1989) *Shakespeare's Personality.* Berkeley: University of California Press.

Honigmann, E. A. J. (ed.) (1986) *Shakespeare and his Contemporaries: Essays in Comparison.* Manchester; Manchester University Press.

Hosley, R. (1964) "The Staging of the Monument Scenes in *Antony and Cleopatra*," *Literary Chronicle* 30: 62–71.

Howard, J. (1988) "Crossdressing, the Theatre, and Gender Struggle in Early Modern England," *Shakespeare Quarterly* 39,4: 418–40.

—— (1994) *The Stage and Social Struggle in Early Modern England.* London: Routledge.

Hughes-Hallett, L. (1990) *Cleopatra: Histories, Dreams, and Distortions*. New York: Harper.

Hulse, S. C. (1979) "Wresting the Alphabet: Orality and Action in *Titus Andronicus*," *Criticism* 21: 106–18.

Humphreys, A. R. (ed.) (1984) "Introduction," in W. Shakespeare, *Julius Caesar*.

Hunter, G. K. (1977) "A Roman Thought: Renassance Attitudes to History Exemplified in Shakespeare and Jonson," in B. S. Lee (ed.), *An English Miscellany: Presented to W. S. Mackie*. Capetown and New York: Oxford University Press, 93–115.

—— (1984) "Sources and Meanings in *Titus Andronicus*," in J. C. Gray (ed.) *Mirror up to Shakespeare: Essays in Honor of G.R. Hibbard*. Toronto: University of Toronto Press.

Huston, N. (1986) "The Matrix of War: Mothers and Heroes," in Suleiman (ed.), 119–36.

Ingleby, C.M., Toulmin-Smith, L. and Furnivall, F. J. (1932) *The Shakespeare Allusion-Book: A Collection of Allusions to Shakespeare from 1591 to 1700*. London: H. Milford and Oxford University Press, 2 vols.

Jacobus, M. (1982) "Is There a Woman in This Text?" *New Literary History* 14,1: 117–41.

—— (1986) "Judith, Holofernes, and the Phallic Woman," in *Reading Women: Essays in Feminist Criticism*. New York: Columbia University, 110–36.

James, H. (1990) "Virgil, Ovid, and Empire in *Titus Andronicus*," in *Themes in Drama*, J. Redmond (ed.), 123–40.

Jardine, L. and Grafton, A. (1990) "'Studied for Action': How Gabriel Harvey Read his Livy," *Past and Present* 129: 30–78.

Jarrell, R. (1969) "The Death of the Bell Turret Gunner," in *The Complete Poems*. New York: Farrar, 144.

Jed, S. H. (1989) *Chaste Thinking: The Rape of Lucretia and the Birth of Humanism*. Bloomington, IN: Indiana University Press.

Jones, A. R. and Stallybrass, P. (1991) "Fetishizing Gender: Constructing the Hermaphrodite in Renaissance England," in Straub (ed.), 80–113.

Joplin, P. K. (1984) 'The Voice of the Shuttle Is Ours', *Stanford Literature Review* 1,1 (spring): 25–53. Reprinted in Higgins and Silver (eds) (1991), 35–66.

—— (1990) "Ritual Work on Human Flesh: Livy's Lucretia and the Rape of the Body Politic," *Helios* 17,1: 51–70.

Kahn, C. (1976) "The Rape in Shakespeare's *Lucrece*," *Shakespeare Studies* 9: 45–72.

—— (1981) *Man's Estate: Masculine Identity in Shakespeare*. Berkeley: University of California Press.

—— (1985) "'The Cuckoo's Note': Cuckoldry and Male Bonding in *The Merchant of Venice*," in Erickson and Kahn (eds), 104–12.

—— (1987) "'Magic of bounty': *Timon of Athens*, Jacobean Patronage, and Maternal Power," *Shakespeare Quarterly* 38,1 (spring): 34–57.

—— and Greene, G. (eds) (1985) *Making a Difference: Feminist Literary Criticism*. New York and London: Routledge.

Kahn, V. (1986) "Virtù and the Example of Agathocles," *Representations* 13 (winter): 63–83.

Kastan, D. (1986) "'Proud Majesty Made a Subject': Shakespeare and the Spectacle of Rule," *Shakespeare Quarterly* 37: 459–75.

Kelly, J. (1977, rpt. 1984) "Did Women Have a Renaissance?" in *Women, History and Theory: The Essays of Joan Kelly*. Chicago: University of Chicago Press.

Kendall, G. M. (1989) "'Lend me thy hand': Metaphor and Mayhem in *Titus Andronicus*," *Shakespeare Quarterly* 40,3: 299–316.

Kinney, C. (1990) "The Queen's Two Bodies and the Divided Emperor: Some Problems of Identity in *Antony and Cleopatra*," in Haselkorn and Travitsky (eds), 177–86.

Kittredge, G. L. (1936) *The Complete Works of Shakespeare*. Boston: Ginn & Co., 971–2.

Knight, G. W. (1931) *The Imperial Theme: Further Interpretations of Shakespeare's Tragedies Including the Roman Plays*. London and Humphrey Milford, Oxford University Press.

Kristeva, J. (1986) "Stabat Mater," in Suleiman (ed.), 99–118.

Laqueur, T. (1990) *Making Sex: Body and Gender from the Greeks to Freud*. Cambridge, MA: Harvard University Press.

Latham, A. M. C. (1939) "Sir Walter Raleigh's Farewell Letter to His Wife in 1603 . . ." *Essays and Studies* 25: 39–58.

Law, R. A. (1943) "The Roman Background of *Titus Andronicus*," *Studies in Philology* 40: 145–53.

Lefkowitz, M. R. and Fant, M. B. (1982) *Women's Life in Greece and Rome*. Baltimore: Johns Hopkins University Press.

Leggatt, A. (1988) *Shakespeare's Political Drama: The History of the Roman Plays*. London and New York: Routledge.

Levine, L. (1994) *Men in Women's Clothing*. Cambridge: Cambridge University Press.

Lewis, C. T. (1890) *An Elementary Latin Dictionary*. New York: American.

Liebler, N. C. (1981) "'Thou Bleeding Piece of Earth': The Ritual Ground of *Julius Caesar*," *Shakespeare Studies* 14: 175–96.

Logan, G. M. and Teskey, G. (eds) (1989) *Unfolded Tales: Essays on Renaissance Romance*. Ithaca: Cornell University Press.

Loomba, A. (1989) *Gender, Race, Renaissance Drama*. Manchester: University of Manchester Press.

Loraux, N. (1981) 'Le Lit, La Guerre', *L'Homme* 22,1: 37–67.

—— (1987) *Tragic Ways of Killing a Woman*. Cambridge MA: Harvard University Press.

Lowe, L. (1986) "'Say I play the man I am': Gender and Politics in *Coriolanus*," *Kenyon Review* 8,4: 86–95.

McAlindon, T. (1973) *Shakespeare and Decorum*. New York: Harper & Row.

MacCallum, M. W. (1910) *Shakespeare's Roman Plays and their Background*. London: Macmillan.

McCoy, R. C. (1983) "'A dangerous image': The Earl of Essex and Elizabethan Chivalry," *Journal of Medieval and Renaissance Studies* 13: 313–29.

—— (1989) *The Rites of Knighthood: The Literature and Politics of Elizabethan Chivalry*. Berkeley: University of California Press.

MacDonald, M. and Murphy, T. R. (1990) *Sleepless Souls: Suicide in Early Modern England*. Oxford: Oxford University Press.

MacDougall, H. A. (1982) *Racial Myth in English History: Trojans, Teutons, and Anglosaxons*. Hanover, NH: University Press of New England.

Mack, P. (1992) *Visionary Women: Ecstatic Prophecy in Seventeenth-century England.* Berkeley/Los Angeles: University of California.

Maclean, I. (1980) *The Renaissance Notion of Women: A Study in the Fortunes of Scholasticism and Medical Science in European Intellectual Life.* Cambridge: Cambridge University Press.

McLuskie, K. (1985) "The Patriarchal Bard: Feminist Criticism and Shakespeare: *King Lear* and *Measure for Measure,*" in Dollimore and Sinfield (eds).

Mallin, E. (1990) "Emulous Factions and the Collapse of Chivalry: *Troilus and Cressida,*" *Representations* 29 (winter): 145–79.

Marshall, C. (1993) "Man of steel done got the blues: Melancholic Subversion of Presence in *Antony and Cleopatra,*" *Shakespeare Quarterly* 44,4 (winter): 385–408.

Martindale, C. and M. (1990) *Shakespeare and the Uses of Antiquity: An Introductory Essay.* London and New York: Routledge.

Maus, K. E. (1984) *Ben Jonson and the Roman Frame of Mind.* Princeton: Princeton University Press.

—— (1986) "Taking Tropes Seriously: Language and Violence in Shakespeare's *Rape of Lucrece,*" *Shakespeare Quarterly* 37,1: 66–82.

Mikalachki, Jodi (1995) "The Masculine Romance of Roman Britain: Cymbeline and Early Modern English Nationalism," *Shakespeare Quarterly* 46,3: 301–22.

Miles, G. B. (1989) "How Roman Are Shakespeare's 'Romans'?" *Shakespeare Quarterly* 40,3 (fall): 257–83.

Miola, R. S. (1983) *Shakespeare's Rome.* Cambridge: Cambridge University Press.

—— (1990) "Othello *Furens,*" *Shakespeare Quarterly* 41,1: 49–64.

Montrose, L. A. (1980) "'The Purpose of Playing': Reflections on a Shakespearean Anthropology," *Helios* 7,2: 51–74.

Mowatt, B. A. (1981) "Lavinia's Message: Shakespeare and Myth," *Renaissance Papers*: 55–69

Mullaney, S. (1988) *The Place of the Stage: License, Play, and Power in Renaissance England.* Chicago: University of Chicago Press.

Mulvey, L. (1988) "Visual Pleasure and Narrative Cinema", in Penley (ed.), 57–68.

Nearing, H. (1949) "The Legend of Julius Caesar's British Conquest," *PMLA* 64: 889–929.

Neely, C. T. (1985) *Broken Nuptials in Shakespeare's Plays,* New Haven and London: Yale University Press.

Neill, M. (1994a) "A Note on the Staging of 4.16 and 5.2," in W. Shakespeare, *The Tragedy of Antony and Cleopatra,* M. Neill (ed.).

—— (1994b) "Introduction," in M. Neill) (ed. and intro.), Shakespeare, W., *The Tragedy of Antony and Cleopatra,* Oxford: Oxford University Press.

Newey, V. and Thompson, A. (eds) *Literature and Nationalism.* Savage, MD: Barnes & Noble.

Newman, J. O. (1994) "'And let mild women to him lose their mildness': Philomela, Female Violence, and Shakespeare's *The Rape of Lucrece,*" *Shakespeare Quarterly* 45,3 (fall): 304–26.

Newman, K. (1986) "Renaissance Family Politics and Shakespeare's *The*

Taming of the Shrew," *English Literary Renaissance* 16,1 (winter): 86–100.

—— (1991) *Fashioning Femininity and English Renaissance Drama*. Chicago: University of Chicago Press.

Noon, G. (1978) "On Suicide," *Journal of the History of Ideas* 39: 371–86.

Novy, M. (1984) *Love's Argument: Gender Relations in Shakespeare*. Chapel Hill, NC: University of North Carolina Press.

O'Dair, S. (1993) "'You cannot see yourself so well as by reflection': Social Role and the Making of Identity in *Julius Caesar*," *Studies in English Literature 1500–1900*, 33,2: 289–307.

Ong, W. J. (1959) "Latin Language Study as a Renaissance Puberty Rite," *Studies in Philology* 56: 93–110.

Oxford English Dictionary, 1989 edn.

Palmer, H. R. (1911) *List of English Editions and Translations of Greek and Latin Classics Printed before 1641*. London: Blades.

Parker, P. (1989) "Romance and Empire: Anachronistic *Cymbeline*," in Logan and Teskey (eds.), 189–207.

—— and Hartman, G. (eds) (1985) *Shakespeare and the Question of Theory*. London: Methuen.

Paster, G. K. (1985) *The Idea of the City in the Age of Shakespeare*. Athens: University of Georgia Press.

——(1989) "'In the spirit of men there is no blood': Blood as Trope of Gender in *Julius Caesar*," *Shakespeare Quarterly* 40,3: 284–98.

—— (1993) *The Body Embarrassed: Drama and the Disciplines of Shame in Early Modern England*. Ithaca: Cornell University Press.

Payne, R. (1962) *The Roman Triumph*. London: Robert Hale.

Pechter, E. (1986) "*Julius Caesar* and *Sejanus*: Roman Politics, Inner Selves, and the Powers of the Theatre," in Honigmann (ed.), 60–72.

Penley, C. (ed.) (1988) *Feminism and Film Theory*. New York: Routledge.

Phillips, J. E. Jr (1940) *The State in Shakespeare's Greek and Roman Plays*. New York: Columbia University Press.

Pietz, W. (1985) "The Problem of the Fetish I," *Res* 9 (spring): 5–17.

—— (1987) 'The Problem of the Fetish II', *Res* 13: 23–45.

Pitkin, H. F. (1984) *Fortune Is a Woman: Gender and Politics in the Thought of Niccolo Machiavelli*. Berkeley: University of California Press.

Platt, M. (1975) "*The Rape of Lucrece* and the Republic for which it Stands," *Centennial Review* 19,2 (spring): 59–79.

—— (1983) *Rome and Romans according to Shakespeare* (1976) Salzburg Studies in English Literature, JDS, no. 51, Salzburg: Institute für Englishe Sprache und Literatur.

Pocock, J. G. A. (1975) *The Machiavellian Moment: Florentine Political Thought and the Atlantic Republican Tradition*. Princeton: Princeton University Press.

Prince, F. T. (1969) "Introduction," in W. Shakespeare, *The Poems*, Arden Shakespeare Paperbacks. London: Methuen.

Prior, M. E. (1969) "The Search for a Hero in *Julius Caesar*," *Renaissance Drama* n.s. 2: 81–101.

Proser, M. (1965) *The Heroic Image in Five Shakespearean Tragedies*. Princeton, NJ: Princeton University Press.

Raab, Felix. (1964) *The English Face of Machiavelli: A Changing Interpretation, 1500–1700*, H. Trevor-Roper (intro.). London: Routledge.

Rabkin, N. (1967) *Shakespeare and the Common Understanding*. New York: Free Press.

Rackin, P. (1983) "*Coriolanus*: Shakespeare's Anatomy of *Virtus*," *Modern Language Studies* 13,2: 68–79.

—— (1990) *Stages of History: Shakespeare's English Chronicles*, Ithaca: Cornell University Press.

Rebhorn, W. A. (1990) "The Crisis of the Aristocracy in *Julius Caesar*," *Renaissance Quarterly* 43,1 (spring): 75–111.

Reiter, R. (ed.), *Toward an Anthropology of Women*. New York: Monthly Review.

Ronan, C. (1995) "*Antike Roman*": *Power Symbology and the Roman Play in Early Modern England, 1585–1635*. Athens, GA: University of Georgia Press.

Rooney, E. (1983) "Criticism and the Subject of Sexual Violence," *Modern Language Notes* 98,5, (December): 1269–77.

Rose, M. B. (ed.) (1986) *Women in the Middle Ages and the Renaissance: Literary and Historical Perspectives*. Syracuse: Syracuse University Press.

Rozett, M. T. (1985) "The Comic Structures of Tragic Endings: the Suicides in *Romeo and Juliet* and *Antony and Cleopatra*," *Shakespeare Quarterly* 36: 152–64.

Rubin, G. (1975) "The Traffic in Women: Notes on the 'Political Economy' of Sex," in Reiter (ed.), 157–210.

Rudick, M. and Battin, M. P. (eds and intro.) (1982) John Donne, *Biathanatos*. New York: Garland.

Rupp, L. (1978) *Mobilizing Women for War: German and American Propaganda, 1939–1945*. Princeton: Princeton University Press.

Schanzer, R. (1963) *The Problem Plays of Shakespeare*, New York: Schocken Books.

Schor, N. (1986) "Female Fetishism: The Case of George Sand," in Suleiman (ed.), 363–72.

Schwartz, M. and Kahn, C. (eds) (1980) *Representing Shakespeare: New Psychoanalytic Essays*. Baltimore: Johns Hopkins University Press.

Scott, J. W. (1987) "Rewriting History", in Higonnet *et al.* (eds) 21–30.

—— (1988) "Gender: A Useful Category of Historical Analysis," in *Gender and the Politics of History*. New York: Columbia University.

Sedgwick, E. K. (1985) *Between Men: English Literature and Male Homosexual Desire*. New York: Columbia University.

Shuger, D. K. (1993) "Review," *Shakespeare Quarterly* 44,4 (winter): 488–93.

Siegel, P. N. (1986) *Shakespeare's English and Roman History Plays: A Marxist Approach*. London and Toronto: Associated University Presses.

Siemon, J. E. (1976) "Noble Virtue in *Cymbeline*," *Shakespeare Survey* 29: 51–61.

Simmons, J. L. (1973) *Shakespeare's Pagan World: The Roman Tragedies*. Charlottesville, VA: University of Virginia Press.

Singh, J. (1989) "Renaissance Antitheatricality, Antifeminism, and Shakespeare's *Antony and Cleopatra*," *Renaissance Drama* 20: 99–121.

Skura, M. (1980) "Interpreting Posthumus's Dream From Above and Below: Families, Psychoanalysts, and Literary Critics," in Schwartz and Kahn (eds), 203–16.

Smith, B. (1991) *Homosexual Desire in Shakespeare's England: A Cultural Poetics*. Chicago: University of Chicago Press.

Smith, G. R. (1959) "Brutus, Virtue, and Will," *Shakespeare Quarterly* 10,3 (summer): 367–79.

Snyder, S. (1980) "The Challenge to Single Combat in Shakespeare: Ourselves Alone," *Studies in English Literature 1500–1900* 20: 201–16.
Spencer, T. J. B. (1957) "Shakespeare and the Elizabethan Romans," *Shakespeare Survey* 10: 27–38.
—— (ed. and intro.) (1964) *Shakespeare's Plutarch*. Harmondsworth: Penguin.
Sprengnether, M. (1986) "Annihilating Intimacy in *Coriolanus*," in Rose (ed. and intro.), 89–101.
—— (1989) "The Boy Actor and Femininity in *Antony and Cleopatra*," in Holland *et al.* (eds).
Sprott, S. E. (1961) *The English Debate on Suicide: from Donne to Hume*. La Salle, IL: Open Court.
Stallybrass, P. (1986) "Patriarchal Territories: The Body Enclosed," in Ferguson *et al.* (1986b), 123–42.
Stampfer, Judah. (1968) *The Tragic Engagement A Study of Shakespeare's Classical Tragedies*. New York: Funk & Wagnalls.
Stirling, B. (1958) "'Or else this were a savage spectacle," in *Unity in Shakespearean Tragedy: The Interplay of Theme and Character*. New York: Columbia University Press.
Stone, L. (1967) *The Crisis of the Aristocracy 1558–1660*, abridged edn. London: Oxford University Press.
Straub, K. (ed.) (1991) *Body Guards: The Cultural Politics of Gender Ambiguity*. London and New York: Routledge.
Strong, R. (1977) *The Cult of Elizabeth: Elizabethan Portraiture and Pageantry*. London: Thames & Hudson.
Suleiman, S. R. (ed.) (1986) *The Female Body in Western Culture: Contemporary Perspectives*. Cambridge MA: Harvard University Press.
Tarn, W. W. and Charlesworth, M. P. (1965) *Octavius, Antony, and Cleopatra*. Cambridge: Cambridge University Press.
Taylor, L. R. (1949) *Party Politics in the Age of Caesar*. Berkeley: University of California Press.
Tennenhouse, L. (1986a) "*Coriolanus*: History and the Crisis of Semantic Order," in Davidson *et al.*, (eds), 217–35.
—— (1986b) *Power on Display: The Politics of Shakespeare's Genres*. London: Routledge.
Thomas, V. (1989) *Shakespeare's Roman Worlds*. London and New York: Routledge.
Thompson, A. (1991) "Person and Office: The Case of Imogen, Princess of Britain," in Newey and Thompson (eds), 76–87.
—— and Thompson, J. O. (1987) *Shakespeare: Meaning and Metaphor*. Savage, MD: Barnes & Noble.
Thomson, L. (1989) "*Antony and Cleopatra*, Act 4, Scene 16: 'A Heavy Sight'," *Shakespeare Survey* 41: 77–90.
Traub, V. (1992) *Desire and Anxiety: Circulations of Sexuality in Shakespearean Drama*. London: Routledge.
Traversi, D. A. (1963) *Shakespeare: The Roman Plays*, Stanford: Stanford University Press.
Tricomi, A. H. (1974) "The Aesthetics of Mutilation in *Titus Andronicus*," *Shakespeare Survey* 27: 11–19.
—— (1976) "The Mutilated Garden in *Titus Andronicus*," *Shakespeare Studies* 9: 89–105.

Velz, J. W. (1968a) "'If I were Brutus now': Role-playing in *Julius Caesar*," *Shakespeare Studies* 4: 149–59.

—— (1968b) *Shakespeare and the Classical Tradition: a Critical Guide to Commentary 1660–1960*. Minnesota; Minnesota University Press.

—— (1978) "The Ancient World in Shakespeare: Authenticity or Anachronism: A Retrospect," *Shakespeare Survey* 31: 1–12.

—— (1982) "Orator and Imperator in *Julius Caesar*: Style and the Process of Roman History," *Shakespeare Studies* 15: 55–75.

Vickers, N. (1985) "'The blazon of sweet beauty's best': Shakespeare's *Lucrece*," in Parker and Hartman (eds).

—— (1986) "'This Heraldry in Lucrece's Face'," in Suleiman (ed.), 209–22.

Waith, E. W. (1962) *The Herculean Hero in Marlowe, Chapman, Shakespeare and Dryden*. New York: Columbia University Press.

Warner, M. (1985) *Monuments and Maidens: The Allegory of the Female Form*. New York: Pantheon.

Warren, L. B. (1970) "Roman Triumph and Etruscan Kings: The Changing Face of the Triumph," *Journal of Roman Studies* 60: 49–66.

Watson, R. N. (1984) *Shakespeare and the Hazards of Ambition*. Cambridge MA: Harvard University Press.

Wayne, V. (ed.) (1991) *The Matter of Difference: Materialist Feminist Criticism of Shakespeare*. Ithaca: Cornell University Press.

Wells, S. J. and Taylor, G. (1987) *William Shakespeare: A Textual Companion*. Oxford: Clarendon Press.

West, G. S. (1982) "Going By the Book: Classical Allusions in Shakespeare's *Titus Andronicus*," *Studies in Philology* 79,1 (winter): 62–77.

Wheeler, R. P. (1980) "'Since first we were dissevered': Trust and Autonomy in Shakespearean Tragedy and Romance," in Schwartz and Kahn (eds), 150–69.

Whigham, F. (1984) *Ambition and Privilege: The Social Tropes of Elizabethan Courtesy Theory*. Berkeley: University of California Press.

Whitney, J. (1993) "The Sword Cuts Both Ways: Antony and the Role of Mardian, the Eunuch." Unpublished paper.

Willbern, D. (1978) "Rape and Revenge in *Titus Andronicus*," *English Literary Renaissance* 8,2: 159–82.

Winkler, J. (1991) "The Education of Chloe," in Higgins and Silver (eds), 15–34.

Woodbridge, L. (1991) "Palisading the Body Politic," *Texas Studies in Language and Literature* 33,3: 327–54.

Worthen, W. (1986) "The Weight of History: Staging 'Characters' in *Antony and Cleopatra*," *Studies in English Literature 1500–1900* 26: 295–308.

Wymer, R. (1986) *Suicide and Despair in the Jacobean Drama*. New York: Saint Martin's Press.

Wynne-Davies, Marion. (1991) "'The swallowing womb': Consumed and Consuming Women in *Titus Andronicus*," in Wayne (ed.), 129–51.

Yates, F. A. (1975) "Elizabethan Chivalry: The Romance of the Accession Day Tilts," in *Astraea: The Imperial Theme in the Sixteenth Century*. London: Routledge & Kegan Paul, 88–111.

Ziegler, G. (1990) "My Lady's Chamber: Female Space, Female Chastity in Shakespeare," *Textual Practice* 4,1: 73–90.

Index

185

gender difference: construction of
15; in *Julius Caesar* 77–8
Goldberg, J. 5, 28, 29
Goux, J.–J. 33
Grafton, A. 7, 8, 12
Grafton, R. 3, 4
Greek tragedy, deaths of women in
139
Green, D.E. 48, 56
Greenblatt, S. 128
Greene, G. 78, 81
Greene, T.M. 4
Griffin, M. 121, 122, 124
Grisé, Y. 121, 122
Gulf War 144

Halpern, R. 7, 11–12, 16
Hampton, T. 11, 13
Hartsock, N. 144
Harvey, G. 8, 12, 91
Hector 150, 151
Hecuba 63, 150, 151
Helms, L. 138, 139
Henry VIII, King of England 3–4
Hercules 129
Herodian 47
heroic discourse, in *Lucrece* 29–32
Heywood, T. 4, 14, 122
Higgins, L.A. 58
Higonnet, M.R. 145
Holinshed, R. 3, 164
honor: preservation of, through
suicide 122–3, 131, 132;
Roman ideology of 36–7
Horace 127
Horatius 164
Howard, J. 9, 13
Hughes-Hallett, L. 111, 112
humanistic education 7, 11–12,
16, 19–20, 47, 91
Humphreys, A.R. 79
Hunter, G.K. 3, 10, 13–14, 47, 49,
169
Huston, N. 145, 146

Iliad, The (Homer) 145
Imogen 160–1, 164
incest taboo 50
Ingleby, C.M. 12

Irigaray, L. 38

Jacobus, M. 18, 28
Jardine, L. 7, 8, 12
Jarrell, R. 144
Jed, S.H. 20, 66
Joan of Arc 145
Johnson, S. 1
Jones, A.R. 15
Jonson, B. 122
Joplin, P.K. 20, 39, 46, 63, 64, 67,
72, 98
Julius Caesar 5, 13, 17, 103, 104,
105
Julius Caesar 77–105, 132;
anachronism in 3; Brutus as
exemplar of Roman virtus in
79–81; feminization/the
feminine in 77–8, 96–9, 103,
104–5; Plutarch as source for
10; public–private opposition in
78–9, 80, 99; structures of
emulation in 88–96, 163

Kahn, C. 28, 32, 42, 53, 156
Kastan, D. 9
kingship, repudiation of 81
Kinney, C. 112, 115
Kirk, R. 97
Kristeva, J. 150, 157

Latham, A.M.C. 123
Lavinia 19, 47–72, 161
Lefkowitz, M.R. 147, 149
Lévi-Strauss, C. 49–50
Lewis, C.T. 150
Liebler, N.C. 90
Life of Cato Utican, The (Plutarch) 124
Life of Julius Caesar, The (Plutarch)
98
Life of Marcus Brutus, The (Plutarch)
81, 98, 102
Life of Paulus Aemilius, The (Plutarch)
128
Life of Romulus, The (Plutarch) 103,
104
Lipsius, J. 97, 98
Livy 10, 12, 47, 65, 70, 72, 156,
164

INDEX

Lodge, T. 4–5, 8, 14, 98
Loraux, N. 139, 146
Love's Labor's Lost 13
Lucrece 10, 13, 27–43, 53, 161
Lucrece 17, 19, 65–6, 72, 133

MacCallum, M.W. 2
McCoy, R.C. 93
MacDonald, M. 121, 122, 123
MacDougall, H.A. 3–4
Machiavelli, N. 83, 84, 85
Maclean, I. 98
McLuskie, K. 19
Maecenus 135
male relationships, rivalrous 15–17, 89–90; between Antony and Caesar 112–21, 128–9, 135, 137
Mallin, E. 16, 92, 93, 94
Marcus 57–9, 66
marriage 37
Marshall, C. 116, 121, 132
masculinity 127, 297; ideology of 2; Volumnia and the masculine in *Coriolanus* 149–50, 154–5; the wound as fetish of 17–18
Massinger, P. 11
Merchant of Venice, The 53
Merry Wives of Windsor, The 6–7
Metamorphoses (Ovid) 47, 63–5, 67
Mikalachki, J. 160, 163
Miles, G.B. 79, 90
mimeticism 38
Miola, R.S. 52, 160
Monmouth, Geoffrey of 3
Montaigne, M. 123, 125, 127, 139
Montrose, L.A. 9
More, Sir Thomas 82
motherhood: and patriarchy, in *Coriolanus* 155–7; and power in Roman culture 147, 157; and war–making 144–54
Mullaney, S. 9, 13
Mulvey, L. 31–2
Murphy, T.R. 121, 122, 123

Neely, C.T. 137, 138
Neill, M. 110, 116, 121
Newman, J.O. 20

Newman, K. 8, 38
Octavia 115
Octavius 105
oikos 77, 84, 146
Ong, W.J. 6, 16
Ovid 10, 32, 39, 46, 47, 63–5, 67

Painter, W., Pallace 66
Pandion 63
Parallel Lives of the Greeks and Romans (Plutarch) 13, 16–17, 92
Paster, G.K. 101, 151, 155
patriarchy 2, 27, 29; and control of female sexuality 47–8, 49–50, 55, 66, 71; motherhood and 155–7
Peacham, H. 4
Peele, G. 93
Petrarch 50–1
Philomel, myth of 20, 38–9, 57–8, 63–5
pietas, tradition of 47, 48, 89, 160
Pietz, W. 18
Pitkin, H.F. 85
the pit, as image of female genitalia, in *Titus Andronicus* 54–5
Platt, M. 42
Plutarch 86, 99, 102, 111–12, 117, 133, 148, 156; *The Life of Cato Utican* 124; *The Life of Julius Caesar* 90, 98; *The Life of Marcus Brutus* 81, 98, 102, 103; *The Life of Paulus Aemilius* 128; *The Life of Romulus* 103, 104; *The Parallel Lives of the Greeks and Romans* 13, 16–17, 92; *The Sayings of Spartan Women* 146, 147; as source for Shakespeare's plays 9–10;
Pocock, J.G.A. 84, 85
polis 77, 83–4, 146
politics, as masculine sphere 83–4
Politics (Aristotle) 82, 83–4
Pompey 13, 85, 89, 114
Ponet, J. 82
Portia 77, 80, 97, 99, 101, 102–3, 133

188